Partisan Balance

Princeton Lectures in Politics and Public Affairs

Cosponsored with Woodrow Wilson School
of Public and International Affairs,
Princeton University

*Partisan Balance: Why Political Parties Don't Kill
the U.S. Constitutional System*
by David R. Mayhew

Partisan Balance

Why Political Parties Don't Kill the U.S. Constitutional System

David R. Mayhew

PRINCETON UNIVERSITY PRESS ■ PRINCETON AND OXFORD

Jacket illustration by BB Sams, © *SEPS, licensed by*
Curtis Licensing, Indianapolis, IN

Library of Congress Cataloging-in-Publication Data

Mayhew, David R.
Partisan balance : why political parties don't
kill the U.S. Constitutional system /
David R. Mayhew.
p.   cm.
ISBN 978-0-691-14465-8
Includes bibliographical references and index.
1. Executive-legislative relations—United States.
2. Political parties—United States.   I. Title.
JK585.M39   2011
328.73′07456—dc22
2010044113

British Library Cataloging-in-Publication Data is available

This book has been composed in Janson Text LT Std
Printed on acid-free paper. ∞
press.princeton.edu
Printed in the United States of America
1 3 5 7 9 10 8 6 4 2

To my wife
Judith

CONTENTS

LIST OF ILLUSTRATIONS

TABLES

FIGURES

ACKNOWLEDGMENTS

Many people assisted me in this work. Jon Menitove supplied the basic material for chapter 1 and is listed as coauthor there. Joe Sempolinski brought valiant service to the project—fact-checking, data analysis, and policing of the logic and style. The Institution for Social and Policy Studies at Yale funded the work by Menitove and Sempolinski. Peter Aronow brought his skills to the statistical calculations. Lew Irwin as a graduate student wrote an insightful paper. Gary Jacobson supplied an election dataset. Scott Adler, Sarah Anzia, David Brady, and Matt Levendusky helped me hunt for data. Insights came from Steve Ansolabehere, Charles Cameron, Justin Fox, Alan Gerber, Matt Green, Karol Kucinski, Joel Middleton, Eric Patashnik, and Luke Thompson. Eric Schickler offered exceptionally constructive advice on the whole manuscript, as did two anonymous reviewers. I profited from comments at a Princeton conference by Doug Arnold, Nolan McCarty, Tom Romer, Keith Whittington, and Julian Zelizer. In the background are many conversations over the years with Bob Dahl. Of great help were the libraries at Yale University and Boston College.

In the United States, the presidency, the House, and the Senate have their own independent electoral bases. A separation-of-powers system thus rooted in voters can generate patterns of both *dissonance* and *skew* in the conduct of government. Dissonance can occur when different sectors of society enjoy special favor in different institutions. Skew can occur when the summary favor of the government tilts to one side. In modern times, the sectors or sides of chief relevance are the political parties. Politics tends to sort into an us versus them contest between two parties (or, in some countries, coalitions of parties) associated with ideologies. This being the case, a constitutional system that is not perceived to accommodate its party sides fairly may run into legitimacy trouble. A government needs to be poised appropriately on an electoral base.

How does the United States stack up in these considerations? In this book, I weave a complicated argument. Perhaps it is best characterized as an exploration. At least during recent times, I argue, using a particular diagnostic lever, both the dissonance and skew at the core of the American government as regards the parties have been very small, perhaps surprisingly small. Beneath everything else that we see, the governmental system has bent toward both *convergence* and *symmetry*. Notwithstanding its separation-of-powers arrangements, the United States has bent toward being a typical democratic country.

That is the skeleton of my argument. But there are complexities and qualifications. I dwell on the parties in this account, but at times I reach beyond contestation between the parties to discuss other coalitional frictions. I probe into congressional processes that are not found in the Constitution. Most important, I advance the idea of *corrigibility* to go along with those of convergence and symmetry. In the realm of policymaking, significant impediments can arise to the working out of these latter two logics. But, given time, many such impediments are tackled and overcome. This process of overcoming is an additional key aspect of the American regime.

What are the implications? One is the following. If the U.S. Constitution and the country's party system are more or less in sync, we might expect to see a scarcity of discontent with the Constitution. A century ago, that old institutional blueprint of 1787 came under considerable fire. One of the sides of that time, the Progressive left, targeted it. Thanks to Charles Beard and others, its class origins came to be suspect.[1] The Senate and federal courts were said to be fundamentally biased. At the least, they needed to be overhauled. We have forgotten the force of this old Progressive-era case. In our own time, nothing like this oppositional drive exists. Thoughtful critiques of the Constitution are being written, but they do not seem to resonate.[2] For the general American public, constitutional reform as a pressing concern seems to rank somewhere near vanishing polar bears and rising cable TV prices. Now in its third century, the U.S. Constitution is riding high. I cannot prove it, but I would guess that one reason is its congruence with the party system. A seriously disgruntled party—or, as in the case of a century ago, an ideological side—can raise a major ruckus.

That is my conceptual rubric. My time span in this work is the decades since World War II. Dwelling on relations among the presidency, the House, and the Senate, I address in sections of

[1] See Richard Hofstadter, *The Progressive Historians—Turner, Beard, Parrington* (New York: Knopf, 1968), chs. 5–8; John Patrick Diggins, "Class, Classical, and Consensus Views of the Constitution," *University of Chicago Law Review* 55 (1988), 555–70.

[2] Robert A. Dahl, *How Democratic Is the American Constitution?* (New Haven: Yale University Press, 2002); Sanford Levinson, *Our Undemocratic Constitution: Where the Constitution Goes Wrong (And How We the People Can Correct It)* (New York: Oxford University Press, 2006).

the analysis a particular topic: the fortunes of domestic legislative proposals that the various American presidents during those decades have championed and cared about. This is a somewhat narrow focus. A great deal of governmental activity is left out. Congress and the presidency can clash otherwise: consider Watergate.[3] Governments pursue foreign as well as domestic policies. The courts can have their own policy agendas. Presidents often make policy by themselves: Truman installed a strict antiespionage program and desegregated the armed services; Eisenhower desegregated the District of Columbia and sent troops to Little Rock; Obama has reorganized the auto industry.

Yet the realm I address is large and important. Domestic legislating at the behest of government leaders is probably as close to the heart of politics as one can get, and a system that does not get it right in this sphere, that does not win substantial legitimacy for what it does, is probably a system in trouble. The specifics in my treatment range from Truman's Fair Deal in 1949 through the Great Society of the 1960s, the Reagan revolution of the early 1980s, and George W. Bush's drives to cut taxes and partly privatize Social Security in the 2000s. Note that lawmaking is not just a domain of Democrats or welfare-state builders. From Alexander Hamilton's bank, Calvin Coolidge's tax cuts, and Eisenhower's spur to a private atomic energy industry through the Bush–Paulson bailout of Wall Street in 2008, the leaders of a capitalist economy have seen need to keep making laws. My analysis does not reach systematically into 2009, yet the centrality of the Obama administration's drives for an economic stimulus package, cap-and-trade regulation, and health insurance reform will be obvious.

My argument in these pages is coherent, I hope, even if it is complicated. It draws on two original datasets. In chapter 1, I present a dataset comparing in a particular way the electoral bases of the presidency, the House, and the Senate as evidenced in the sixteen presidential elections since World War II. I use as an

---

[3] For a treatment of clashes between Congress and the presidency in general, see David R. Mayhew, *America's Congress: Actions in the Public Sphere, James Madison through Newt Gingrich* (New Haven: Yale University Press, 2000), chs. 3, 6.

indicator the split of the major-party popular vote cast for president. Four values come into play for any election—the split of that presidential vote share in the nation at large, the split of it in the pivotal Electoral College unit once those units (there are now 51) are laid end to end according to their presidential vote share, and, analogously, the split of it in the median House district and the median Senate district (that is, state). Thus measured, how have the vote splits in the three districted universes deviated from the national popular vote split for president taken straight? Do partisan tilts appear? In the case of the Electoral College, the partisan bias has been, on average, zero. On the congressional side, using the same yardstick, partisan tilts in a Republican direction have existed—on average a 1.1 percent tilt in the case of the House, 1.3 percent in the case of the Senate. These chamber tilts have been chronic and detectable but they have been small. Perhaps surprisingly, the House and Senate tilts have differed from each other only trivially. Also, the Senate, notwithstanding its common image as Wyoming, Utah, and Idaho writ large, has not loomed as much of a Republican outlier when measured in these terms against the House or the system in general.

Given this data demonstration, the account proceeds, what might we expect in the way of policymaking relations among the three elective institutions? In chapter 2, a second dataset affords one line of insight into this question. I present a list of 184 high-priority domestic legislative proposals that the presidents from Truman through George W. Bush sent to Congress during their first two years after winning election or reelection. Analysis ensues in the chapter. What can be said about the achievements of the presidents as requesters? At issue is the performance of Congress taken as a whole. In the cases of these requests, did the presidents finally get what they wanted or not? In particular, given the small, to be sure, Republican tilts on Capitol Hill, is there any sign of partisan bias in the final legislative results? On balance, have Democratic presidents had a harder time on Capitol Hill than Republican presidents? This is a question fraught with all kinds of analytic perils, but one facet of it seems to be theoretically

plain and, at least in principle, empirically tractable. The answer seems to be: possibly yes. It is indeed possible that the Democrats have carried an additional burden. Yet the pattern I come up with is clouded in a statistical sense, it is probably not widely perceived, and it may be otherwise accounted for. The result is something of a Rorschach. It is ambiguous. It may match the pattern of small but nonzero values in the representational tilts—the 1.1 and 1.3 percent. It may bring episodic puzzlement and frustration without being seriously delegitimizing.

In chapters 3 and 4 I examine presidential success in the House as opposed to the Senate. Here I take up the success records of Democratic presidents as opposed to Republican presidents, but also the success records of all presidents, period, regardless of party. The former and latter concerns are very similar in their empirics although not identical. When White House initiatives have ended up blocked on Capitol Hill, has either of the two chambers stood out as chief blocker? If everything else averages out, the small 1.1 versus 1.3 percent partisan tilts of the House and Senate would predict small or no chamber-specific biases toward Democratic as opposed to Republican presidents, as well as small or no chamber-specific biases toward presidents, period. Of course, everything else does not average out—consider the Senate filibuster—and a wealth of analytic perils arises here, too. Yet a pattern of near-parity seems to shine through. Surprisingly, across the full sixty years through George W. Bush, when White House requests—of Democratic or Republican presidents, or alternatively of all presidents—have ended up buried on Capitol Hill, the House and Senate have served as nearly equal-opportunity buriers.

In analyzing this dataset of White House requests, I consider a range of theories—or perhaps more broadly, causal accounts—that political scientists and others have offered regarding Congress, the presidency, or relations between them. The theoretical line extends from Woodrow Wilson in the 1880s through James MacGregor Burns in the 1940s through Keith Krehbiel and Gary Cox and Mathew McCubbins in recent times. Journalists have chimed in. In chapters 3 and 4, I juxtapose these various bents of theorizing to the legislative experience of the recent sixty years. Why is it that analysts once asked the question: "Why is the Senate more liberal than the House?" In lawmaking terms, did the districting revolution of the 1960s make any difference? Is it really true that southern committee barons—Judge Howard Smith of Virginia and the rest—once kept House majorities from getting their way? In the sphere of White House requests, what has been the role of "party cartels" in the House? As a theoretical matter, what can be said about the classic civil rights filibuster? Have assertive presidents been thwarted by a House Agriculture Committee flexing its jurisdictional sovereignty? It may take sixty votes for a measure to clear the Senate today, but how important was the Senate cloture pivot in thwarting White House aims before the 1990s? Has the Senate, as some critics allege, played a long-term role as a hidebound enemy of progress?

My general assessment on this front is that a number of theories have turned out to be partly, or, in a time sense, locally, valid. But that is all. Perhaps that is the best that can be expected of theories in this complicated and evolving subject area.

Four themes infuse the ensuing chapters. The idea of a *public sphere* pertains throughout. This is the idea that political activity takes place before the eyes of an appraising public—not in a Washington, D.C., realm that can be theoretically or empirically isolated. In its elective bodies, the American regime is relentlessly transparent. We keep a pretty good bead on what the politicians would like to achieve (although they may be vague even in their own minds), what they aim to achieve, what they take steps to achieve, and what they succeed in achieving. Strategies as well as behavior can be documented. Strategizing *is* a kind of behavior. This transparency is theoretically important. Whether the opposing sides in politics are being fairly treated is a matter of perception. The public can watch and judge. It is probably no accident that sports and party competition grew up together in the English-speaking world. In the sports realm, we know what the teams are up to, and if one side in a football game enjoys twelve

players on the field and five downs, those bonuses and their likely consequences will be noticed. So it is in politics. Consider the play-out of the election of 2000.

In chapter 1, a theme of *microcosm*—the idea that the median constituencies of the House and Senate have approximated the presidential constituency as well as each other—seems to provide illumination. At a limit, this theme blends the connotations of convergence and symmetry that were introduced earlier. Yet approximation is not the same thing as identity, and the persistent, if small, space between the presidential vote-share taken by itself and its manifestation in the congressional medians may have policy significance. Also, as will be seen in chapter 3, leverage may derive from calculating the medians for the congressional constituencies according to an alternative principle.

A theme of *majoritarianism* emerges in chapters 3 and 4.[4] That is, at the level of policy interaction considered here embracing the full sixty years, all three of the elective institutions seem to have behaved at least usually in majoritarian fashion—even the Senate. That is the anchoring default. The qualifier "usually" emerges from, and I hope survives, a range of analysis I undertake in these chapters. Yet deviations from majoritarianism have played a role too, as is suggested by the cascade of theories in that vein offered by the political scientists named above and many others. I explore several antimajoritarian intricacies in chapters 3 and 4.

Finally, the theme of *corrigibility*, or, to put it another way, *reform*, makes its appearance in chapter 5. That is, failing all else, institutional or procedural reform is endogenous to the American system. All else can certainly fail, at least for awhile. Chapters 3 and 4 offer summary data regarding White House victories and losses, but they also supply generous evidence of wrinkles, distortions, or peculiarities that can invest the policy process during particular times or in particular policy areas. The civil rights filibuster and a rural skew in the House, to cite two examples, were once

---

[4] See the idea of the "majoritarian postulate" in Keith Krehbiel, *Information and Legislative Organization* (Ann Arbor: University of Michigan Press, 1991), p. 16.

real. But reform is out there as an option. Any of the elective institutions that deviates from the others in its policy stances as a result of alleged defects of representation runs the risk of getting cuffed into place by elements of the other institutions or the public. Ample history backs up this idea. Cuffing happens. Yet reform has its limits. It can be sluggish, it can itself fail, and the processes embedded in the Constitution are an especially difficult target.

Notwithstanding the qualifications, these organizing themes seem to do useful work. In a nutshell, an interlock of companion elective institutions whose representative bases are similar, whose processes in possibly the most salient range of policy action are basically, or at least ordinarily, majoritarian (thus cutting down on obstreperous outlier behavior), and where corrective reform is a real option, is not likely to run into serious legitimacy problems—at least for the reasons of relevance here. Whatever else may be said about it, and of course much can be, the American system of recent generations has enjoyed these characteristics and has probably been bolstered by them. Yet this is not an unasterisked case. The deviations of a correctable sort have been real and consequential, and the possible penalty to Democratic presidents adumbrated in chapter 2 hangs out there as a question mark.

CHAPTER 1

The Electoral Bases

coauthored with *Jonathan Menitove*

Even in a system of just one elected institution, it can be tricky to poise a government on an electorate. Nineteenth-century Britain is the textbook case. Beyond questions of suffrage expansion, apportioning the House of Commons geographically proved to be a continuing, often tense project. Skew was the problem.[1] According to one account, "Britain has never in modern times been closer to revolution than in the autumn of 1831"—a run-up to the Great Reform Act of 1832, which targeted the "rotten boroughs" of the House of Commons and gave parliamentary voice to the new industrial cities of the North in answer to their processions, petitions, and riots.[2] Skew arose in another major constituency overhaul in the 1880s testing whether "the varying opinion of the country was to be fairly represented in the House of

[1] Dissonance also enters the discussion if the nonelective House of Lords of the nineteenth-century is brought into the picture.
[2] Eric J. Evans, *The Great Reform Act of 1832*, second ed. (London: Routledge, Lancaster Pamphlets, 1994), on the revolutionary potential pp. 1, 54–56, quotation at p. 54; Charles Seymour, *Electoral Reform in England and Wales: The Development and Operation of the Parliamentary Franchise, 1832–1885* (Hamden, Conn.: Archon Books, 1970).

Commons."[3] A goal of that new reform was "a general correspondence between the support in [popular] votes and the representation of the two great parties."[4]

In American history, again bypassing questions of suffrage, the national government during the decades after the Civil War may offer the best case of a representational question mark. Both skew and dissonance figured in a mix highlighting the Senate.[5] Starting in the 1860s, Republicans in control of the government created a series of new states small in population and friendly to their party. Republicans in control of most of those states' legislatures (as well as others in the North) followed the party line in choosing senators.[6] A Republican edge in Senate membership came to jar against a better Democratic showing in the membership of the House and the presidential popular vote.[7] A near miracle seemed to be required for the Democrats to win the Senate.[8] Tension built up. Keynoting the Progressive era, the muckraker David Graham Phillips in his celebrated essay of 1906, "The Treason of the Senate," assailed that body as "the eager, resourceful, indefatigable agent of interests as hostile to the American people as any invading army could be, and vastly more dangerous; interests that manipulate the prosperity produced by all, so that it heaps up riches for the few."[9] This harsh language is worth reading twice.

---

[3] Seymour, *Electoral Reform*, p. 499.

[4] Peter Catterall, "The British Electoral System, 1885–1970," *Historical Research* 73: 181 (June 2000), 156–74, quotation at 160, attributed to *Report of the Royal Commission Appointed to Enquire into Electoral Systems*, 34.

[5] In this discussion, I treat the nineteenth-century Senate as an elective body.

[6] Charles Stewart III and Barry R. Weingast, "Stacking the Senate, Changing the Nation: Republican Rotten Boroughs, Statehood Politics, and American Political Development," *Studies in American Political Development* 6:2 (1992), 223–71.

[7] Ibid., 242–59.

[8] During the thirty-six years between the midterm election of 1874, which dented the Republican supremacy of the Civil War and Reconstruction era, and that of 1910, which ushered in the Democratic-centered phase of the Progressive era, the Democratic party controlled the House for sixteen years, the Senate for only four years. Four of the nine presidential elections during those thirty-six years brought Democratic edges in the national popular vote, although only two of them yielded Electoral College victories for the Democrats.

[9] David Graham Phillips, "The Treason of the Senate," *Cosmopolitan Magazine* 40, essay # 5 (March 1906), 6.

The Senate was running into legitimacy trouble. Reform came in the adoption of the Seventeenth Amendment in 1911–13 requiring direct election of senators.[10] According to one analysis, this shift to direct Senate elections erased that chamber's outlier Republican edge in the government once the electorates of the northern states proved to be less lockstep Republican in their choice of senators than their legislatures had been.[11]

That was a century ago. What is the record more recently? More specifically, how has the American mix of national elective institutions—the presidency, the Senate, and the House—connected to the nation's electorate during the decades since World War II?

To pursue this question here, I make heavy use of a particular statistic, the division of the major-party popular vote cast for president—the Bush versus Gore vote in 2000, the Nixon versus Humphrey vote in 1968, the Eisenhower versus Stevenson vote in 1952, and so on. Without much doubt, the popular vote for president is the most important formal expression of political opinion in American public life. A presidential election seems to tell where the country stands. The stakes are high, turnout and interest peak, and the voting behavior of states, regions, and demographic groups is analyzed and accorded significance. Noted are the shape of the vote (Kansas voted one way, Rhode Island the other) as well as the thrust of the vote (the Republicans had a good year). All this has been true since the 1830s. When American elections are compared with those in parliamentary systems,

[10] David E. Kyvig, *Explicit and Authentic Acts: Amending the U.S. Constitution, 1776–1995* (Lawrence: University Press of Kansas, 1996), 208–15. Congressional approval of the amendment in 1912 during the Taft administration was followed by state ratification in 1913. The Senate of the early twentieth century presented a joint problem. Its membership was both indirectly elected *and*, in a partisan sense, skewed. Democratization offered a remedy for this mix that was both practical and traditional.

[11] See Ronald F. King and Susan Ellis, "Partisan Advantage and Constitutional Change: The Case of the Seventeenth Amendment," *Studies in American Political Development* 10:1 (1996), 69–102. "The Republican party during the late nineteenth and early twentieth centuries was consistently favored under the indirect election of senators by the state legislatures. The pattern was eliminated, even reversed, after the shift to direct election in 1913" (90–92). See also King and Ellis, "Inter-Party Advantage and Intra-Party Diversity: A Response to Wirls," *Studies in American Political Development* 13:1 (1999), 31–45, at 40–44.

the presidential vote is ordinarily used. In addition, the popular vote for president seems to possess a moral authority beyond whatever may happen in the Electoral College. We often hear that Al Gore "really won" the election of 2000.

Granted, as a diagnostic of "where the country stands," the major-party vote-share statistic does pose difficulties. There are at least six. First, the measure ignores an often sizable third-party vote for president as in 1968, 1980, and 1992. Second, tens of millions of people do not vote at all in American elections. Third, there is the Electoral College. We cannot know what kinds of appeals and mobilizing drives the parties would employ in any imaginable counterfactual system—say, to cite the most obvious alternative, one of direct national voting for president. The voting patterns, as well as the parties' win-loss outcomes, might differ in an alternative system. Fourth, again regarding the Electoral College, a particular distortion arises: owing to strategies induced by that system, voter turnout tends to slump a bit in nonbattleground states relative to battleground states.[12] Fifth, a pinch of salt has to accompany summary election returns in a decentralized system like the American one where states and locales have their own customs and procedures. Exact correctness is an unwise expectation. In 2000 Florida had its hanging chads and butterfly ballot. In 1960 Illinois had a clouded count,[13] and Alabama in that same year staged a vote for individual electors, not directly for presidential candidates, in a fashion that has spurred discussion then and since about how the state's votes should have counted toward a national popular vote total that year, and indeed, in light of the Alabama complexity, whether Kennedy really did win a national vote plurality over Nixon. To award the national vote edge to Kennedy "involves a moderate amount of license," the political

[12] On this subject, see for example Ron Shachar and Barry Nalebuff, "Follow the Leader: Theory and Evidence on Political Participation," *American Economic Review* 89 (1999), 525–24; Alan S. Gerber et al., "Using Battleground States as a Natural Experiment to Test Theories of Voting," paper presented at the annual conference of the American Political Science Association, 2009.

[13] See Edmund F. Kallina, "Was the 1960 Presidential Election Stolen? The Case of Illinois," *Presidential Studies Quarterly* 15:1 (Winter 1985), 113–18.

scientist V. O. Key, Jr., concluded in 1961.[14] Sixth, to raise a different kind of point, the presidential popular vote can offer obvious idiosyncrasies associated with candidates. Reagan's landslide 59–41 win over Mondale in 1984 and Nixon's 62–38 win over McGovern in 1972 were, in this sense, distortions of where the country really stood. Also, the Kennedy vote in 1960 had a signature Roman Catholic flavor, the Carter vote in 1976 a southern flavor, the Reagan vote in 1980 a possibly southwestern flavor, and so on.

There is another possible kind of difficulty. Whether, in a normative sense, the presidential popular vote *should* be seen as indexing "where the country stands" is a separate matter. For one thing, American "policy mandates," for all the claims about them, do not seem to enjoy very sure empirical roots.[15] Also, the style of contestation in American presidential elections has aspects of both plebiscitarianism and vacuousness that have left some observers uneasy.[16] The less flashy link of legislative representation has its own kind of integrity.[17] But this is a road we do not need to go down. I am engaging here in positive analysis, not normative assessment.

Notwithstanding all its impurities, distortions, and possible dubiousness, the presidential vote is out there as an exceptionally prominent artifact. It can be used as an analytic wedge.[18]

[14] V. O. Key, Jr., "Interpreting the Election Results," in Paul T. David (ed.), *The Presidential Election and Transition 1960–61* (Washington, D.C.: Brookings, 1961), 150–75 at 150. See the testimony of Neal R. Peirce in U.S. Congress, Senate Committee on the Judiciary, Subcommittee on Constitutional Amendments, Hearings on the Nomination and Election of President and Vice President and Qualifications for Voting, 87th Cong., 1st Sess., 1961, 391–99; Neal R. Peirce, *The People's President* (New York: Simon and Schuster, 1968), 102–7; Brian J. Gaines, "Popular Myths about Popular Vote-Electoral College Splits," *PS: Political Science and Politics* 34 (March 2001), 71–75; George C. Edwards III, *Why the Electoral College Is Bad for America* (New Haven.: Yale University Press, 2004), 48–51.

[15] See Robert A. Dahl, "Myth of the Presidential Mandate," *Political Science Quarterly* 105:3 (1990), 355–72.

[16] See James Burnham, *Congress and the American Tradition* (New Brunswick, N.J.: Transaction, 2003), ch. 22; Willmoore Kendall, "The Two Majorities," *Midwest Journal of Political Science* 4:4 (1960), 317–45.

[17] See Richard F. Fenno, Jr., *Home Style: House Members in Their Districts* (Boston: Little, Brown, 1978); Kendall, "The Two Majorities."

[18] See, for example, its use in Lew Irwin, "A 'Permanent' Republican House? Patterns of Voter Performance and the Persistence of House Control," *The Forum*, Berkeley Electronic Press, http://www.bepress.com/forum, 2:1 (2004), article 4.

Conveniently, the presidential major-party vote-share statistic is available for the country at large but also in calculations for individual House districts (at least since 1952), individual Senate districts (that is, states), and the District of Columbia (starting in 1964 when voters there were enfranchised for presidential contests). For purposes here, I ask a "general correspondence" question of a special sort: How does the presidential vote-share statistic play through the universes of House districts, Senate districts, and the Electoral College as compared with its performance in the country taken as a whole? More specifically, as will be discussed, I home in on the presidential vote-share statistic in the *median* district for the House, the Senate, and the Electoral College once the units of each of these universes are ranked for any election according to that value. This analytic course is a way around many of the impurities or distortions outlined above. The nonvoters and the counterfactual electoral systems lose relevance: in question is how American opinion formally registers itself in the system that actually exists. The problem of presidential landslides recedes: in question is the *relation* between the presidential vote share in the country as a whole and the presidential vote share strained through the various systems of subunits, regardless of whether the national results were close or one-sided. The third-party problem remains, but there is no way to manage it well and it does not seem to vitiate the analysis.

An intuition lurks behind this plan. It is that the political texture of constituencies is fundamentally important. Constituencies express their tastes by, for one thing, electing officials of one party or another, and those officials once in office tend to behave as partisans, but that is not the end of the story of representation. Party still has to struggle with constituency.[19] In Congress, a Maine Republican is not likely to compile the same kind of voting record

---

[19] Works that make this case include Julius Turner, *Party and Constituency: Pressures on Congress* (Baltimore: Johns Hopkins University Press, 1951); David R. Mayhew, *Party Loyalty among Congressmen: The Difference between Democrats and Republicans, 1947–1962* (Cambridge: Harvard University Press, 1966).

as a Texas Republican. We are not surprised when Republican Senator Susan Collins of Maine disagrees with Republican Senator James Inhofe of Oklahoma. In a pattern that transcends party, politicians tend to tailor themselves to—or at least to match—their constituencies. This can be for reasons of electoral calculation, principled deference to home opinion, or, for that matter, accurate sampling of constituencies in the selection of candidates. No doubt all these factors have a role.

Enter the presidential vote-share statistic. As an *indicator* of the political texture of a constituency—the whole nation, a state, or a congressional district—it seems to be very good. At the congressional level, political scientists have increasingly used the statistic as such an indicator. It seems to capture a blend of partisanship and ideology. For any election, states and districts can be scored and ranked according to their presidential performance. For any constituency, the statistic can supply information to an outside observer trying to predict how an office-holder will behave, and it can supply information to an office-holder trying to figure out how to behave. To be sure, presidential landslides can pitch the statistic up and down, which makes for a kind of distortion in one sense yet in another sense, it is not: Even in 1984, "Reagan carried my state" could supply nontrivial political cues to, say, a senator from Massachusetts.[20]

For an exhibit of the independent illumination that can be supplied by the presidential vote-share statistic—that is, independent of the party memberships of office-holders—see figure 1.1, a scatterplot designed by Paul Frymer.[21] Plotted here are the roll-call records of House members elected in 1988 according to the share of the presidential vote won by George H. W. Bush in their

[20] For a general argument that the "honeymoon" legislative fortunes of new presidents since 1932 have corresponded on the Senate side to those presidents' just-achieved electoral performances in the individual states, see Matthew N. Beckmann and Joseph Godfrey, "The Policy Opportunities in Presidential Honeymoons," *Political Research Quarterly* 60:2 (2007), 250–62.
[21] This exhibit appears in Paul Frymer, "Ideological Consensus within Divided Party Government," *Political Science Quarterly* 109:2 (1994), 287–311, at 296.

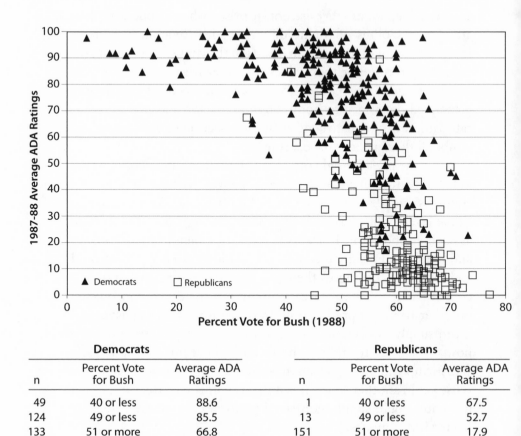

	Democrats			Republicans	
n	Percent Vote for Bush	Average ADA Ratings	n	Percent Vote for Bush	Average ADA Ratings
49	40 or less	88.6	1	40 or less	67.5
124	49 or less	85.5	13	49 or less	52.7
133	51 or more	66.8	151	51 or more	17.9
32	60 or more	56.8	134	60 or more	12.8

1.1. Bush vote in 1988 in House districts according to their members' ideologies. *Source*: Paul Frymer, "Ideological Consensus within Divided Party Government," *Political Science Quarterly* 109:2 (1994), 287–311, at 296.

districts that year. Americans for Democratic Action (ADA) scores are the roll-call measure. For the mass of incumbents who ran again in 1988 and won, the roll-call scores here are from the preceding Congress of 1987–88. For newcomers they are from the succeeding Congress of 1989–90—a second-best solution in Frymer's design. In principle, Frymer's question was: Relying on information at hand, do voters in the same district on the same day tend to select the same ideological flavor across offices?[22] Democratic members appear in figure 1.1 as filled-in triangles, Republicans as hollowed-out rectangles. A summary of the data appears below the scatterplot. The first lesson from this display is that, yes, Democrats certainly do have higher ADA scores than Republicans. But a second lesson is that the parties vary within as well as between. In general, within each party, the higher the Bush vote the lower the ADA score. These figures are for 1988. The patterns of these within-party relationships would no doubt vary in a fuller study extending across the last half century, but the relationships would always be there to some degree. On offer, it seems likely, is a performance of the presidential vote-share statistic as an independent indicator of the political texture of the constituencies.

In Congress, defections from party ranks in a direction predicted by presidential vote-share can be important. For some illustrative instances, see table 1.1, which presents roll-call summaries for one or both of the House or Senate parties in five congressional showdowns of recent decades. These votes were chosen to bear out the "can be important" claim rather than as a representative sample of congressional decisions. But confrontations of the sort included here are rare and significant. In all five cases, new presidents had just been elected in close-fought contests. In a side effect, the patterns of their election victories had helped to update everyone's information about the political texture of the country and its various subunits.[23] The new presidents had ambitious policy aims. Now they were testing them on Capitol Hill. Whether they could get what they wanted came down to one or more highly salient, vigorously contested drives for congressional votes. It is a familiar story.

In early 1961, the first instance, the drive by the Kennedy White House and the House Democratic leadership to pack the House Rules Committee with liberals, a move central to the

---

[22] See ibid., 293–301.
[23] In its longitudinal (updating) aspect, the premise of this analysis differs somewhat from Frymer's above.

Table 1.1.
Roll-Call Votes by House or Senate Parties on Selected Major Issues

		Aye	Nay	Percent aye
House, 1961—reform of Rules Committee—total chamber vote 217–212				
Democrats	district won by Kennedy	138	32	81%
	district won by Nixon	55	25	69%
	district won by Dixie Dems	3	7	30%
Republicans	district won by Kennedy	14	14	50%
	district won by Nixon	9	136	6%
Senate, 1969—Haynsworth nomination—total chamber vote 45–55				
Democrats	state won by Humphrey	2	14	13%
	state won by Nixon	7	24	23%
	state won by Wallace	10	0	100%
Republicans	state won by Humphrey	2	8	20%
	state won by Nixon	24	9	73%
House, 1981—Gramm–Latta budget cuts—total chamber vote 217–211				
Democrats	district won by Carter	9	101	8%
	district won by Reagan	20	108	19%
House, 1993—Clinton budget—total chamber vote 218–216				
Democrats	district won by Clinton	185	20	90%
	district won by Bush 41	32	21	60%
Senate, 2001—Bush tax cut—total chamber vote 62–38				
Democrats	state won by Gore	3	27	10%
	state won by Bush 43	9	11	45%

party's policy aims, sagged among Democrats from districts that Kennedy had failed to carry in 1960,[24] but it was apparently lofted

[24]In table 1.1, for purposes of scoring who won the 1960 presidential election, ten Alabama and Mississippi districts are credited to slates of conservative anti-Kennedy Democrats running for Electoral College victories. Mississippi is straightforward, but

to victory by defecting Republicans from districts that Kennedy *did* carry. A striking 50 percent of Republicans from such districts, including ex-Speaker Joseph Martin of Massachusetts, voted to pack the committee. In 1969 the Senate vote on Nixon's nomination of the conservative Clement Haynsworth to the Supreme Court was complicated, yet the presidential vote-share statistic shines through. For one thing, Haynsworth would apparently have commanded a Senate majority if the Republicans from states carried by Humphrey in 1968 had voted in his favor. In 1981 Reagan's major spending cuts bundled in the Omnibus Budget Reconciliation Act (OBRA, or Gramm-Latta II) would have foundered absent helpful defections by twenty-nine House Democrats—disproportionately from districts that Reagan had carried in 1980. In 1993 Clinton's omnibus budget package narrowly made it through the House— almost, yet not quite, a casualty of defections by Democrats from particularly districts carried by George H. W. Bush in 1992.[25]

---

scoring Alabama posed a problem. In November 1960 that state's voters could vote for up to eleven individual electors, not directly for presidential candidates. All the state's electors were elected statewide, although returns for each candidate for elector proved to be available at the district level. The Republicans ran a statewide slate of eleven Nixon electors. The Democrats ran a slate of six anti-Kennedy and five pro-Kennedy electors nominated earlier in a spiritedly contested statewide primary. Statewide, each of the anti-Kennedy Democratic candidates for elector won more popular votes in November than did any of the pro-Kennedy or Nixon candidates. (All eleven Democratic electors won victories in November statewide.) In coding for table 1.1, I scored the Alabama districts according to whether the mean vote for the Nixon electors, the mean vote for the pro-Kennedy Democratic electors, or the mean vote for the anti-Kennedy Democratic electors came out on top in a district. Following that model, Nixon carried one of the state's districts (the Birmingham district), Kennedy carried one district (the Huntsville district represented at that time by Democratic party loyalist Bob Jones), and the anti-Kennedy Democrats carried the other seven districts. This is an improvised way of proceeding, but to agree that Kennedy carried all the Alabama districts, a solution implied by the canonical judgment of the 1960 Alabama vote, would make little sense given the purposes of table 1.1. The district statistics for Alabama in 1960 appear in Peter A. Brannon (Director), State of Alabama Department of Archives and History, *Alabama Official and Statistical Register 1963* (Montgomery.: Walker Printing Co., 1963), pp. 637, 647–50, 663–70. See also regarding the nomination and election of the Democratic electors: "States Rightists Lead in Alabama," *New York Times*, May 4, 1960; "Alabama Loyalists Win by Only 6 to 5," *New York Times*, June 3, 1960 (this report was off by one); "Democrats Score Alabama Victory: Win Control of 11 Electoral Votes, but Only 5 Are Sure for Senator Kennedy," *New York Times*, November 9, 1960; "Six Electors Bar Kennedy Support," *New York Times*, December 11, 1960.

[25] Republicans voted unanimously or nearly so on OBRA in 1981 and the Clinton budget in 1993. There is not much point in exhibiting their votes.

Finally in table 1.1, the new George W. Bush administration won its choice tax cut in 2001 with Democratic help. As a practical matter, the White House calculated, an ingredient of cross-party aid was needed in the Senate.[26] Bush himself, in a transparent move to pressure Democratic senators from states he had just carried, toured Arkansas, Florida, Louisiana, Nebraska, North Dakota, and South Dakota in early 2001 merchandising the tax cut.[27] Key to the outcome was Max Baucus of Montana, ranking Democrat on the Senate Finance Committee, who helped package the final deal.[28] Bush had carried Montana by twenty-five points in 2000. "To satisfy Montana's unpredictable mix of conservatism and populism," a more recent assessment of the veteran senator goes, "Mr. Baucus must consider when to stick to the Democratic line and when to side with Republicans."[29] In the end, the tax cut in 2001 drew the support of 10 percent of the Senate Democrats from Gore states, 45 percent of those from Bush states.[30]

In the spirit of table 1.1, although the relevant defections were few, President Obama carried his $789 billion (the final figure)

[26] The measure was protected, or at least probably it was protected, against minority obstruction in the Senate since it fell under budget reconciliation rules. It did not require sixty votes to stave off a filibuster. A simple majority would apparently have been sufficient. See the account in Andrew Taylor, "Law Designed for Curbing Deficits Becomes GOP Tool for Cutting Taxes," *Congressional Quarterly Weekly* (CQW), April 7, 2001, 770–71. But the coalitional situation was somewhat cloudy. Solid Republican support was apparently not a sure bet.

[27] On the Republican strategies and actions to advance the tax cut, see Eric Schmitt, "G.O.P. Tax-Cut Ads Take on Senators from Big Bush States," *New York Times*, January 17, 2001; Frank Bruni and Alison Mitchell, "Bush Pushes Hard to Woo Democrats over to Tax Plan," *New York Times*, March 5, 2001; Shailagh Murray, David Rogers, and Jim VandeHei, "House Prepares to Pass Tax-Rate Cut, but Full Package Will See Long Debate," *Washington Post*, March 5, 2001; Mike Allen, "Senate Fight Opens in S.D.," *Washington Post*, March 9, 2001; Marc Lacey, "Bush Deploys Charm on Daschle in Pushing Tax Cut," *New York Times*, March 10, 2001; Marc Lacey, "In Heartland, Bush Savors His Victory on Tax Cut," *New York Times*, March 9, 2001.

[28] On Baucus's role, see Helen Dewar, "Baucus Deal on Tax Cut Upsets Senate Democrats," *Washington Post*, May 12, 2001; John Mercurio, "Taxing Time for Baucus: Bush Plan's Popularity in Montana Gives Democrat Headaches," *Roll Call*, May 14, 2001, 15, 22; John F. Harris and Dan Balz, "Delicate Moves Led to Tax Cut," *Washington Post*, May 27, 2001; Shailagh Murray, "Baucus Finds His New Stature Presents Him with Fresh Peril," *Washington Post*, July 2, 2001.

[29] Sarah Lueck, "Key Senate Figure Walks Fine Line," *Wall Street Journal*, April 11, 2007.
[30] The fifty Republican senators voted unanimously aye.

stimulus package in February 2009 with the critical help of Republican senators Arlen Specter of Pennsylvania (then still a Republican) and Olympia Snowe and Susan Collins of Maine.[31] These two states had voted solidly for Obama three months earlier. These senators offered a mirror image to Max Baucus on the tax cut in 2001.

What are the terms of conflict and coexistence among the presidency, the Senate, and the House? One obvious answer to that question lies in the formal statistics of party affiliation—one party may control the presidency, another may control Congress, and so forth. A scholarship exists on the subject of unified as opposed to divided party control of the government.[32] But an additional and competing consideration, I am arguing here, is the array of political textures inhering in each institution's collection of constituencies—as plausibly indexed by presidential vote-share. This consideration may even be more basic than it looks. The parties continually need to devise positions for themselves on issues, after all—those do not exist in nature—and in devising such positions they no doubt take into account the array of political textures in each of the various universes in which they need to bid for majorities.

In the study of unified versus divided party control of the government, an obvious kind of logic or arithmetic involving the party affiliations of office-holders is deployable to plumb the relations among the three institutions. The Republicans have the presidency, the Democrats have a 233-seat majority in the House,

[31] The Senate vote was 61 to 37. In this case, sixty votes were needed to preclude a filibuster. This key vote was on the Senate's $838 billion version of the plan, which ended up a $789 billion plan after a conference committee decision. David M. Herszenhorn and Jeff Zeleny, "Senate Approves Stimulus and Begins Intense Talks," *New York Times*, February 11, 2009, p. A20; Carl Hulse, "No Ordinary Republicans: Maine Senators Break with Party on Stimulus," *New York Times*, February 11, 2009, A20; David M. Herszenhorn and Carl Hulse, "House and Senate in Deal For $789 Billion Stimulus," *New York Times*, February 12, 2009, A1.

[32] See, for example, Morris P. Fiorina, *Divided Government* (New York: Longman Classics, 2002); David R. Mayhew, *Divided We Govern: Party Control, Lawmaking, and Investigations, 1946–2002* (New Haven: Yale University Press, 2005); Sarah A. Binder, *Stalemate: Causes and Consequences of Legislative Gridlock* (Washington, D.C.: Brookings Institution Press, 2003).

and so on. In an alternative approach emphasizing the political textures of arrays of constituencies, it seems to make sense to dwell on *medians*. The national presidential vote-share taken by itself is not a median, but it can plausibly be compared with the median expression of itself in any districted universe where victory requires a majority. Here, that means the Electoral College, the Senate, and the House. In the House, for example, the presidential vote-share in the 218th of the chamber's 435 districts, once those districts are ranked according to presidential vote-share, becomes an important marker. In the House, it takes 218 votes to win. That is a basic fact. Here is the pitch of this argument: to the degree that the three districted universes, as indexed by their median presidential vote-shares, are *microcosms* of the national electorate, as indexed by the national presidential vote-share taken by itself, the overall system is centripetalized, so to speak. In a limiting case, perfect microcosms would mean zero difference between any of the medians and the national vote-share taken alone. In that scenario, the various parties, coalitions, interests, and politicians would need to reckon with identical winning-location political textures thus envisioned as they go about their business of governing, and we could expect minimal friction, all else equal, among the institutions. To be sure, the idea of microcosm used here could hinge in principle on alternative indicators, but in terms of the operation of the political system the presidential vote-share indicator seems like a good one.

What would *non*microcosmic representation look like? As discussed earlier, Britain before the Reform Act of 1832 is a classic instance. Leaving aside suffrage restrictions, British opinion (imagine it as a notional equivalent of the U.S. presidential vote-share) was not being mirrored very well in the median constituency of the House of Commons during that era of south-coast rotten boroughs. The late-nineteenth-century U.S. Senate offers a likely instance.

Also, the American states before the redistricting revolution of the 1960s offer a wealth of instances. It may help to take a look at certain of those prereform states. The extreme among them can place the contemporary U.S. national system in relief. Rhode Island and Connecticut qualify as good examples. In the conventional wisdom of American politics, those two New England states in their prereform days stand out for their skewed representation. Small towns had a leg up. In both cases, traditional plans of representation gave grandly disproportionate power to small towns in one legislative chamber (in Rhode Island, the state senate; in Connecticut, the state assembly), often making for tense political relations between that chamber, on the one hand, and the governorship and the other chamber on the other.[33]

In those states, the election of 1934 in Rhode Island offers a peak instance, and that of 1954 in Connecticut a good instance, of the kinds of split institutional results that the old systems could yield. I analyze the two elections here in a fashion tailored to match a median-driven analysis of the national system. The question at the state level becomes: How does the major-party vote-share for governor, rather than for president as in the national case, play through a state's universes of assembly and senate elections? (Neither state had anything like an electoral college for choosing governors.)

The results appear in table 1.2. As the New Deal impulse surged in Rhode Island in 1934, Democratic Governor Theodore Francis Green won reelection with a triumphant 57.2 percent of the vote and scored a vote-share of 55.1 percent in the median assembly district (with those districts arrayed according to Green's vote-share), but of only 47.9 percent in the median senate district.[34] At the outer bounds, that amounts to a difference of 9.3 percent—a kind of structural dissonance score for the system.

[33] See Duane Lockard, *New England State Politics* (Princeton: Princeton University Press, 1959), 178–80, 190–96, on Rhode Island; 228–29, 271–75, on Connecticut. The pronounced Republican tilt of the Connecticut lower chamber of those times has been discussed recently in Stephen Ansolabehere and James M. Snyder, Jr., *The End of Inequality: One Person, One Vote and the Transformation of American Politics* (New York: W. W. Norton, 2008), 249–50.

[34] The calculations here were straightforward with one qualification. Vote-share for governor was not available for any of the four senate districts located within the city of Providence. Each of them was awarded here the citywide value for Providence. This seems a plausible judgment. The city was quite Democratic.

TABLE 1.2.
Democratic Major-Party Vote-Share for Governor in Two
State Elections (in percent)

	Rhode Island 1934	Connecticut 1954
Statewide	57.2	50.2
In median assembly district	55.1	43.2
In median state senate district	47.9	50.9
Maximum disparity	9.3	7.7

Source: State of Rhode Island and Providence Plantations, *Official Count of the Ballots Cast, 1934* (Providence: E. L. Freeman, 1934), pp. 11–46.

The Rhode Island Republicans, in that historically dismal year for their party, still managed to keep control of the state's senate. Yet that was not to last. In January 1935 the Democrats seized the upper chamber in what amounted to a coup. They called in state troopers to corral a few Republicans toward a chamber quorum, rigged a recount of two senate district contests to their advantage, and, in a decision-laden fourteen minutes, packed the state supreme court with friendly new judges and collapsed more than eighty state agencies into eleven departments accommodating to Democratic programs and job-seekers. The state's long Republican era was over.[35]

The Connecticut election of 1954 brought a comparable dissonance score of 7.7 percent. Democrat Abraham Ribicoff won the state's governorship with 50.2 percent and scored a vote-share of 50.9 percent in the median senate district, but of only 43.2 percent in the median assembly district.[36] The assembly

[35] See Lockard, *New England State Politics*, 190–92; V. O. Key, Jr., *American State Politics: An Introduction* (New York: Knopf, 1956), 63; "Democrats Seize Legislature Rule in Rhode Island," *New York Times*, January 2, 1935; "Democratic Coup Aids Rhode Island," *New York Times*, January 13, 1935.
[36] These calculations were straightforward with two qualifications. Most of the assembly districts elected two members at large; the rest elected one member. For purposes of

stayed overwhelmingly Republican. There was no sign of a coup in Connecticut. The state muddled through. Yet across the years, it was speculated, unbroken Republican control of the Connecticut assembly from 1876 into the 1950s had warded off enactment of a state income tax.[37]

These old New England scores of 9.3 percent and 7.7 percent are extreme. They fall somewhere near the outer limit of what one would expect to find in an analysis of the full range of American separation-of-powers universes. They can be kept in mind as yardstick limiting-cases in an analysis of the national system.

Dissonant representation, let it be remembered, is a live possibility in the American national system, offering as it does the Electoral College, a universe of House districts subject to gerrymandering, and a two-members-per-state Senate whose largest unit, California, had sixty-nine times the population of its smallest unit, Wyoming, as of the 2000 census. The Supreme Court's one-person-one-vote standard has never applied to the Senate. In a recent survey of legislatures around the world, the U.S. Senate came out as more malapportioned than *any* of seventy-eight lower chambers, and the fifth most malapportioned of twenty-five upper chambers.[38]

Next is my national-level analysis. It features four time-series beginning after World War II. The first is simply the share—here the Democratic share—of the major-party popular vote cast for president nationwide in each election through 2008. The second is the median value of that presidential vote-share in the Electoral

---

pinpointing a district with the median gubernatorial vote-share, the two-member districts were counted twice side by side, the single-member districts once, in a ranking of all the districts. Also, the gubernatorial vote-share statistic was not available for any of twelve senate districts located within the state's big cities. The party vote-share for state senate was used as a proxy in these districts. This is a sensible move. Party-line voting was very tight among Connecticut voters in those days. In addition, it is easy to see that these cities were Democratic territory on that party's side of the state balance. Source: State of Connecticut, *Register and Manual, 1955* (Hartford: Published by the State, 1955), 439–41, 451–59, 476–83, 502–9.

[37] Key, *American State Politics*, 66–67, 78.

[38] David Samuels and Richard Snyder, "The Value of a Vote: Malapportionment in Comparative Perspective," *British Journal of Political Science* 31 (2001), 651–71, at 660–62.

College's system of, so to speak, districts. That is, if the states, plus beginning in 1964 the District of Columbia, are weighted according to their Electoral College votes and laid end to end according to presidential vote-share, what is the vote-share value in the unit that turns out to be pivotal—that is, to contain the median elector—in the Electoral College vote? What is the vote-share of the tipping unit? In 2004, for example, the answer was 48.9 percent for Kerry in Ohio. In 2000 it was 49.995 percent for Gore in the final Florida count. The third time-series tracks the value of the Democratic presidential vote-share in the median House district.[39] The fourth series tracks that value in the median Senate district—that is, state.[40] For reasons of data availability, the values for the House districts start with the 1952 election. All the other values start with the 1948 election.[41]

An array of numbers follows in table 1.3. Figure 1.2 presents the same data in graph form. Mean values for the columns in table 1.3—means of the medians in the cases of the last three columns—appear at the bottom. Look first at the first two columns of percentages, which compare the popular vote with the electoral vote. Across the sixteen elections, accepting the measurement technique, has the Electoral College shown an overall partisan bias of any sort? The answer is no. On average, the bias is zero—or as close to zero as one can practically get. Starting in 1948, the mean Democratic share of the popular vote for president

---

[39] Many thanks to Gary Jacobson for making available a dataset of presidential returns by House district for 1952 through 2004. It was gathered from diverse published sources. For purposes of this project, I checked the dataset item-by-item for possible mistakes and found some, although the dataset in the form received is basically sound. The proposed corrections are available through http://press.princeton.edu/titles/9432.html. The returns for 2008 are from *Congressional Quarterly*.

[40] At each presidential election time since World War II, the number of states has been even. Today, the median value for the states on any dimension is taken to be the mean of the values for the twenty-fifth and twenty-sixth states. For the elections before 1960, when Alaska and Hawaii voted for the first time, the states numbered forty-eight, and the median values here hinge on the twenty-fourth and twenty-fifth states.

[41] In all the calculations here for 1960, following well-ingrained if questionable custom, all the popular vote for Alabama's Democratic electors is credited to Kennedy, regardless of whether those electors had pledged to vote for Kennedy (five of them) or ran unpledged and eventually voted against him (six of them).

TABLE 1.3.
Democratic Share of Major-Party Presidential Vote (in Percent)

			Median share of vote in electoral units		
Year	Winner	Nationwide	Electoral College units	House districts	Senate districts (states)
1948	Truman	52.3	50.5	–	52.2
1952	Eisenhower	44.5	44.2	44.0	44.1
1956	Eisenhower	42.2	42.6	42.1	41.8
1960	Kennedy	50.1	50.4	49.3	49.4
1964	Johnson	61.3	62.4	61.2	60.3
1968	Nixon	49.6	48.7	48.2	47.4
1972	Nixon	38.2	38.7	36.3	36.7
1976	Carter	51.1	50.9	50.1	49.5
1980	Reagan	44.7	45.7	44.6	44.4
1984	Reagan	40.8	40.5	39.4	39.0
1988	Bush 41	46.1	46.0	44.7	44.2
1992	Clinton	53.5	52.8	52.3	52.2
1996	Clinton	54.7	55.2	53.6	53.6
2000	Bush 43	50.3	49.995	49.0	48.1
2004	Bush 43	48.8	48.9	46.3	46.9
2008	Obama	53.7	54.7	52.3	51.9
Mean including 1948		48.9	48.9	–	47.6
Mean without 1948		48.6	48.8	47.6	47.3

has been 48.9 percent, and the mean of the medians of that vote-share in the distributions of Electoral College units has been 48.9 percent also.[42] Eight times, including in 2004 and 2008, the Democrats have scored a shade better in the Electoral College median than in the popular vote; eight times, including in 2000,

[42] Another recent assessment came up short in a search for significant statistical bias in the Electoral College since World War II. See Bernard Grofman, Thomas Brunell, and Janet Campagna, "Distinguishing between the Effects of Swing Ratio and Bias on Outcomes in the US Electoral College, 1900–1992," *Electoral Studies* 16:4 (1997), 471–87, at 473, 478–79, 484.

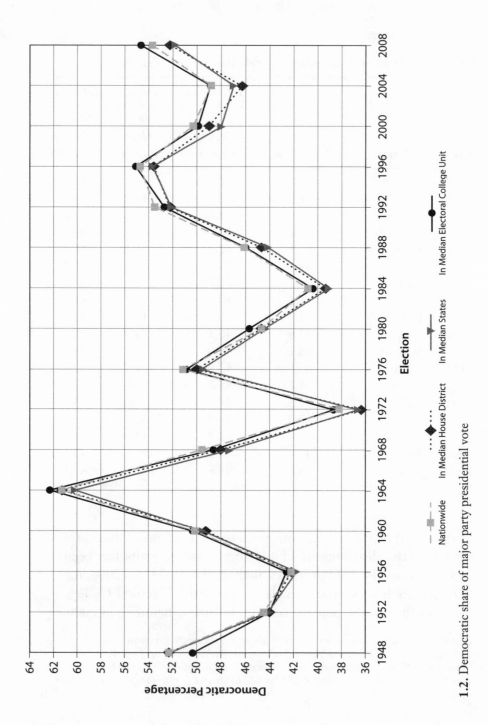

1.2. Democratic share of major party presidential vote

the Republicans have done that.[43] In absolute terms—that is, ignoring plus and minus signs—the mean difference between the two vote-share values across the sixteen elections has been 0.6 percent. In temporal terms, no sign of trend appears in either the size or the directionality of the differences.

To be sure, this overall correspondence has not warded off question marks or incongruities in extremely close elections. It is unwise to pursue this matter very far into decimal points in a search for sure ground. Local customs and procedures for counting votes, behavioral gaps between battleground and nonbattleground states, and other factors can cause too much ambiguity or counterfactual clutter. Yet there have been two anomalous instances. In 1960 Kennedy won a clean Electoral College median, but his national popular-vote edge, given the unsolvable difficulty in counting Alabama's popular vote, was clouded. Perhaps Kennedy should be credited with a national vote edge that year; perhaps Nixon should. Possibly Kennedy enjoyed a slight advantage in the Electoral College due to fortuitous distributions of Catholics and Protestants in the states.[44] In 2000 the Bush–Gore election brought its well-known divergence of popular and Electoral College outcomes. Yet generally speaking, Florida's electoral processes rather than the Electoral College have taken the blame for that dissonance. For one thing, to put it simply: no "butterfly ballot" in Palm Beach

[43] On the 2000 tilt versus the 2004 tilt, see Ron Johnston, David Rossiter, and Charles Pattie, "Disproportionality and Bias in US Presidential Elections: How Geography Helped Bush Defeat Gore but Couldn't Help Kerry Beat Bush," *Political Geography* 24 (2005), 952–68. There were slight biases in both cases. "In 2000, that bias favoured George W. Bush—and because of it he won in the Electoral College despite getting fewer popular votes than his opponent, Al Gore. Four years later, the bias operated against Bush and favoured his opponent, but not sufficiently to deliver victory to John Kerry" (967).

[44] In effect, religious balances could have helped generate a small popular-vote edge for Kennedy in a state like New Jersey but a large edge for Nixon in a state like Oklahoma. See the discussion in Ithiel de Sola Pool, Robert P. Abelson, and Samuel Popkin, *Candidates, Issues and Strategies: A Computer Simulation of the 1960 and 1964 Presidential Elections* (Cambridge: M.I.T. Press, 1965), 117–18. For other discussions of the considerable crosscutting effects of religion in the 1960 election, although these sources do not take up the question of the Electoral College, see Key, "Interpreting the Election Results"; Philip E. Converse et al., "Stability and Change in 1960: A Reinstating Election," *American Political Science Review* 55:2 (1961), 269–80.

County, no dissonance. Absent just that anomaly, Gore would almost certainly have won Florida and the election.[45]

Occasionally, academics and journalists express concern about the Electoral College. Perhaps for good reason. It has other difficulties. But given the college's overall lack of partisan bias during recent generations, we should not be surprised that criticisms of the institution have enjoyed scant resonance among political operatives or the general public. Of course, that quiescence is subject to change. In particular, notwithstanding the summary arithmetic, a new instance favoring the Republicans framed by the memory of 2000 might bring on a strong movement targeting the Electoral College. Currently, that memory may be at the back of a move on the reform Left to have the states precommit their electoral votes to whichever presidential candidate wins a national plurality of the popular vote.[46] But this impulse seems faint, and it is not clear that Democratic party operatives aware of the electoral geography of 2004 and 2008 will want to buy in.

How about the House and Senate? For those institutions, table 1.4 offers a reorganization of the data that is perhaps easier to read. For each election, the Democratic share of the national presidential popular vote *minus* that value's instantiation in the median House, or median Senate, district is supplied in the last two columns, respectively. Two patterns jump out. First, for both institutions across the sixteen (or, in the case of the House, fifteen) elections, the values in both columns are all at least slightly positive. That is, all thirty-one of the House and Senate medians have bent to the Republican side of the national popular vote-share.

Second, the values in the two congressional columns are small. On average they are just over 1 percent. That is, on average the Democratic share of the presidential popular vote has exceeded its instantiation in the median House or Senate district by just over

[45] See Henry E. Brady et al., "'Law and Data': The Butterfly Ballot Episode," *PS: Political Science and Politics* 34 (2001), 59–69.

[46] See John R. Koza et al., *Every Vote Equal: A State-Based Plan for Electing the President by National Popular Vote* (Los Altos, Calif.: Popular Vote Press, 2006); Akhil Reed Amar and Vikram David Amar, "How to Achieve Direct National Election of the President without Amending the Constitution: Part Three of a Series on the 2000 Election and the Electoral College," FindLaw, http://writ.news.findlaw,com/amar/20011228.html.

TABLE 1.4.
Democratic Share of Major-Party Popular Vote Minus Its Median in
House and Senate Districts (in percent)

Year	Winner	National popular vote-share	House districts	Senate districts (states)
1948	Truman	52.3	–	0.1
1952	Eisenhower	44.5	0.5	0.4
1956	Eisenhower	42.2	0.1	0.4
1960	Kennedy	50.1	0.8	0.7
1964	Johnson	61.3	0.1	1.0
1968	Nixon	49.6	1.4	2.2
1972	Nixon	38.2	1.9	1.5
1976	Carter	51.1	1.0	1.6
1980	Reagan	44.7	0.1	0.3
1984	Reagan	40.8	1.4	1.8
1988	Bush 41	46.1	1.4	1.9
1992	Clinton	53.5	1.2	1.3
1996	Clinton	54.7	1.1	1.1
2000	Bush 43	50.3	1.3	2.2
2004	Bush 43	48.8	2.5	1.9
2008	Obama	53.7	1.4	1.8
Mean including 1948		48.9	–	1.3
Mean without 1948		48.6	1.1	1.3

1 percent. How to evaluate these disparities is a matter of judgment. On the one hand, an average difference of zero, as in the
Electoral College match, is available as a standard. On the other
hand, prereform Rhode Island and Connecticut offer real-world
outlier dissonance standards of 9.3 percent and 7.7 percent. By
comparison with outliers like those, the national system has approached zero.

In the case of the House, the unbroken differentiation in a Republican direction shown here may cause surprise.[47] What has

[47] For an additional take on the Republican bias in House elections, see David A. Hopkins,
"Whatever Happened to Moderate Republicans? Party Asymmetry in the U.S. Congress,

been going on? The District of Columbia offers little help (either here or regarding the Senate). Voting for president but not for Congress in the heavily Democratic district has accounted for less than a tenth of the mean 1.1 percent House Republican tilt in table 1.4. Is Republican gerrymandering a cause? It is interesting that the House value for the 2004 election—2.5 percent off the presidential popular vote—exceeds any other value for the House or Senate in table 1.4. Perhaps that party's unusually deft gerry-mandering of House districts in Florida, Michigan, Ohio, and Pennsylvania after the 2000 census, capped by Texas after the 2002 midterm, raised the 2004 value here a bit. Yet the value for the 2008 Obama election conducted in the same set of districts does not stand out. In general, Republican gerrymandering is an un-promising explanation for the post–World II era taken as a whole. On balance, it seems a good bet that Democrats have drawn self-serving maps at least as often and as effectively as Republicans.[48]

The more general consideration seems to be that Democratic voters have tended toward geographic concentration. At the level of congressional districts, landslide vote-shares for presidential candidates have routinely turned up in greater quantity on the Democratic side than on the Republican side. See figure 1.3 for three more or less typical examples of that skew in presidential elections spaced since World War II—1952, 1976, and 2000. The outsized Democratic vote-shares appear in the tails to the right. Major contributors to these tails have included southern rural districts in the days of the solid Democratic South, majority-minority districts recently, big-city districts in general, and New York City districts in particular. New York City has always been a

---

1972–2008," paper presented at the annual conference of the American Political Science Association, 2009.

[48] Generally speaking, the Democrats have enjoyed an edge in the control of state govern-ments during the postcensus redistricting phases of the last half century. See Bill Pascoe, "Why Republicans Should Get on the Redistricting Reform Bandwagon," http://www.centerforpolitics.org/crystalball, January 14, 2010. Yet the particular outlier value for 2004 evident in table 1.4 is consistent with a result regarding the influence of post-2000 Republican gerrymandering presented in Nolan McCarty, Keith T. Poole, and Howard Rosenthal, "Does Gerrymandering Cause Polarization?" *American Journal of Political Science* 53:3 (July 2009), 666–80, at 678.

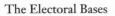

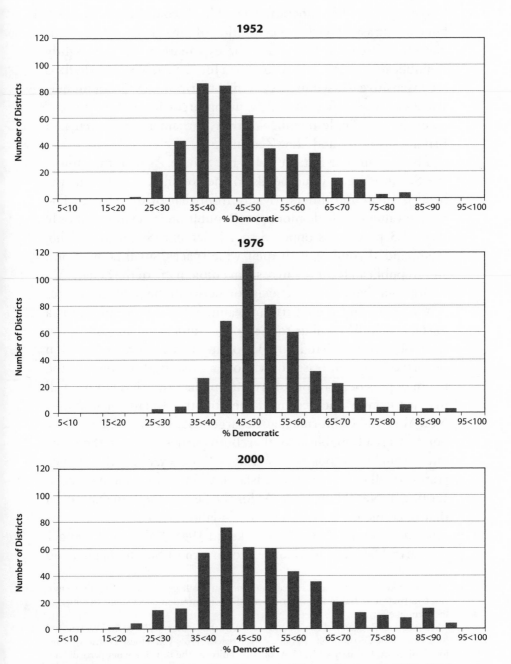

1.3. Democratic share of presidential vote in House districts in 1952, 1976, and 2000

heavy supplier of Democratic skew. This is complicated terrain,[49] but chronic asymmetric concentration of the parties' voters seems like the source—if not exactly the explanation—of the slightly Republican-leaning values for the House in table 1.4. Medians are insensitive to asymmetries. This American skew is not unique. Parties of the Left centered in urban areas have also "wasted" votes in the single-member-district parliamentary systems of Britain, Australia, and New Zealand.[50]

The big surprise in table 1.4 is the Senate. As with the House, the Senate's mean value bends to the Republican side, but the bend is small and differs trivially from that of the House. The Senate value is a shade more pro-Republican in texture, but only that—1.3 percent as opposed to 1.1 percent. States like Idaho, Utah, and Wyoming, with their wide spaces, small populations, and Republican leanings, may seem emblematic of the Senate. Yet it turns out that any easy association between the population sizes of the states and their partisan leanings for the presidency is a mistake. The Wyoming to California dimension in population size does not translate into a Wyoming to California dimension in partisanship—at least not without a great deal of noise. In the realm of presidential vote-share, the median state has not been all that far from a microcosm of the country. Today, for example, New York and California may be large-state Democratic outliers, but Texas is a Republican outlier. Both parties have had their rotten boroughs. In today's New England, for example, the Democrats do well in Maine, Rhode Island, and Vermont and have been surging in New Hampshire. As for the Senate itself, an institution that once included Glen Taylor of Idaho (Henry Wallace's running mate on the Progressive ticket in 1948), "Will Bill" Langer of North Dakota, and George McGovern of South Dakota, and

---

[49] One reason it is complicated is that voter turnout has flagged in these heavily Democratic districts, too. But in the patterns here, the concentration effect seems to outweigh the turnout effect.

[50] See Jonathan Rodden and Chris Warshaw, "Why the Democrats Need Boll Weevils and Blue Dogs: The Distribution of Political Preferences across U.S. House Districts," Stanford University, February 2009, 13. As of 2010, however, the British Labour party did not seem to be suffering any such penalty.

now includes Patrick Leahy and Bernard Sanders of Vermont, it is no mystery what a vest-pocket Left would look like in that chamber.

The cross-institutional pattern shown here is one framework against which American government is conducted. Broadly speaking, it seems like a pattern of commonality. The term "general correspondence" seems apt. This commonality is probably one of the more basic and important features of American political life. Yet dissonances and skews appear here too. The perpetual, if slight, Republican tilts of the House and Senate medians may have policy significance. Both the commonality and the dissonances will be taken up in the succeeding chapters on policymaking.

There is a last point about commonality. It addresses a particular implication of table 1.4. Disregard, for a moment, the presidency. If the House and Senate values in the table are nearly identical, should not the parties' records of electoral success in those institutions be nearly identical also? Should not there be a sameness across the chambers? A specific factual question is: How often have Congress's biennial elections ended in House and Senate seat majorities for the same, as opposed to different, parties? Note that this question implicates the whole postelection memberships of the chambers—not only, in the Senate case, the classes of thirty-three or so senators just elected. In fact, although the matter will not be pursued here, the Senate's classes at immediate electoral risk have played a major role in balancing the parties' membership shares across the *whole* chambers. As in 2006, high party turnover in one Senate class can nudge the partisan arithmetic of the whole Senate in consonance with that of the House.

As posed here, the question about sameness of outcome is a simple binary one. The best answer, starting in 1914, when direct election of senators began, seems to be forty-five instances of sameness out of forty-eight outcomes—the exceptions being three consecutive disparate outcomes during the Reagan era. Judgment calls about coding were needed here. On the House side, strictly speaking, the Democrats won a plurality of seats in the 1916 election, not a majority. Following convention, let that plurality count as a majority. On the Senate side, one party or the other has occasionally needed an acquiescent independent member or a tie-breaking vice president to form a majority, as in 2000–2001. Let such instances count as majority-party victories. The outcome of the midterm of 1930 is often scored as dissonant, with the Democrats capturing the House but not the Senate that year, yet on close inspection that interpretation turns out to be incorrect. It is true that the Democrats succeeded in organizing the post-1930 House (although not the Senate) once the resulting new Congress met for the first time thirteen months later in December 1931. Yet it required member deaths followed by special House elections favorable to the Democrats in late 1931, a Depression-wracked time under Hoover, to make that organization possible.[51] As of late 1930, the new Senate and House rosters following that year's election stood as 48 Republicans, 47 Democrats, and one Farmer-Laborite from Minnesota in the Senate; and 218 Republicans, 216 Democrats, and one Farmer-Laborite from Minnesota in the House.[52] A closer correspondence is scarcely imaginable.

If the immediate results of biennial elections, rather than what might have happened between them, are taken as determinative,[53] the House of Representatives—designed in 1787 to be the popular body—has shifted party control eight times since 1912. Those

[51] "Control of House Hangs on One Vote: Should One Republican District in 5 Pollings Tuesday Be Upset, Democrats Will Lead," *New York Times*, November 1, 1931; "Republicans Lose Seat: Upset in Michigan District Gives Foes a Congress Lead," *New York Times*, November 4, 1931; "Democratic Trend Next Year Is Seen in Election Results; Switching of House Control Causes Some Republicans to Welcome the Outcome; Responsibility Is Shifted," *New York Times*, November 5, 1931; "Kleberg, Democrat, Wins Texas House Seat; Succeeds Wurzbach, Former Lone Republican," *New York Times*, November 25, 1931; "Democratic Majority of Three in the House Now Is Assured," *New York Times*, December 2, 1931.

[52] "House Seesaw Continues: Shifts in Illinois and Indiana Give 218 Seats to the Republicans," *New York Times*, November 8, 1930; "Revised Results in Detail of the Election of 1930," *New York Times*, November 9, 1930.

[53] This coding steers around the postelection developments of 1931 in the House's coalitional arithmetic, as well as the Senate's switch in majorities in mid-2001 when the pivotal James Jeffords, Jr., of Vermont defected from organizing with the Republicans to organize with the Democrats.

shifts came in 1918, 1932, 1946, 1948, 1952, 1954, 1994, and 2006. Each time the Senate simultaneously shifted control in the same direction also. To be sure, the perfection of this Senate matching pattern can be destroyed by one future event, but the trend is striking. The 1980s marred the tradition of commonality in a different way. While the House stayed Democratic, the Senate switched twice by itself, to the Republicans in 1980 and back to the Democrats in 1986, yielding three Congresses divided by party in between.[54] The House may sometimes be volatile, as was envisioned in 1787, but shock Senate sweeps are a part of history also. Distortions, so to speak, in Senate seat balances and probably also in policymaking can result. Such distortions may occur even without switches in party control—as in the still unrivaled addition of fifteen Democratic seats to an already Democratic Senate in the midterm of 1958 under Eisenhower.[55]

The Republican Senates of the 1980s tilted that chamber's post-1912 score sheet, compared with that of the House, three victories to the Republican side. Yet that tilt was apparently partnered, or more accurately nonpartnered, during the surrounding era in a strange notional way. On the House side, a historic surge during the 1960s in incumbency electoral advantage accruing to individual members seems to have aided the Democratic party that controlled that chamber then with a large majority. The bulk of the incumbent members who gained were Democrats— profiting from the newly augmented advantage, whatever the causes of that augmentation exactly were. In the face of this context, serious Republican challenges for House seats came to sag. The wind went out of Republican national campaigns for the

[54] On the electoral arithmetic of those years, see Bruce I. Oppenheimer, "Split Party Control of Congress, 1981–86: Exploring Electoral and Apportionment Explanations," *American Journal of Political Science* 33:3 (1989), 653–69.
[55] As compared with 1956, the Democrats' seat edge in the Senate surged from 49–47 to 64–34. One of those gains came in 1957 when Democrat William Proxmire succeeded the deceased Republican Joseph McCarthy in a special election in Wisconsin. Two more Democratic gains came from the admission of Alaska. Yet even without Alaska, the seat swing to the Democrats between 1956 and 1958, a year of economic recession, stands out as the largest in Senate history since the Civil War. The Republicans in the Reagan election of 1980 gained twelve Senate seats.

House. In the end, the Democrats managed to keep control of the chamber for a record forty years until 1994.

It is plain that a Democratic edge in party identification among voters helped keep the party on top in the House during those decades. Yet suppose that the House's seats–votes translation ratio—a standard tool in the study of legislative elections—had kept functioning as usual. That is, suppose that party shifts in the share of the House national popular *vote* between biennial elections had kept translating into party shifts in the share of House *seats* between elections—say, between 1964 and 1966—according to the formula that had obtained before the 1960s. In that event, it has been estimated, the Republicans would have won control of the House in at least 1966 (a time of the Vietnam War and city disorders), 1968 (more of the same), and 1984 (the year of Reagan's "Morning in America" reelection).[56] Incumbency advantage in the new era seems to have muffled the seat shifts—benefiting the Democrats in years like these three when the Republicans were generally soaring. On the House side of Capitol Hill, there would have been three takeover victories for the Republicans matching their wins of 1980, 1982, and 1984 on the Senate side. In this counterfactual scenario, the parties' overall victory scores for House and Senate control from 1914 through 2008 would have been identical.

In this chapter, I have dwelt on the similarity among the House, Senate, and presidency in their electoral bases. What can explain this similarity? All in all, given the variety in the sizes and other characteristics of the states, it seems almost eerie. I do not have clear answers, but I offer two observations.

The first involves the geography of the states—a key factor in the Senate and the Electoral College. Where did the states come from, and so what? In fact, neither in its design nor in its effects has the historical coining of the American states amounted to a gigantic gerrymander favoring one side. Yes, the moves by the

[56]And possibly in 1980 and 1990. See Stephen Ansolabehere, David Brady, and Morris Fiorina, "The Vanishing Marginals and Electoral Responsiveness," *British Journal of Political Science* 22:1 (1992), 21–38, at 33.

late-nineteenth-century Republicans had that aspect, but they need to be placed in perspective. For one thing, much of the statehood map still owes to pre–Civil War balancing across the regions. Also, admission of states under divided or Democratic control of the government—not just Republican control—has played a role. Many other considerations have figured in admission politics. Constraints on chicanery have not been lacking. Generally speaking, the map of the states west of the Mississippi resembles a stately march of rectangles to the Pacific Coast if it is compared with, say, the Georgia congressional map of today, which brings to mind a basket of eels.

On the effects side, to admit states with partisan intent has approached—at least in the middle or long run—writing in the sand. Since the Republicans arose to rival the Democrats in the mid-1850s, nineteen states have joined the Union. Let us see how each one voted in its first fifteen presidential elections after being admitted (thirteen in the cases of Alaska and Hawaii). Let admission mean the official passage of a congressional enabling act. Arizona, New Mexico, Alaska, and Hawaii came in under generic circumstances of divided party control, and their summary record afterward is an even-up twenty-eight verdicts for Democratic presidential candidates, twenty-eight for Republicans. This is a nice result. Ten states came in under unified party control (three Democratic, seven Republican), and another five in circumstances of one-sided Republican influence. Those five are Kansas, which entered in early 1861 thanks to the Republicans when the Democrats still sharing formal power gave up as civil war loomed and their southerners decamped; and Montana, Washington, and both Dakotas, which entered in early 1889 under formally divided control, but the Republicans victorious in the election of 1888 had the upper bargaining hand in a lame-duck session where the Democrats faced exile from all three elective branches.[57]

[57] To summarize, since the mid-1850s four states have entered in unasterisked circumstances of divided party control: Arizona, New Mexico, Alaska, and Hawaii. Three have entered under formal Democratic control of all three branches: Minnesota, Oregon, and Utah. Seven have entered under formal Republican control: West Virginia, Nevada,

The Democrats struck the best deal they could. Joining the ten and the five cases of party domination, in how many of these fifteen instances did the party dominant at admission carry a state in a majority of that state's succeeding fifteen presidential elections? The answer is eight instances out of fifteen—no better than a coin flip.[58] Of the 225 postadmission voter verdicts—that is, multiply the fifteen states times their fifteen performances in elections— just 106, or 47 percent, brought victory for the party that had dominated the admission.[59]

There is an awful lot of slack here. Things happen. History rises up and bites—as the Civil War bit the Democrats who had admitted Minnesota and Oregon, or the Populist movement bit the Republicans who had admitted plains and mountain states. Issues change. Party coalitions change. Party fortunes wax and wane. Americans move around. A century ago, who would have envisioned a Vermont loaded with Democrats? Flux and contingency are bad news for any theory of overall design.

My closing observation is that the two major parties have no doubt adapted themselves to the U.S. constitutional system in waging elections and governing. At that task, they have had a century and a half of practice. They have needed to craft coalitions and issue portfolios that maximize their policymaking influence in an existing system. That has meant paying some heed to the Senate and the House, not just to the presidency, even if the presidency ranks first. In Darwinian terms, adaptation has meant attunement to a constellation of niches, not just one niche. On demand has been a certain heterogeneity of appeal and reach. In the Senate, the Republicans have needed their Borahs, the Democrats

Nebraska, Colorado, Idaho, Wyoming, and Oklahoma. Five have entered under formally divided control but the Republicans had the clear upper hand: Kansas in 1861, and North Dakota, South Dakota, Montana, and Washington in 1889. In the 1889 lame-duck deal, Montana was thought to lean Democratic, the other three admittees to lean Republican.
[58] The eight: Kansas, West Virginia, Nevada, Nebraska, Colorado, North Dakota, South Dakota, Wyoming. The seven: Minnesota, Oregon, Montana, Washington, Idaho, Utah, Oklahoma.
[59] Without Montana, the record is 8 instances out of 14, and 100 instances out of 210, or 48 percent.

their Borens.[60] There is no way around it. There is a companion implication. A party's route to the presidency is through the Electoral College, where the states have weight. As a result, to devise ideological or issue appeals to a presidential constituency may be to appeal, as a side effect, to the Senate's added-up all-states-are-equal base a bit more than would be the case if presidential elections were directly popular. Operating this way may be baked into party custom. More than they might otherwise be, the Senate and the White House are part of the same cake.

[60] William Borah of Idaho was a classic Republican renegade of the Progressive Left during the 1910s through the 1930s. David Boren of Oklahoma gave President Clinton trouble from the conservative side in the 1990s.

CHAPTER 2

President and Congress

Presidents ask Congress to enact laws. That is not the only spur
to lawmaking. Congress can supply the energy and initiative
itself—as seen in a line of enactments from the Bill of Rights in
1789 and the Missouri Compromise in 1820 through the Taft–
Hartley Act of 1947, the Clean Air Act of 1970, and the McCain–
Feingold campaign finance reform of 2001.[1] Congress has carried
its own major tax plans against White House reluctance or opposition in, for example, 1938, 1948, 1969, and 1978.

Yet presidents are major requesters. This is not a new development. George Washington, or more precisely his secretary of the
treasury, Alexander Hamilton, asked for debt and banking measures. Abraham Lincoln pressed for the Thirteenth Amendment
abolishing slavery, Grover Cleveland for tariff reform. Although
spotty in the nineteenth century, this White House role surged
toward routinization in the early twentieth century and reached
that status in the 1940s.[2] Congress and the public have come to

---

[1] On this subject, see, for example, Mayhew, *Divided We Govern*, 35, 81–91, 102–12.
[2] See Richard E. Neustadt, "Presidency and Legislation: Planning the President's Program," *American Political Science Review* 49 (1955), 980–1021.

rely on the White House to set a legislative agenda. The moves are familiar. Electoral mandates are claimed. Problems and crises are pointed to. Programs are announced. Congresses are appealed to. Sometimes, long-running legislative campaigns are conducted before our eyes—as with Reagan's drive for tax and expenditure cuts in 1981, Clinton's for health-care reform in 1993–94, George W. Bush's for tax cuts in 2001, and Obama's for health-care reform in 2009–10. Little is more central to the conduct of American politics and policymaking.

Here, I use presidential requesting and Congress's reaction to it as a template for investigating separation of powers. Given especially the electoral commonalities elaborated in the preceding chapter, what has been the nature of the interaction among the branches in this high stratum of legislative activity? I start by specifying the factual material I rely on in the analysis and then go on to questions of theory.

I have compiled a dataset of 184 legislative proposals that presidents beginning with Truman and ending with George W. Bush asked Congress to enact. Within certain boundaries, it is a complete dataset. In principle, it includes all White House legislative proposals during that time span that met all three of the following criteria: A proposal had to be advanced during the first two years of a freshly elected, or reelected, president's term. It had to be in the area of domestic policy. And it had be a proposal that a president was really interested in advancing.

Given the rhythm and expectations of American politics, the first two years of a presidential term seem like the right place to investigate. It is then that presidents are chiefly relied on as domestic policy innovators. The president, the new House, and a new third of the Senate have been elected on the same day, experiencing the same political winds. There may exist a mandate. There may be a honeymoon. A burst of innovative lawmaking may ensue.[3] The congressional seat attrition, pileup of problems, political disquiet, and next-election excitement that ordinarily

[3] On the distinctive policy productivity of the first two years of a presidential term, see Mayhew, *Divided We Govern*, 175–77; Keith Krehbiel, *Pivotal Politics: A Theory of U.S. Lawmaking* (Chicago: University of Chicago Press, 1998), chs. 2, 3.

accompany the third and four years of a presidential term have not arrived yet. The result for this dataset is a focus on fifteen two-year intervals just after presidential elections, starting with the Eighty-first Congress of 1949–50 and ending with the One Hundred Ninth Congress of 2005–06. I have steered clear of President Ford as a requester (for one thing, he was busy otherwise) during the last post-Watergate months of 1974 when he assumed office. Ford has no role at all in the dataset, nor does Truman as a nonelected president during 1945–48 or Johnson as a fresh president during late 1963 and calendar 1964 in the wake of Kennedy's assassination.

Generally speaking, newly elected presidents bunch their legislative programs in their first year rather than their second year, but that is not uniformly true. Eisenhower waited until his second year in 1954.[4] The full two-year spans are worth examination. There is an additional wrinkle. Far from all legislative proposals grow out of elections, party programs, and claimed mandates. Presidents are managers with in-boxes. Problems and events come along during the first two years, as afterward, that seem to call for legislation, and the presidents ask for it—as during the oil shock in the winter of 1973–74 and after the 9/11 attack in 2001. There is no easy way to wall off event-induced proposals. The National Defense Education Act of 1958, for example, was at once a domestic reform and a response to an exogenous event—Sputnik. The Voting Rights Act of 1965 ensued from demonstrations in Selma, Alabama. Whatever the stimuli might have been, legislative proposals of the pre-midterm years that seem to qualify as domestic are caught in the net here.

In principle, I confine the analysis to domestic policy. Foreign policy and military matters tend to have their own dynamics and raise their own kinds of analytic questions. Still, judgments were needed about what is domestic and what is not. A bright line does not exist. I have excluded all presidential requests for foreign

[4] Gary W. Reichard, *The Reaffirmation of Republicanism: Eisenhower and the Eighty-third Congress* (Knoxville: University of Tennessee Press, 1975), chs. 5–7.

aid, treaty ratifications, resolutions such as the Tonkin Gulf Resolution of 1964 (regarding the Vietnam War) and the Iraq Resolution of 2002, weapons systems, and military provision as in the
Defense Production Act of 1950 (financing the Korean War) and
the switch to the draft lottery in 1969. Yet, I have included requests regarding immigration and international trade. Policies
in those areas have substantial domestic impact, and they are not
event-driven to the same degree as typical foreign and military
policies. I have included requests to reorganize the government—
even those regarding the Defense and Homeland Security departments. I have included requests to regulate or restructure
the economy or society, even if those requests were spurred by
external crisis. On this terrain it is hard to know what to leave out.
Yes, of course, Carter's energy program in 1977 was domestic. But
if that, why not Nixon's energy-related proposals in 1973–74?
And if those, why not certain proposals emanating from 9/11 in
2001? Airline security needed to be beefed up. On the ground
that they entailed regulation of society, I allowed the requests for
the USA Patriot Act of 2001 and military tribunals in 2006 to
make the cut. On balance, I was possibly generous in defining
"domestic."

Now for the hard part—the identification of proposals that
the presidents were really interested in advancing. Let me start
with a detour. One often-used lens into relations between the
White House and Congress on legislation is summary roll-call
data. I skirt that method entirely. It has at least two defects. It
tends to group the important with the unimportant, and it fails
regarding proposals that generate no roll calls. This latter defect
is not minor. In the dataset of 184 presidential proposals I am
about to describe, 38 drew no roll calls at all—not even procedural
ones—in the House, 30 drew none in the Senate, and an overlap-
ping 20 drew none in either chamber. In 1958, for example, the
measure creating the National Aeronautics and Space Administration sailed through both houses on voice votes. That is one
route to no roll calls. More often, a White House proposal never
makes it to the floor. George W. Bush's plan to partly privatize

Social Security in 2005, for example, never made it to the floor of either chamber. Truman's plan for federal aid to education never reached the floor of the House. In the half-century before Obama, four presidents—Truman, Eisenhower, Nixon, and Clinton—asked for national health insurance in various ambitious designs. Three of these plans (the exception is Eisenhower's) never reached the roll-call stage in the House, and three of them (the exception is Clinton's) never got that far in the Senate.[5] An indicator that bypasses cases like these has limits.[6]

Lists of presidential proposals sent to Congress are a standard tool. *Congressional Quarterly* has run a "presidential box score" based on such lists. In personal testimony, President Eisenhower noted in his memoirs that he submitted 232 "specific requests for legislation to Congress" in 1954.[7] In the accepted professional scholarship, one line of analysis has hinged on lists that are lengthy and comprehensive. George C. Edwards III, for example, considers 206 presidential requests in 1957, 358 in 1961, 469 in 1965, 171 in 1969, and 183 in 1973.[8] Mark Peterson samples from a list of 5,069 domestic requests stretching from 1953 through 1984—an average of 244 per year for Democratic presidents, 107 for Republicans.[9] Andrew Rudalevige samples from a list of 6,926 proposals stretching from 1949 through 1996.[10] At a much reduced level, Paul C. Light, basing his work on interviews with White House staff from Kennedy through Carter, addresses an average of 36 new domestic requests during the first halves of

---

[5] In the Clinton case, the roll calls in the Senate reflected just preliminary maneuvering.
[6] For an elaboration of this argument, see David R. Mayhew, "Clinton, the 103rd Congress, and Unified Party Control: What Are the Lessons?," ch. 10 in John G. Geer (ed.), *Politicians and Party Politics* (Baltimore: Johns Hopkins University Press, 1998), 281–82.
[7] Dwight D. Eisenhower, *Mandate for Change, 1953–1956* (Garden City, N.J.: Doubleday, 1963), 298.
[8] George C. Edwards III, *Presidential Influence in Congress* (San Francisco: W. H. Freeman, 1980), 14.
[9] Mark A. Peterson, *Legislating Together: The White House and Capitol Hill from Eisenhower to Reagan* (Cambridge: Harvard University Press, 1990), 95.
[10] Andrew Rudalevige, *Managing the President's Program: Presidential Leadership and Legislative Policy Formation* (Princeton: Princeton University Press, 2002), ch. 4. Treaties are excluded from consideration.

presidential terms, 17 during the second halves.[11] Light has an eye for "the President's personal priorities, the ideas discussed and refined in the Oval Office. These are the items that absorb the President's time and expend the greatest resources. They are uniquely 'presidential.'"[12]

As quoted here, Light's standard seems to me exemplary. It empiricizes the matter in a particular way. It is true that we may never be sure what went on secretly in a president's mind. Yet, given suitable witnessing and reporting, we can hope for fly-on-the-wall evidence from a president's "refine and discuss" sessions in the Oval Office or other close-in behavioral clues like this to presidential aims.

My standard here resembles Light's, but I went about compiling my request lists differently and they are shorter. On the first count, I needed a practical way to cover presidential administrations across sixty years. Interviews with White House staff were not an option. I needed a executable blueprint. On the second count, I aimed for just the very high points. What have the presidents *really* wanted? This is a theory-driven question. The U.S. system may risk special strain in the extreme circumstance where maximal presidential demand meets possible congressional supply—and where as a consequence the public, the parties, ideological activists, interest groups, and the media often watch and take sides. At an extreme of the extreme, we have seen drives like Clinton's for health-care reform in 1993–94. Haynes Johnson and David S. Broder entitled their work on that drive *The System: The American Way of Politics at the Breaking Point*.[13]

For evidence regarding presidential requests, I relied on the most illuminating accounts I could find by historians, journalists, political scientists, and, in the cases of Truman, Eisenhower, Johnson, Nixon, Carter, Reagan, and Clinton, the presidents

[11] Paul C. Light, *The President's Agenda: Domestic Policy Choice from Kennedy to Carter* (Baltimore: Johns Hopkins University Press, 1982), 42.

[12] Ibid., 5.

[13] Haynes Johnson and David S. Broder, *The System: The American Way of Politics at the Breaking Point* (Boston: Little, Brown, 1996).

themselves, about what went on during the first two years of the presidential terms. The presidents' memoirs offer a taste of personal revelation, and they are often excellent (Eisenhower's, for example), yet it is true that they are tailored hindsight and I have used them cautiously and only as a supplement to the mix. The other sources are standard accounts, direct or indirect, of manifestations of presidential aims.

See the appendix of this volume for a discussion and documentation of the sources consulted.[14] There are eighty-five in all, including twenty-four that address more than one presidential term. At the maximum and minimum, I found ten usable accounts for Clinton's first term in 1993–94, five for Clinton's second term in 1997–98. In canvassing for sources, I came to appreciate careful, clipped accounts like those authored by Louis W. Koenig on the Kennedy presidency, William C. Berman on Clinton's first term, and Barbara Sinclair on George W. Bush's first term.[15] Works on individual presidencies issued by the University Press of Kansas proved especially helpful. Sources like these plus the presidents' memoirs seemed to carry me adequately through 2002. A problem arose regarding 2005–06. I was determined not to lose this recent two-year span, not least because George W. Bush's drive for part-privatization of Social Security in 2005 stands out as one of the more resolute legislative campaigns conducted by the White House during recent times. A half-dozen good accounts proved to be available for calendar 2005, but they do not extend well into calendar 2006. Aiming for a comparable standard of coverage, I fleshed out this full Bush Congress by using supplementary documentation from *Congressional Quarterly Weekly*, a somewhat different kind of source.[16]

[14] This appendix is also available through http://press.princeton.edu/titles/9432.html.
[15] Louis W. Koenig, "Kennedy and the 87th Congress," ch. 5 in Ivan Hinderaker (ed.), *American Government Annual, 1962–1963* (New York: Holt, Rinehart and Winston, 1962); William C. Berman, *From the Center to the Edge: The Politics and Policies of the Clinton Presidency* (Lanham, Md.: Rowman and Littlefield, 2001), ch. 2; Barbara Sinclair, "Context, Strategy, and Chance: George W. Bush and the 107th Congress," ch. 5 in Colin Campbell and Bert A. Rockman (eds.), *The George W. Bush Presidency: Appraisals and Prospects* (Washington, D.C.: Congressional Quarterly Press, 2004).
[16] For the specifics, see the appendix. Of the sixteen requests listed there for 2005–6, eleven have at least some anchoring in the standard accounts. The other five, reflecting coverage

In canvassing for requests worth listing, I sought in any instance a threshold mix of attention, commitment, and energy reported to be applied by a president. I aimed for a balance of evidence across the various sources in each case. Such assessment is of course a matter of judgment, and there were close calls. Not making the cut, for example, were legalization of common-site picketing, a high-priority labor-union aim, in 1977, and corporate account-ability reform in 2001–02, following the collapse of Enron. These were important causes, but I concluded on the evidence that pres-idents Carter and Bush did not respectively do much to make them their own personal causes.[17] The White House did not need to originate a proposal for a president to be credited with the re-quest of it. Actual origins might include the administrative agen-cies or even Congress itself.[18] On the latter count, as in the classic case of Franklin D. Roosevelt and the Wagner Act in 1935, presi-dents by way of their requests can add standing to proposals al-ready otherwise generated and in process on Capitol Hill. Clinton did that with family leave in 1993, which makes the list here. Presidents are not request-prone in anywhere near equal degree. In the dataset here, Johnson led the request ranks with twenty proposals in 1965–66. Reagan hit bottom with only three propos-als in 1985–86, although one of those requests spurred the impor-tant Tax Reform Act of 1986.[19]

See table 2.1 for a complete list of the 184 presidential re-quests.[20] Ignore for a moment the bold typeface on many entries. The table is long, but its full complement of information should

---

of legislative activity stretching across the two years, or just during 2006, rely entirely on accounts in *Congressional Quarterly Weekly* (*CQW*). In length, the resulting list of sixteen presidential initiatives for 2005–6 matches an average of 16.1 for the six previous presi-dencies since World War II that also operated under conditions of unified party control during their full pre-midterm spans.

[17] Common-site picketing died in the Democratic-controlled House of Representatives of 1977. Corporate accountability reform was voted by a Democratic Senate and a Republi-can House and signed by George W. Bush.

[18] For a discussion that distinguishes between the White House and the agencies as origi-nators, see Rudalevige, *Managing the President's Program*.

[19] Only Reagan himself, in his memoirs, addresses any domestic White House initiative during 1985–86 besides tax reform. The seven other sources for those years give consider-able attention to tax reform yet mention no other initiative.

[20] This table is available through http://princeton.edu/titles/9432.html.

TABLE 2.1.
Presidential Requests

Presidency	Legislative proposal	Win	Loss	Later?	Weight
Truman	**Omnibus civil rights**		loss		2
1949–50	**Hike corporate, gift, estate taxes**		loss		1
	Repeal of Taft-Hartley Act		loss		2
	Federal aid to education		loss		2
	National health insurance		loss		2
	Agriculture (Brannan Plan)		loss		2
	Omnibus housing	win			2
	Minimum wage hike	win			1
	Social Security expansion	win			1
	Columbia Valley Authority		loss		1
	Middle-income housing		loss		1
	Rent control	win			1
	Admit displaced persons	win			1
	Executive reorganization authority	win			1
	Reciprocal trade	win			1
	Defense Department reform	win			1
Eisenhower	Extend excess profits tax	win			1
1953–54	**Tidelands oil to states**	win			2
	Revise tax code	win			2
	Housing	win			2
	Social Security expansion	win			2
	National health insurance		loss		1
	Flexible crop prices	win			2
	Revision of Taft-Hartley Act		loss		2
	Spur atomic energy industry	win			1
	St. Lawrence Seaway	win			2
	Post Office reform		loss		1
	Displaced persons	win			1
	Hawaii statehood		loss		1
	Colorado River project		loss	yes	1
	Reciprocal trade		loss	yes	2

TABLE 2.1. (*Continued*)

Presidency	Legislative proposal	Win	Loss	Later?	Weight
Eisenhower	1957 budget		loss		1
1957–58	Civil rights	win			2
	Agriculture	win			1
	National Defense Education Act	win			1
	Alaska statehood	win			1
	Defense Department reform	win			1
	Trade authority	win			1
	Aid for school construction		loss		1
	Space agency (NASA)	win			1
	Hawaii statehood		loss	yes	1
Kennedy	**Extend unemployment benefits**	win			1
1961–62	**Aid to depressed areas**	win			2
	Federal aid to education		loss		2
	Medicare		loss		2
	Minimum wage hike	win			2
	Omnibus housing	win			2
	Cabinet department of housing		loss		1
	Manpower retraining	win			1
	Agriculture		loss		1
	Social Security expansion	win			1
	Trade expansion	win			2
	Investment tax credit	win			1
	Communications satellite	win			1
	Pharmaceutical regulation	win			1
	Civil rights		loss		1
Johnson	**Federal aid to education (ESEA)**	win			3
1965–66	**Medicare/Medicaid**	win			3
	Voting Rights Act	win			3
	Double antipoverty spending	win			1
	Aid to higher education	win			1
	Highway beautification	win			1

TABLE 2.1. (*Continued*)

Presidency	Legislative proposal	Win	Loss	Later?	Weight
	Arts and humanities (NEA/NEH)	win			1
	Heart, cancer, and stroke	win			1
	Aid to Appalachia	win			1
	Repeal of 14b of Taft–Hartley Act		loss		1
	Omnibus housing	win			1
	Agriculture	win			1
	Cabinet department of housing (HUD)	win			1
	Water Quality Act	win			1
	Fund rent supplements	win			1
	Immigration reform	win			1
	Department of Transportation (DOT)	win			2
	Model cities	win			2
	Open housing (civil rights)		loss	yes	2
	District of Columbia home rule		loss		1
Nixon 1969–70	Family Assistance Plan (FAP)		loss		2
	Tax reform		loss		1
	Revenue sharing with states		loss	yes	2
	Supersonic transport		loss		1
	Postal service reform	win			1
	DC crime control	win			1
	Combat illegal drug use	win			1
Nixon 1973–74	**1973 budget cutting poverty programs**		loss		2
	Fast-track trade authority	win			1
	Emergency energy powers to pres		loss		1
	New cabinet department of energy		loss		1
	Alaska pipeline	win			1
	Daylight savings time year-round	win			1
	Energy R&D (including nuclear)		loss		1
	Deregulate natural gas prices		loss		1
	Highway speed limits	win			1
	National health insurance		loss		1

Table 2.1. (*Continued*)

Presidency	Legislative proposal	Win	Loss	Later?	Weight
Carter	Executive reorganization authority	win			1
1977–78	Emergency natural gas supply	win			1
	Eliminate water projects		loss		2
	Omnibus energy plan		loss		4
	Consumer Protection Agency		loss		1
	Ethics-in-government reform	win			1
	Economic stimulus	win			1
	Tax reform		loss		2
	Welfare reform		loss		2
	Agriculture		loss		2
	Create Department of Energy	win			1
	Social Security refinancing	win			1
	Hospital cost containment		loss		1
	Airline deregulation	win			1
	Civil Service reform	win			1
	Create Department of Education		loss	yes	1
Reagan	**Tax cuts (ERTA)**	win			4
1981–82	**Expenditure cuts (OBRA)**	win			3
	New federalism		loss		1
	Deregulation of savings and loans	win			1
	Const amdt to balance budget		loss		1
	IRS rules		loss		1
	Const amdt to allow school prayer		loss		1
	Tuition tax credits		loss		1
	Ban on school busing		loss		1
	Deficit reduction 1982 (TEFRA)	win			1
	Const amdt to curb abortion		loss		1
Reagan	**Tax Reform Act (TRA)**	win			3
1985–86	**Agriculture**		loss		1
	Const amdt to balance budget		loss		1

TABLE 2.1. (*Continued*)

Presidency	Legislative proposal	Win	Loss	Later?	Weight
Bush 41	**Const amdt to ban flag burning**		loss		1
1989–90	Americans with Disabilities Act (ADA)	win			2
	Clean Air Act	win			2
	Savings and loans bailout	win			1
	Education reform		loss		1
	Capital gains tax cut		loss		1
	Combat illegal drug use	win			1
	Deficit reduction	win			3
Clinton	**Omnibus budget package**	win			4
1993–94	**Economic stimulus**		loss		1
	Family leave	win			1
	Motor voter	win			1
	Earned Income Tax Credit hike	win			1
	National service (AmeriCorps)	win			1
	Brady bill (gun control)	win			1
	North American Free Trade (NAFTA)	win			2
	Welfare reform		loss		1
	Goals 2000 (education)	win			1
	Health-care reform		loss		4
	Lobbying reform		loss		1
	Campaign finance reform		loss		1
	Crime	win			2
	World trade (GATT)	win			1
Clinton	Balanced budget deal	win			2
1997–98	**Child health insurance (CHIP)**	win			1
	Tax breaks for higher education	win			1
	Fund 100,000 teachers	win			1
	Fast-track trade authority		loss		1
	Save surplus for Social Security	win			1
	Minimum wage hike		loss		1
	Patients' bill of rights		loss		1

TABLE 2.1. (*Continued*)

Presidency	Legislative proposal	Win	Loss	Later?	Weight
	Immigrant aid givebacks	win			1
	Child-care program		loss		1
	Campaign finance reform		loss		1
Bush 43	**Tax cuts**	win			3
2001–2	No Child Left Behind Act	win			2
	Fund faith-based initiatives		loss		1
	Omnibus energy program		loss		1
	Fast-track trade authority	win			1
	Medicare prescription drugs		loss	yes	1
	Economic stimulus	win			1
	USA Patriot Act after 9/11	win			2
	Airline security after 9/11	win			2
	Reconstruct New York City after 9/11	win			1
	Department of Homeland Security	win			2
Bush 43	**Part-privatization of Social Security**		loss		3
2005–6	**Curb class-action lawsuits**	win			1
	Bankruptcy reform	win			1
	Omnibus energy program	win			1
	Free trade with Central America	win			1
	No Child Left Behind for high schools		loss		1
	Renew USA Patriot Act	win			1
	Deficit reduction	win			1
	Curb medical malpractice suits		loss		1
	Authorize oil drilling in Alaska		loss		1
	Extend 2001 and 2003 tax cuts	win			1
	Rebuild Gulf Coast after Katrina	win			1
	Immigration reform		loss		1
	Military tribunals for terrorists	win			2
	Expansion of Health Savings Account	win			1
	Make estate tax repeal permanent		loss		1

be presented. For many readers, the table will offer memories. There it is again. The Brannan Plan. The Saint Lawrence Seaway, statehood for Alaska, manpower retraining, and aid to Appalachia. The Family Assistance Plan, the supersonic transport, the Alaska pipeline, and the Consumer Protection Agency. The New York City bailout, the Balanced Budget Amendment, motor voter, patients' bill of rights, and faith-based initiatives.

Yet for certain purposes, a request list planned in this include-it-or-not fashion is not enough. The requests that are included cry out for weighting. We know very well, for example, that Johnson went to the wall for voting rights, that Carter emphasized his energy program, that Reagan dwelt far more on his tax cuts than on, say, his proposed constitutional amendment to ban abortion, and that Clinton drove himself over health-care reform, not campaign finance reform.[21] This is settled knowledge about American policy history. It is a kind of knowledge that should not be lost in an analysis of presidential requesting. Weighting requests is a risky enterprise. I have taken a stab at it, consulting the sources listed in the appendix with, again, an eye for mixes of presidential attention, commitment, and energy, yet this time alert also to gradations above a threshold.

Contributing to such judgments was testimony like the following. We are told that Kennedy began his presidency with five "must bills" addressing federal aid to education, Medicare, housing, depressed areas, and a minimum wage hike,[22] that at some point he also identified trade expansion as his "number-one legislative priority,"[23] and that "of all his narrow losses, the most

---

[21] In an alternative methodology, one plausible guide to White House prioritizing is how often a proposal is mentioned in a president's written or spoken public statements. With this as a standard, there can be no doubt about Carter's exceptional interest in his energy program or Reagan's in his 1981 tax cuts. Reagan's proposal for expenditure cuts in 1981 is a clear high-side outlier also. See Patrick J. Fett, "Truth in Advertising: The Revelation of Presidential Legislative Priorities," *Western Political Quarterly* 45:4 (December 1992), 895–920, at 905–8.

[22] James N. Giglio, *The Presidency of John F. Kennedy* (Lawrence: University Press of Kansas, 2006), 99.

[23] Allen J. Matusow, *The Unraveling of America: A History of Liberalism in the 1960s* (New York: Harper and Row, 1984), 35.

discouraging to Kennedy was the defeat of his 'Medicare' bill."
He had devoted a good deal of time and energy to Medicare.[24]
Truman wrote in his memoirs: "I have had some bitter disap-
pointments as President, but the one that has troubled me most,
in a personal way, has been the failure to defeat the organized opposition to a national compulsory health-insurance program."[25]
Reagan wrote in his memoirs: "With the tax cut of 1981 and the
Tax Reform Act of 1986, I'd accomplished a lot of what I'd come
to Washington to do."[26] Regarding Nixon in 1969–70: "Nixon
himself took to the stump for revenue sharing—it was the only
major piece of domestic legislation that Nixon personally cam-
paigned for."[27] Clinton is said to have exclaimed in 1993: "If I
don't get health care done, I'll wish I didn't run for president."[28]

See the last column of table 2.1 for the weightings. I use a
1-to-4 scale. This scheme may underweigh drives like Reagan's
for his tax cuts and Clinton's for his budget, which are scored at
the allowed maximum of 4. In inspecting the requests coded as
3 or 4, note their obviously high substantive significance. It is no
surprise that the presidents and the political community in general focused on them. Certain of these were omnibus measures
that included many ingredients—Carter's energy package, Reagan's expenditure cuts (OBRA), George H. W. Bush's deficit-
reduction package, and Clinton's 1993 budget. Omnibus measures pose counting problems. It is an artifact of process that
Carter's energy program (113 ingredients, it was said) was han-
dled by the White House, the House, and finally the whole Congress as one measure (the Senate tried to break it up), whereas

[24] Theodore C. Sorensen, *Kennedy* (New York: Harper and Row, 1965), 342–44, quotation at 342.

[25] Harry S. Truman, *Memoirs*, vol. 2, *Years of Trial and Hope* (Garden City, N.Y.: Doubleday, 1956), 23. In this passage Truman was not keying on 1949–50 in particular. He had kept proposing national health insurance throughout his nearly two full terms as president. But 1949–50 was the showdown time on the issue.

[26] Ronald Reagan, *An American Life* (New York: Simon and Schuster, 1990), 335.

[27] At least during calendar 1970. John Robert Greene, *The Limits of Power: The Nixon and Ford Administrations* (Bloomington: Indiana University Press, 1992), 62.

[28] John F. Harris, *The Survivor: Bill Clinton in the White House* (New York: Random House, 2005), 20.

Nixon's energy program of 1973–74 sprawled across several requests. The 1-to-4 scaling here has problems, but it seems like a
plausible guide.

As a final feature of the factual presentation, what happened
once these 184 requests were sent to Congress? Case by case, did
the presidents get what they wanted or not? Did they win or lose?
That states the question in binary terms, which is of course a sim-
plification. Ordinarily, the White House does not get everything it
asks for even when it does get something. A more graduated measurement of success or failure can be attempted.[29] Yet that route
offers exceptional complexities, and there is another consideration: The *political* judgment about what happened to a presidential request ordinarily shakes down into binary. Washington, D.C.,
is a city of score-keepers. The political community there seems to
crave win–loss judgments. In the case of Clinton's 1993 budget
package, for example, a good deal of content had been abandoned
by the time that program reached enactment, but few observers
had any trouble perceiving a White House victory. Closer to the
edge, George H. W. Bush in 1990 and Clinton in 1997 had to
strike major compromises with unfriendly Congresses to advance
their deficit reduction and budget-balancing measures of those
years, but effectively compromise they did, and in Washington,
D.C., terms they won victories.[30]

To score the 184 requests for wins and losses, I relied on discussions in the sources listed in the appendix and in supplementary scholarship, but I also searched though *Congressional Quarterly Almanac* case-by-case for assessments. *CQ* ordinarily presents
good summary judgments pinpointing the relative perceived importance of the various ingredients of complicated enactments. In
probably 90 percent of the 184 instances, given the evidence, the
answer to the win–loss question was easy common sense. Yet

[29] See, for example, Andrew W. Barrett and Matthew Eshbaugh-Soha, "Presidential Success on the Substance of Legislation," *Political Research Quarterly* 60:1 (2007), 100–12.
[30] On the compromise of 1997, see Steven M. Gillon, *The Pact: Bill Clinton, Newt Gingrich,
and the Rivalry That Defined a Generation* (New York: Oxford University Press, 2008), ch. 12;
Daniel J. Palazzolo, *Done Deal: The Politics of the 1997 Budget Agreement* (New York: Chatham House, 1999).

there were closer cases needing judgment. In one interesting twist, presidents occasionally sign bills even if they have, in assessments going beyond White House spin, lost. A claim of victory may look better than a concession of loss. Or a president may request $100 billion and be given $100 million—an improvement on the status quo from the standpoint of the White House, yet a sunk program to the eyes of outside observers.

This is difficult territory, but in a serious canvass for wins and losses it needs to be reckoned with. In the area of agricultural policy, for example, presidents have often sent over proposals that foundered once they reached Capitol Hill, but the presidents have suppressed their qualms and signed the eventual every-four-years-or-so farm bills anyway, not least because the customary default outcome in the farm sector absent a legislative renewal is no program at all. Not surprisingly, outside observers have spied White House losses in these cases. In the area of tax policy, the Nixon administration sent proposals in 1969, "but few were adopted by Congress. As it developed, Congress itself wrote almost the entire [eventual] bill."[31] Nixon signed it, even though it was a Democratic-flavored reform seen by the White House to risk an unwelcome revenue drain. Several good accounts exist of this episode, and from the standpoint of the president as requester they seem to add up to loss.[32] "Nixon was never master of the situation."[33] Carter signed on to several apparent losses. Early in 1977, he asked for sharp cuts in pork-barrel water projects and got some of what he wanted, but both houses voted down his main plan, leaving "several of the most expensive and least environmentally friendly ventures," and "Carter himself later remarked that

[31] *Congressional Quarterly Almanac 1969* (Washington, D.C.: Congressional Quarterly Press, 1970), 589. Hereafter cited as *CQA*.
[32] Ibid.; A. James Reichley, *Conservatives in an Age of Change: The Nixon and Ford Administrations* (Washington, D.C.: Brookings, 1981), ch. 10; Rowland Evans, Jr., and Robert D. Novak, *Nixon in the White House: The Frustration of Power* (New York: Random House, 1971), 194–200, 211–23; Melvin Small, *The Presidency of Richard Nixon* (Lawrence: University Press of Kansas, 1999), 205; Allen J. Matusow, *Nixon's Economy: Booms, Busts, Dollars, and Votes* (Lawrence: University Press of Kansas, 1998), ch. 2; Nigel Bowles, *Nixon's Business: Authority and Power in Presidential Politics* (College Station: Texas A&M Press, 2005), ch. 2.
[33] Evans and Novak, *Nixon in the White House*, 216.

he rued the day he had agreed to compromise on 'those worthless projects.'"[34] This one is a close call but arguably a loss. In the energy area, to put it summarily, Carter asked for a tighter regulatory regime; Congress gave him deregulation of natural gas prices. The final bill, which Carter signed, "contained only remnants of the tough plan originally presented by Carter in April 1977."[35] In the tax area, again summarily, Carter asked for a standard menu of liberal reforms; Congress gave him a stiff cut in capital gains taxes. The president "fought a losing battle with Congress." The final legislation, which Carter signed, "bore little resemblance to the tax reform proposals the administration had recommended."[36] In the sense aimed for here, a president can at once sign and lose.

In table 2.1, the wins and losses are designated in separate columns. This win–loss formulation needs an asterisk. In 7 of the 184 cases, a proposal failed during a president's first Congress but did pass under that same president following the midterm.[37] See the column of "yeses" in table 2.1. This is a patternless mix. Eisenhower had a hard time trying to extract a three-year trade

[34] Burton I. Kaufman, *The Presidency of James Earl Carter, Jr.* (Lawrence: University Press of Kansas, 1993), 51. See also Jimmy Carter, *Keeping Faith: Memoirs of a President* (Fayetteville: University of Arkansas Press, 1995), 82–84; Haynes Johnson, *In the Absence of Power: Governing America* (New York: Viking, 1980), 158–59; *CQA, 1977*, pp. 650–51.

[35] *CQA, 1978*, 639–63, quotation at 639. See also Kaufman, *Presidency of James Earl Carter*, 33, 57, 66–68, 107–8; Charles O. Jones, *The Trusteeship Presidency: Jimmy Carter and the United States Congress* (Baton Rouge: Louisiana State University Press, 1988), 135–40; Johnson, *In the Absence of Power*, 184–93, 292–93. Another assessment: "But Congress passed nothing until the very last day of the 1978 session, and then its final product was barely a shadow of Carter's original proposals." The final bill "bore scant resemblance to Carter's original proposals." Rudalevige, *Managing the President's Program*, 120, 121.

[36] Kaufman, *Presidency of James Earl Carter*, 101, 109. See also Randall Strahan, *New Ways and Means: Reform and Change in a Congressional Committee* (Chapel Hill: University of North Carolina Press, 1990), 121–23; *CQW 1978*, 219–48. "Almost all of his proposed 'reforms,' except for a few tokens, had been scrapped, and the cuts were skewed much more towards the upper end of the income scale than he had recommended" (219).

[37] I exclude the welfare reform of the 1990s from this brief list. Clinton sent a proposal that failed during 1994, and welfare reform did pass in 1996, but the latter instrument was enacted under chiefly Republican impetus and was significantly different and not really Clinton's. Also excluded is civil rights during 1961–64. Kennedy sent a somewhat perfunctory proposal that sank in 1962. The later Civil Rights Act of 1964 was enacted under Johnson, not Kennedy, in the wake of the Kennedy assassination and the Birmingham demonstrations of 1963 in a quite different political environment.

authorization from the Republican Congress of 1953–54, and, if anything, the Democratic takeover of Capitol Hill in November 1954 probably helped his cause.[38] The Upper Colorado project was caught in controversy as of late 1954 but succeeded under the Democrats.[39] Statehood for Hawaii seemed on a sure road to passage in late 1958, given the favorable treatment then of Alaska, but it had not quite happened yet.[40] Under Lyndon Johnson, an ambitious open housing proposal sank dramatically in 1966, and it would probably have stayed sunk absent the backing of a group of moderate Republican senators newly elected in November 1966 and the crystallizing assassination of the Rev. Martin Luther King, Jr., in April 1968.[41] Nixon's revenue-sharing plan went nowhere during 1969–70, but a version of it carried in 1972 thanks apparently to backing by Governor Nelson Rockefeller of New York and big-city mayors.[42] Carter's plan to create a Department of Education was obstructed to death by a resistant House minority in late 1978, but it won passage after the midterm.[43] George W. Bush's plan for prescription drugs through Medicare failed in 2001–2, but the surprising Republican gains in the 2002

[38] Raymond A. Bauer, Ithiel de Sola Pool, and Lewis Anthony Dexter, *American Business and Public Policy: The Politics of Foreign Trade* (New York: Atherton, 1963), 53–54, ch. 5; Eisenhower, *Mandate for Change*, 195, 203, 292–93; Michael Barone: *Our Country: The Shaping of America from Roosevelt to Reagan* (New York: Free Press, 1990), 267; *CQA 1954*, 265–72; *CQA 1955*, 289–99.

[39] *CQA 1954*, 508–10; *CQA 1956*, 408–10.

[40] *CQA 1958*, 285–86; *CQA 1959*, 173–75.

[41] Robert Dallek, *Flawed Giant: Lyndon Johnson and His Times, 1961–1973* (New York: Oxford University Press, 1998), 322–29; Matusow, *Unraveling of America*, pp. 206–8; Hugh Davis Graham, *The Civil Rights Era: Origins and Development of National Policy* (New York: Oxford University Press, 1990), 258–62, 270–73; Hugh Davis Graham, "The Surprising Career of Federal Fair Housing Law," *Journal of Policy History* 12:2 (2000), 215–32, at 217–19 ("Lyndon Johnson, Congress, and the Surprising Open Housing Act of 1968"); *CQA 1966*, 450–72; *CQA 1968*, 152–68.

[42] Greene, *Limits of Power*, 62–64; *CQW 1969*, 961–65; *CQW 1970*, p. 923; *CQW 1971*, 698–709; *Congressional Quarterly, 1972*, 636–52; Samuel H. Beer, "The Adoption of General Revenue Sharing: A Case Study in Public Sector Politics," *Public Policy* 24:2 (Spring 1976), 127–95, at 171–95.

[43] *CQA 1978*, 571–76. In the context of a tight late-session agenda, the House Democratic leadership pulled the plan once a Republican member aiming to block it insisted that a lengthy conference report on another subject be read word for word on the House floor. On 1979: *CQA 1979*, 465–74.

midterm following 9/11 helped grease it to victory in 2003.[44] These diverse cases need to be kept in mind in the ensuing discussion, yet I code them as losses. That is because for any president the first two years are the propitious years. In general, a loss then is a real loss. It may not be retrievable. The day needs to be seized. Given the rhythms of American politics, who knows what difficulties a midterm may bring?

As a theoretical matter, what can be made of these 184 requests and their win-loss designations? I am aiming for a particular exploration of the data, but a general discussion should come first.

Why does a president make a legislative request at all?[45] The obvious answer is: to get a law passed.[46] Documentation of the point is scarcely needed, although insider testimony could easily supply it. Backhand evidence is available in the behavior of presidents operating in varying circumstances. In 1965, for example, President Johnson "saw his [landslide 1964] electoral victory and current popularity as an unusual opportunity to get a lot of important bills through Congress."[47] Large Democratic majorities on Capitol Hill were available. A stream of requests ensued. On the other hand, the Nixon administration in 1969 had no wish for "an enervating and ultimately heartbreaking struggle to pry legislation out of a Democratic Congress."[48] Nixon, in his own words, did not see a "coalition I could tap for support on domestic policy."[49] A White House staffer reflected, "No one felt we could send a large number of programs to Congress."[50] Similarly, according to one account, George H. W. Bush in 1989 judged that "four years of

[44] Sinclair, "Context, Strategy, and Chance," 127; *CQA 2002*, 10:3–7; *CQA 2003*, 11:3–8.
[45] Illuminating discussions of this question appear in Light, *The President's Agenda*, pp. 106–7, and Peterson, *Legislating Together*, ch. 2.
[46] "The underlying premise of agenda-setting research is that the president should be able to package policy priorities so as to increase the likelihood of their adoption." Matthew Eshbaugh-Soha, "The Politics of Presidential Agendas," *Political Research Quarterly* 58:2 (June 2005), 257–68, quotation at 257.
[47] Dallek, *Flawed Giant*, 190.
[48] Evans and Novak, *Nixon in the White House*, 12.
[49] Richard M. Nixon, *The Memoirs of Richard Nixon* (New York: Grosset and Dunlap, 1978), 351.
[50] Light, *The President's Agenda*, 53.

stalemate" would issue from an "attempt to confront a Democratic Congress with a distinctly Republican program."[51] "It would have been foolhardy for Bush to have sent a massive, not to mention costly [there was a deficit problem, too] domestic package to the hill. So he didn't."[52] To generalize at least across conditions of party control, using this study's dataset, the presidents serving under unified party control sent an average of sixteen requests, those serving under divided control an average of nine.[53] With weightings as in table 2.1, the gap rises to twenty-three versus twelve. These disparities are understandable.

Yet such eyes-on, do-it-now instrumentalism is not the whole story. The instrumentalism can shade off into an uncalculating request-proneness, or it can accommodate aims beyond legislative victory in the short term. In the production of requests, a presidential mindset of "This should be done, so please do it" seems to be rather common whatever the congressional odds, which at any rate a president may discount. Carter, who tended to shuck off information about unpromising Capitol Hill climates, is the prize instance.[54] "It's almost impossible for me to delay something that I see needs to be done," remarked the president after one week in office, and his record in making legislative requests seems to bear out that reflection.[55] Presidents have their

---

[51] Michael Duffy and Dan Goodgame, *Marching in Place: The Status Quo Presidency of George Bush* (New York: Simon and Schuster, 1992), 58.

[52] John Robert Greene, *The Presidency of George Bush* (Lawrence: University Press of Kansas, 2000), 61.

[53] The Congress of 2001–2, during which party control shifted, is excluded from these calculations.

[54] On the shucking off, see, for example, Kaufman, *Presidency of James Earl Carter*, p. 28; Erwin C. Hargrove, *Jimmy Carter as President: Leadership and the Politics of the Public Good* (Baton Rouge: Louisiana State University Press, 1988), 21.

[55] Quotation cited in Kaufman, *Presidency of James Earl Carter*, 28; Hargrove, *Jimmy Carter as President*, 16. In Light, *The President's Agenda*, 17, a White House aide recollected about Carter: "He liked to make a decision on the merits and check the decision box that seemed to him the best direction for the nation to go and that was an enormous strength and has an enormous amount of intellectual integrity. It was also however a liability at times because you can't always simply check the right box." In general, on Carter's approach to leadership as it entailed making proposals, see Hargrove, ch. 2; Jones, *The Trusteeship Presidency*, chs. 1, 4; Stephen Skowronek, *The Politics Presidents Make: Leadership from John Adams to George Bush* (Cambridge: Belknap, Harvard University Press, 1993), 364, 389.

hobbyhorses. Throughout his two terms, Eisenhower kept asking for pay-as-you-go postal reform without result.[56] Reagan kept asking for a constitutional amendment to require a balanced budget.[57]

Especially the earlier presidents of the postwar era seem to have taken their parties' platforms seriously. Whatever the odds, advancing them was a duty. "To me," Truman wrote in his memoirs, "party platforms are contracts with the people, and I have always looked upon them as agreements that had to be carried out."[58] Eisenhower recalled from his opening meeting with Republican congressional leaders in 1953: "I said first that it was my intention to redeem the pledges of the platform and the campaign. To my astonishment, I discovered that some of the men in the room could not seem to understand the seriousness with which I regarded our platform's provisions, and were amazed by my uncompromising assertion that I was going to do my best to fulfill every promise to which I had been a party."[59] Carter, once in office, dwelt on his own personal campaign pledges (as distinguished from those in the Democratic platform)—notably, to cut down on pork-barrel spending and reorganize the government.[60] At a level more exalted than platform planks or personal pledges, presidents may commit themselves to long-standing party programs and pursue those. One theme in the accounts, for example,

---

[56] Eisenhower, *Mandate for Change*, 199–201. From a meeting in mid-1953 with Republican congressional leaders: "When one senator volunteered that there was but dim hope that the Congress would enact the [postal] increase that summer, I said that perhaps the congressmen should give up their vacation, stay in Washington, and get the job done. Several faces around the table turned ashen" (200). In general, before 1970 when a Nixon-generated reform distanced the postal system from congressional influence, members of the relevant House and Senate committees catered jointly to postal employees by conferring benefits and to consumers by keeping rates low. Pay-as-you-go accounting was not a likely consequence of such a politics. See Richard F. Fenno, Jr., *Congressmen in Committees* (Boston: Little, Brown, 1973), 5–9, 35–43, 64–69, 90–91, 110–14, 135–37, 139–40, 152, 170–71, 180–84, 242–55, 281–83.
[57] Reagan, *An American Life*, 338.
[58] Truman, *Years of Trial and Hope*, 182.
[59] Eisenhower, *Mandate for Change*, 194–95.
[60] See Carter, *Keeping Faith*, p. 66; Kaufman, *Presidency of James Earl Carter*, 30; Johnson, *In the Absence of Power*, 155.

is the persisting force of Franklin D. Roosevelt's "Economic Bill of Rights" of wartime 1944, soon repackaged as Truman's "Fair Deal," once Truman and later Kennedy got a chance at postelection power in their presidencies of 1949 and 1961.[61]

Although the evidence gets cloudy, it is also claimed that presidents may use their legislative requests to try to educate the public,[62] speak out for the people,[63] articulate the common good,[64] arouse the national conscience,[65] set the national agenda,[66] or, if the going gets rough today, pave the way for lawmaking at some favorable tomorrow.[67] Additionally, even if the next election is a distant haze as a new presidency begins, today's requests may be seen to possess backup utility as future campaign issues even if they fail right now.[68]

What should we expect in the way of presidents' success rates on their initiatives? If the presidents were always pure instrumentalists aiming at near-horizon legislative victories, and if they could operate with perfect information about their political environments, they would never lose on Capitol Hill. They would attune themselves perfectly to their environments. They would always score 100 percent success rates. That is a plausible default way to approach this matter. But of course they often do lose.

[61] See Richard E. Neustadt, "Congress and the Fair Deal: A Legislative Balance Sheet," 15–42, in Alonzo L. Hamby (ed.), *Harry S. Truman and the Fair Deal* (Lexington, Mass.: D. C. Heath, 1974), 18–21, 40–42; Giglio, *Presidency of John F. Kennedy*, p. 99. This Roosevelt program emerged in the closing phase of World War II, which was a major seedbed of party programs in the United States and elsewhere. See David R. Mayhew, "Wars and American Politics," *Perspectives on Politics* 3:3 (2005), 473–93, at 478–80.

[62] Regarding Kennedy: Arthur M. Schlesinger, Jr., *A Thousand Days: John F. Kennedy in the White House* (Cambridge, Mass.: Houghton Mifflin, 1965), 170; Light, *The President's Agenda*, 106.

[63] Regarding Truman: William W. Lammers and Michael A. Genovese, *The Presidency and Domestic Policy: Comparing Leadership Styles, FDR to Clinton* (Washington, D.C.: Congressional Quarterly Press, 2000), 142.

[64] Regarding Carter: Hargrove, *Jimmy Carter as President*, 13.

[65] Regarding Truman: Neustadt, "Congress and the Fair Deal," 41. Regarding Carter: Kaufman, *Presidency of James Earl Carter*, 28.

[66] Regarding Truman: Lammers and Genovese, *The Presidency and Domestic Policy*, 148, 154. Regarding Kennedy: Sorensen, *Kennedy*, 353.

[67] Regarding Truman: Neustadt, "Congress and the Fair Deal," 40–42. Regarding Kennedy: Schlesinger, *A Thousand Days*, 709–10.

[68] Regarding Kennedy: Sorensen, *Kennedy*, 353.

Across the 184 requests documented here, the presidential success rate is 59.8 percent—or, with weighting, 60.9 percent. As a side note, the near identity of these figures is perhaps a surprise. Why don't presidents do better when they care more and try harder? One reason, I would guess, is that the opposition mobilizes too. An intense White House tends to spur an intense reaction.

As it happens, these results match virtually exactly an average 61.6 percent success rate reported for chief executives pursuing legislative initiatives in a wide range of presidential democracies.[69] Strategic attunement is not a mirage, of course. An excellent piece of evidence for it is the near equivalence of White House success rates, once the presidents actually make requests, under conditions of unified as opposed to divided party control. Those rates are 64.0 percent as opposed to 52.9 percent taken straight, yet a nearly identical 61.3 percent versus 60.0 percent if the requests are, as in table 2.1, weighted.[70] The latter convergence of the figures owes notably to Reagan's major victories on his tax cuts (ERTA), expenditure cuts (OBRA), and tax reform (TRA) under conditions of divided control in 1981 and 1986.

Yet 60 percent or so is the general picture, not 100 percent. What are we to make of this? Why the losses? There are the considerations introduced in the previous paragraphs. There is also uncertainty—a major hazard for presidents even in many exercises of instrumentalism.[71] Who can be sure what Congress will

---

[69] Reported in José Antonio Cheibub, *Presidentialism, Parliamentarism, and Democracy* (New York: Cambridge University Press, 2007), 87–92.

[70] In this and subsequent calculations, here is the coding plan for 2001–2. For numerator and denominator purposes, the Bush tax cut is assigned to unified party control. All other White House proposals during that two-year span are assigned to divided party control, even if Bush introduced them during January through June 2001, before the defection of Senator James Jeffords, when the Republicans still controlled all three of the elective institutions (albeit via a "power-sharing" design in the Senate with Vice President Cheney breaking 50–50 ties). Any coding of 2001–2 has vulnerabilities. Favoring this one is that the Bush tax cut dominated the politics of early 2001 and was wrapped up in June, whereas all the other White House proposals at issue here received their decisive congressional consideration after Jeffords's switch had given the Senate formally to the Democrats.

[71] For an argument that accents unpredictability in the politics of presidential requesting (although not specifically the U.S. case), see Sebastian M. Salegh, "Political Prowess or 'Lady Luck'? Evaluating Chief Executives' Legislative Success Rates," *Journal of Politics* 71:4 (October 2009), 1342–56.

do? Uncertainty can hit a peak when a president needs to merchandise a proposal to the public in order to build support for it on Capitol Hill. At least in the cases of Carter and Clinton, that long march through the public to victory is reported to have been a conscious strategy.[72]

I think I see one pattern in the loss column of table 2.1 that has a theoretical basis. It is not this book's concern, so I will just take note of it and move on, although a similar idea regarding the parties appears at the close of this chapter. It has to do with the *nature* of proposals. On balance, presidents tend to favor grand rationalizing schemes, whereas Congress is more at home with shapeless compromises agreeable to interest groups and geographic constituencies. This is not a surprise. Two distinct reasons for it come to mind, although in practice their footprints are hard to distinguish. First, presidents, being accountable to the public all by themselves, are more likely to be tied by the nationwide election system to the general downstream effects of policies—such as unemployment rates or consumer prices at some future time. Members of Congress are more likely to gain points for piecemeal credit-claiming as legislative measures are forged and carried out.[73] Second, a president is one person; members of Congress are 535 persons. Possibly every human being has a fancy for grand rationalizing schemes, at least to some degree.[74] But, whereas on Capitol Hill such individual fancies may get their logic rubbed away in nonlinear compromises, presidents are free to scheme on alone.

[72] On Carter: "Carter saw his own approach to leadership as antithetical to the tactics of compromise and bargaining practiced by legislators." "Interest groups [a force in Congress] might be able to defeat an incremental proposal because the public could not be easily mobilized to support it. But the public might rally behind a comprehensive proposal that appealed to public goods." Hargrove, *Jimmy Carter as President*, 16. On Clinton: "The massive Clinton health care reform plan of 1993–1994 was based on the underlying, and unquestioned, assumption within the White House that the president could sell his plan to the public and thus solidify congressional support." George C. Edwards III, *On Deaf Ears: The Limits of the Bully Pulpit* (New Haven.: Yale University Press, 2003), 7.

[73] This argument is worked out in David R. Mayhew, *Congress: The Electoral Connection* (New Haven: Yale University Press, 1974).

[74] The limiting case among executives may be the Emperor Seth in Evelyn Waugh's *Black Mischief* (Boston: Little, Brown, 1977), from whom rationalizing schemes emanated in great number.

In this regard, free trade, which presidents have routinely championed, is a grand rationalizing scheme rooted in economic theory whose effects are friendly to dispersed unorganized consumers and now voiceless future producers (Congress is more likely to favor already established producers who are organized and feel threatened).[75] In agricultural policy, Republican presidents have often pressed free-market theories, Democratic presidents tightly coiled regulatory plans, aiming in both cases for economic efficiency and consumer welfare, yet commodity interests on Capitol Hill have impartially balked. All the national health insurance plans advanced by Truman, Eisenhower, Nixon, and Clinton were rationalizing intrusions into complicated markets. Carter's campaign against water projects was an application of cost–benefit principle. Truman's Columbia Valley Authority and Nixon's Family Assistance Plan were flourishes of elaborate design. It is a solid bet that White House plans like the above will encounter adverse winds on Capitol Hill.[76] That can make for losses.

Here is the question I am interested in exploring at this juncture. It harks back to chapter 1. Peering past the idiosyncrasies of individual presidents, the inevitable strategic uncertainty, and any built-in differences in institutional taste regarding effects-oriented

[75] Regarding the distinctive pro–free trade stance of the White House and the possible reasons for it, see William R. Keech and Kyoungsan Pak, "Partisanship, Institutions, and Change in American Trade Politics," *Journal of Politics* 57:4 (1995), 1130–42, at 1136–39. Independent of all else, one reason is White House responsibility for foreign policy. See also Orin Kirshner, "Superpower Politics: The Triumph of Free Trade in Postwar America," *Critical Review* 19:4 (2007), 523–42.

[76] In early 2009 the Obama administration proposed a grand rationalizing "cap and trade" plan in the area of energy policy. Its joint aims were to raise considerable revenue and to spur the reduction of carbon dioxide emissions by requiring culpable industries to buy permits in order to emit. The permits, purchased in auctions, could be traded. In House hands, however, the plan became in large degree a distributive subsidy measure lean in revenue and blurry in its incentive effects. Singled-out industries would be given free permits in a pattern friendly to individual member districts and to the assembling of a winning coalition. "Cap and Trade, with Handouts and Loopholes," *The Economist*, May 22–29, 2009, online; John M. Broder, "Adding Something for Everyone, House Leaders Won Climate Bill," *New York Times*, July 1, 2009, A1, A17; Steven Pearlstein, "For the Farm Lobby, Too Much Is Never Enough," *Washington Post*, June 26, 2009, online; Jim Tankersley, "House Climate Bill Was Flooded with Last-Minute Changes," *Los Angeles Times*, July 20, 2009, online.

abstraction versus shapeless particularism, is there any sign of a theoretically predictable *party asymmetry* in the win–loss rates of the presidents? Specifically, have Republican presidents on balance done better than Democrats in getting their requests passed? If so, such an edge could owe to what might be called, in line with the presentation in chapter 1, a Max Baucus effect. This phrase draws on the key boost that that Democratic senator from the one-sided Bush state gave to the Bush tax cut in 2001.[77] The textures of constituencies can matter. For that reason, to generalize and speculate regarding 2001, holding all else equal insofar as that can be imagined, a counterfactual Gore in the White House at that time might have fared a bit worse in his congressional dealings than did the real Bush. Spread this idea over the sixty years. Any such effect would be small. In chapter 1, the just over 1 percent average pro-Republican tilt of the House and Senate medians, juxtaposed to the split in the nationwide presidential popular vote or the Electoral College median, is small. Granted, the primal propensity of presidents to attune themselves to their Capitol Hill environments, whatever those environments may be, makes any statistical analysis on the request front perilous. Also, as chapters 3 and 4 will show, there are ample competing considerations. Yet sixty years is a long time over which anomalies might even out and a small real persisting effect might show.

The intuition is as follows. On average, Democratic presidents, as compared with Republicans, have possibly suffered a slightly greater dissonance between the commitments they made in winning elections and, once in office, the odds of performing on those commitments on Capitol Hill. Presidential candidates seem to promise whatever they think they need to promise in order to win elections. Following a familiar blueprint, they need to capture the political center in a context of energizing their own bases. It is a tricky business. No doubt they aim for both a national popular vote edge, which has political importance and normative

[77] In 2009 Baucus headed a Senate committee effort to write a centrist health-care reform bill, a stance that did not please the Democratic party's liberal base, although eventually he signed on to a party plan stripped of a "public option."

authority—"Gore really won"—and an electoral vote edge, which has legal authority.[78] Exactly how in practice the candidates and their armies of operatives balance these two aims is difficult to say. At once they seem to glue themselves to the national polls—how could anyone not do that?—and to accent the battleground states.[79] For purposes here, this dual realms question can be bypassed, since on average since World War II, as was shown in table 1.3, each party's share of the presidential vote in the popular realm has equaled its share in the median Electoral College unit. On average, the two metrics have shared an identical Democratic-side distance from the Republican-tilting House and Senate medians.[80]

Thus are campaign promises made. Yet once a campaign is over, the promises remain. They do not go away. Ordinarily they morph into legislative requests. The new presidents are locked in. "Obama is, quite simply, stuck with these programs [health care and the rest] as a result of his campaign promises," one analysis went in mid-2009.[81] Over the years, an effect of the just over 1 percent Republican tilt in the congressional medians has possibly been to *pry apart* the campaign commitments from their congressional enactment odds a bit more in the cases of Democratic presidents than in the cases of Republicans.

All this is hypothetical. Is there anything to back it up? There is suggestive testimony in the cases of especially Truman and Kennedy. Truman's surprising victory in the 1948 election "nevertheless left the Democrats, and especially the Administration,

---

[78] For Clinton in 1996, a third aim seems to have had nontrivial importance. He wanted to win more than 50 percent of the total popular vote. He fell short.

[79] For an analysis of campaign strategies geared to the Electoral College during recent elections in which state-specific polling information has become especially rich, see Daron R. Shaw, *The Race to 270: The Electoral College and the Campaign Strategies of 2000 and 2004* (Chicago: University of Chicago Press, 2006).

[80] Also, as table 1.3 demonstrates, in every election except one since World War II, the Democratic share of the presidential vote in the median Electoral College unit has always exceeded the party's share of the presidential vote in either the median House district or the median Senate district (that is, state). The exception is 1948 on the Senate side. (That election lacks House data.) Possibly the 1948 election was anomalous because the third-party Strom Thurmond and Henry Wallace candidacies of that year bit into the major-party presidential vote in various important ways in various states.

[81] Dick Morris, "GOP: Stand Your Ground," http://www.realclearpolitics.com, July 1, 2009.

a legacy of other problems," the political scientist David B. Truman commented.

> During the campaign . . . , President Truman had in effect
> committed himself to a program of legislation that was not
> only extensive but also heterogeneous and at a good many
> points highly controversial. Truman was almost inevitably a
> prisoner of the kind of campaign he had conducted. . . . He
> had endorsed the civil rights program with renewed vigor,
> and his attacks on the Republicans had all but obliged him
> to seek repeal of the Taft–Hartley Act and passage of legisla-
> tion on public housing, rent and price control, education,
> and farm prices, to list only the most conspicuous domestic
> matters. The diversity and controversiality of these commit-
> ments were a standing threat to the solidarity of an already
> divided party, and the size of the program meant that the
> most favorable conditions would be required if legislation
> were to be taken on any considerable number of the items.[82]

True to this diagnosis, the reelected Truman asked for an immense program in 1949. And then he kept taking losses—notably
on civil rights, national health insurance, federal aid to education,
repeal of Taft–Hartley, and his Brannan Plan for agriculture.
"Why did he keep asking?" Richard E. Neustadt mused in an
analysis covering the full span of Truman's presidency. Resolute
commitment to an unfulfilled party program was Neustadt's leading interpretation.[83]

In the Kennedy case, according to Mark A. Peterson, the pre-
sident's "activism at the initiative stage came despite the fact that
President Kennedy recognized the limits of his political base."[84]
"He could never escape the political arithmetic," Arthur M.
Schlesinger, Jr., has written; the president "knew that he just
did not have the votes for his more controversial proposals."[85]

[82] David B. Truman, *The Congressional Party: A Case Study* (New York: Wiley, 1959), 17–18.
[83] Neustadt, "Congress and the Fair Deal," 18–21, 40–42, quotation at 40.
[84] Peterson, *Legislating Together*, 240.
[85] Schlesinger, *A Thousand Days*, 708, 712.

According to Theodore C. Sorensen, "After November, 1960, [Kennedy] was counting Congressional votes, and this time he could not make the sums come out right."[86] Yet according to James L. Sundquist, the president, notwithstanding at best a wafer-slim coalitional edge on Capitol Hill, "methodically sent forward to Congress in 1961 most of the program measures to which his party was committed."[87] Medicare and federal aid to education went down to defeat. Richard Bolling, the liberal congressional leader, estimated that in general terms the House of Representatives of 1961 contained 213 "Democratic program-oriented votes" (including 10 Republican liberals) and 224 "conservative-oriented votes."[88]

James MacGregor Burns, theorizing two generations ago about the national system as it existed from Franklin Roosevelt through Kennedy, saw a dissonance something like the one I am exploring here. Presidential campaigns could bring a unique "dramatization of epochal national questions."[89] The presidential party was distinctively "the 'popular' party." Congress had other fish to fry. The difference was systematic: in particular, Democrats in the White House could be counted on to position themselves on the New Dealish side of the Democratic party in Congress—not to mention on that side of Congress as a whole.[90]

Is there any sign of the hypothesized party asymmetry across the sixty years? Let me step back. Animating this study is an interest in tension between political sides heightened by separation-of-powers institutions. Consider the frustrated Rhode Island Democrats of the 1930s. Of special interest is the circumstance in which

[86] Sorensen, *Kennedy*, 339.

[87] James L. Sundquist, *Politics and Policy: The Eisenhower, Kennedy, and Johnson Years* (Washington, D.C.: Brookings Institution, 1968), 473. Kennedy held off on civil rights until 1962.

[88] Richard Bolling, *Power in the House: A History of the Leadership of the House of Representatives* (New York: E. P. Dutton, 1968), 207. Admission of Alaska and Hawaii had briefly raised the House membership to 437.

[89] James MacGregor Burns, *Congress on Trial: The Legislative Process and the Administrative State* (New York: Harper and Brothers, 1949), 12.

[90] James MacGregor Burns, *The Deadlock of Democracy: Four-Party Politics in America* (Englewood Cliffs, N.J.: Prentice-Hall, 1963), 199. Burns's interpretation of the dissonance he saw differs somewhat from my account. Burns's account will be taken up in chapter 3.

one political party tries to advance its core ideological positions and is blocked by the other party. Combine that kind of blockage with allegations of process illegitimacy and a particular kind of trouble may result. In canvassing for party asymmetry, therefore, I confine the analysis at this point to a particular subset of presidential requests. Those are the ones that in each case satisfied two conditions: presidents aimed to advance the core ideological principles of their own parties *and* those aims clashed with the core ideological principles of the opposite party. That strips down the analysis to, at the ultimate, requests like Truman's for national health insurance in 1949 and George W. Bush's for part-privatization of Social Security in 2005.

To be ignored accordingly, for the purpose at hand, are some three-eighths of the 184 requests listed in table 2.1. Of relevance here—the survivors—are the 114 requests listed in boldface type in that table. These are the proposals advancing the parties' core ideologies as stipulated. The reader may wish to scan the table to see which proposals made it into boldface and which did not. Gone from consideration here—that is, not in boldface—are presidential fancies like Carter's curb on water projects. Gone are crisis moves like Nixon's call for a national speed limit in 1973–74 and Bush's for tightening of airline security in late 2001. Gone are requests largely innocent of party principle such as Eisenhower's for the Saint Lawrence Seaway, Carter's for Civil Service reform, and George H. W. Bush's for deficit reduction. Gone also are requests in which presidents jarred against their own parties' ideological type as in Nixon's for his Family Assistance Plan, George H. W. Bush's for the Americans with Disabilities Act, and Clinton's for NAFTA.

To survive the weeding, a request needed to map onto one or more of the party principles specified in table 2.2. Stylized, and I would hope uncontroversial, knowledge is the basis for this categorization.[91] Accommodating the parties' terms of combat in the

<hr/>

[91] I have steered clear of using roll-call data to discern the parties' core ideological positioning. The problem is that roll-call cleavages or dimensions can pick up simple partisanship as well as core ideology. On Capitol Hill, the parties are capable of turning many kinds of matters into party versus party questions. To take a revealing if extreme case, although not one involving roll calls, when the baseball pitcher Roger Clemens faced a

request politics of the last six decades, the principles in the table seem like a plausible list.[92] For example, the Democrats appear as champions of unions, social provision, and progressive tax reform, the Republicans as champions of business, tax cuts, and crackdowns on crime. I specify instances of relevant requests alongside the principles, although I have not tried to be exhaustive. In general, I list the principles separately by party in chronological order according to their first historical appearance in a relevant request. At the practical level of requests, it will be seen in table 2.2, the parties' ideologies have stayed constant in most areas during these decades, yet they have navigated a 180-degree turn in one area—international trade—and they have added or shed content of various sorts as the concerns of the public have risen and fallen.

See table 2.3 for the summary results. Confining the analysis to the 114 ideology-flavored requests, and weighting those requests as in the foregoing discussion, the table displays presidential success rates in a variety of categories. Note at the bottom of the table, for example, that unified party control has brought slightly higher success rates than divided party control (no great surprise)—60 percent versus 51 percent. Republican presidents have enjoyed slightly better luck than Democratic presidents—59 percent versus 56 percent. An intriguing handhold appears in the better record of Republican presidents operating under conditions of unified party control—71 percent as opposed to the Democrats' 56 percent operating in that circumstance. But these disparities are limited and obviously veered by the peculiarities of presidents—for example, Carter.[93]

House investigation in 2008 for alleged drug use, the Democratic committee members lined up as anti-Clemens, the Republicans as pro-Clemens. See Duff Wilson, "For Clemens, No Joy Found in Testimony," *New York Times*, February 14, 2008, A1; Harvey Araton, "A Day to 'Misremember': Politicians Turn Hearing into a Partisan Squabble," *New York Times*, February 14, 2008, D1.

[92] A similar effort at categorization appears in Frances E. Lee, *Beyond Ideology: Politics, Principles, and Partisanship in the U.S. Senate* (Chicago: University of Chicago Press, 2009), ch. 3.

[93] As a background to Carter's poor success rate on core-ideological requests during 1977–78, it is well to recall that the Democrats enjoyed congressional majorities during those years that approached those of 1965–66 when Johnson pursued his Great Society. The

Table 2.2.
Party Principles Figuring in Presidential Requests

Democratic presidents
    Civil rights (that is, proposals for government intervention into labor and housing markets, as in 1949 and 1966, and DC home rule, but *not* proposals regarding the suffrage since voting-rights drives like those of 1957 and 1965 pitted section against section, not party against party)
    Regional planning (Columbia Valley Authority, aid to Appalachia)
    Pro-union (repeal of Taft–Hartley, repeal of 14b)
    Tax reform in a progressive direction (as in 1949–50, 1977–78, 1993)
    Social provision (Social Security, health insurance, housing, unemployment benefits, aid to education, manpower retraining, antipoverty, Medicare, EITC hike, CHIP, AmeriCorps)
    Regulation of industry (Brannan Plan, rent control, minimum wage hikes, pharmaceuticals in 1962, Carter's energy plan, family leave in 1993)
    Easier immigration (admit displaced persons in 1949, the 1965 reform)
    Free trade through the 1950s (the Democrats' traditional stance on international trade dating back more than a century; the Republicans were more protectionist)
    Consumer protection (pharmaceuticals in 1962, Consumer Protection Agency, patients' bill of rights)
    Creation of new agencies to serve party causes (HUD, Department of Education, Consumer Protection Agency)
    Regulation to protect the environment (highway beautification, Water Quality Act)
    Support culture (Arts and Humanities foundations)
    Process reforms (ethics reform, motor voter, campaign finance reform, lobbying reform)
    Handgun control (Brady bill)

Republican presidents
    Empowering of state and local governments (tidelands oil in 1953, Nixon's revenue sharing, Reagan's new federalism, antibusing for racial balance)

TABLE 2.2. (*Continued*)

Tax cuts or business-friendly tax revisions (tax code in 1953–54, omnibus cuts in 1981 and 2001, Tax Reform Act in 1986, capital gains cuts in 1989, estate tax repeal in 2005–6)

Deregulation of industries or markets (Eisenhower's plans for agriculture, Nixon's for natural gas pricing, Reagan's for agriculture and S&Ls)

Probusiness in labor-management relations (Eisenhower's request regarding Taft–Hartley)

Spurring of new private industries or markets (atomic energy in 1953–54, Medicare prescription drugs in 2001–02, expand Health Savings Accounts in 2005–6)

Privatizing (postal service in 1970, tuition tax credits, Social Security in 2005)

Crackdown on crime (requests by Nixon and Bush 41)

Moral regulation (illegal drugs, school prayer, abortion, faith-based initiatives)

Anti–affirmative action (antibusing for racial balance)

Expenditure cuts (Nixon's antipoverty cuts in 1973, OBRA in 1981)

Smaller government (balanced budget amendment)

Patriotism (anti–flag-burning amendment)

Free trade starting in the 1990s (the GOP's distinctive new position in contrast to the Democrats' new stance of protectionism: fast-track authority, CAFTA)

Antiterrorism (as against the Democrats' concerns about civil liberties and executive power: the Patriot Act, military tribunals)

Protecting business in law sector (bankruptcy reform, curb class-action suits, curb medical malpractice suits)

Energy production (as against the Democrats' concerns about the environment: Alaska drilling, other measures of the 2000s)

I should emphasize both the precariousness and the boundaries of this exercise. Many contestable coding decisions were made

party's House and Senate edges were, respectively, 295–140 and 68–32 under Johnson, 292–143 and 62–38 under Carter. Carter had more northern Democrats in the House than Johnson.

Table 2.3.
Presidential Success Rates on Requests Issuing from Standard Party
Ideologies (with requests weighted according to their importance)

President	Years	Wins	Losses	Success rate
Democrats, Unified Party Control				
Truman	1949–50	7	13	
Kennedy	1961–62	10	5	
Johnson	1965–66	19	4	
Carter	1977–78	3	8	
Clinton	1993–94	9	7	
	Total	48	37	56%
Democrats, Divided Party Control				
Clinton	1997–98	5	4	
	Total	5	4	56%
Republicans, Unified Party Control				
Eisenhower	1953–54	7	2	
Bush 43	early 2001	3	0	
Bush 43	2005–6	10	6	
	Total	20	8	71%
Republicans, Divided Party Control				
Eisenhower	1957–58	1	0	
Nixon	1969–70	3	3	
Nixon	1973–74	0	3	
Reagan	1981–82	8	6	
Reagan	1985–86	3	2	
Bush 41	1989–90	1	2	
Bush 43	late 2001, 2002	3	3	
	Total	19	19	50%
Total Unified Control		68	45	60%
Total Divided Control		24	23	51%
Total Democratic		53	41	56%
Total Republican		39	27	59%

along the way. What is the Patriot Act doing in the dataset? Is it really fair, even after all the weighting, to assign Reagan only an eight-out-of-fourteen success rate in 1981–82 given his immense investment in ERTA and OBRA compared with his reserved stances toward the several smaller items he lost on? Is it fair to assign Reagan and George H. W. Bush losses on constitutional amendments, and Truman and Kennedy on civil rights bills, that needed two-thirds rather than simple majorities in one or both houses?[94] All in all, in light of many canonical judgments, does Kennedy really deserve a ten-out-of-fifteen success score?[95] There is a good deal of coding fragility. The problem of outlier presidents will not go away. On the low-scoring side, Carter was Carter and Truman was Truman. There is the low incidence of unified Republican control. There is the problem of the small, all things considered, Ns of 114 or, with weighting, 160 in the core-ideology dataset I have worked with. Still, I would not expect improvement in a more extensive strategy—that is, one that would expand the dataset into a terrain of less motivated presidential proposals in a reach for larger numbers and thus statistical significance. The stratum of requests dealt with here is in principle a complete universe. It is not a sample.

As for boundaries, a theoretical caveat applies. Legislative requests that the presidents did in fact historically make are the grist for a Baucus effect as I probe for it here. Yet the Republican-side tilts of the House and Senate could have been exacting the Democratic presidents a penalty not discernible through this lens. To substantial degree, after all, as was discussed earlier, the presidents of both parties are let's-win-on-Capitol-Hill instrumentalists. Legislative requests may be designed accordingly. For

[94] In certain respects, the differences between the parties crystallized on civil rights in the 1960s. But on labor-market regulation centering on fair employment practices (FEPC), a principled party cleavage was amply evident in the 1940s under Truman. See Eric Schickler, Kathryn Pearson, and Brian Feinstein, "Congressional Parties and Civil Rights Politics from 1933 to 1972," *Journal of Politics* 72:3 (July 2010), 672–89.

[95] In a different calculation, James L. Sundquist has scored Kennedy three-out-of-eleven on his domestic requests during 1961–62. See *Politics and Policy*, 474–76. Yet Sundquist's own agenda rather than Kennedy's was perhaps at issue in this estimate.

one thing, election promises may be trimmed or abandoned to match congressional realities. Those realities have included the 1.1 and 1.3 percent biases. Thus the White House request list in use here might itself have incorporated, so to speak, a slight tilt toward congressional contexts that has disfavored the policy propensities of Democratic presidents. A Baucus effect as I have canvassed for it here would not pick up any such tilt. This is a difficult matter. The empirics is daunting. Evidence of party-asymmetric White House strategizing would be needed in a data realm of soft evidence where any real systematic dissonance would be tiny. In my experience with the historical accounts, a dissonance like this does not jump out, but it may be there. It may be a hidden ingredient of the environment.

Notwithstanding these limits, the evidence realm that I explore here for a Baucus effect has a theoretical importance all by itself. It is a realm of high-visibility action where the presidents have pressed their core-ideological priorities. It is the public sphere of American politics where the doings of governments, parties, and politicians can be seen and judged for their quality and legitimacy. Also, it is a realm that might connect the promises of elections to the performance of governments.

The material in table 2.3 allows multivariate analysis. I report some results in a brief addendum at the close of this chapter.[96] The question is: Controlling in simple yes–no terms for conditions of unified versus divided party control, have Democratic presidents suffered worse win–loss rates on the core-ideological front than have Republican presidents? Arranging equations is troublesome given the one-through-four weightings of the proposals. I followed a plan that loses some information but is tractable and, it seems, true to the data. There are three equations—one for all 114 proposals unweighted, one for the 82 lower-priority proposals that were weighted one, and one for the 32 high-priority proposals that were weighted two through four (not distinguishing

[96] Thanks to Peter Aronow for advising and conducting this work, Joseph Sempolinski for an earlier version, and Eric Schickler for tips on how to proceed.

among them according to their weights).[97] I present those latter 32 items again in table 2.4 for convenient inspection.

In the 114-item equation, and also the 82-item one, unified party control brings a significant, unsurprising thumbs-up to the White House proposals, yet the variable for which party controls the presidency performs poorly. It is the equation for the 32 high-priority proposals that performs most interestingly. Unified party control drops out, but Democratic control of the presidency perks up. Or rather perks down. Notice in table 2.4 that the record of the Democratic presidents at this high-priority stratum is eight wins and eleven losses, that of the Republican presidents nine wins and four losses. Despite the small size of this distilled dataset, the coefficient in the multivariate equation for Democratic control of the White House edges toward significance. Democratic presidents draw a minus sign; they seem to do worse. Edges is the appropriate term. You would not want to bet too much. Surfacing is a p-value of 0.187 for the coefficient, which means that the odds are roughly one in five that the relationship is a fluke. (The odds become roughly one in ten if a one-tailed statistical test is applied—a plausible move since the negative directional sign of the relationship is theoretically expected). Peering past this caveat, the equation says: under unified party control, Republican presidents have enjoyed a 71 percent probability of winning as against a Democratic probability of 42 percent. Under divided party control, the Republican probability has been 67 percent, the Democratic probability 37 percent.

Where does this leave us? On exhibit is some indication of an "off-center" systemic tilt favoring the Republicans.[98] We may be

[97] Not reported in the addendum are several trials that did not bring appreciably different results. I tried a dependent win–loss variable that coded Nixon's tax cut and Carter's energy plan as 0.5 results rather than as clean losses. I tried a dependent win–loss variable that coded as wins rather than losses the 4 proposals among the 114 that passed in the subsequent Congresses under the same presidents (those were open housing under Johnson, revenue sharing under Nixon, a department of education under Carter, and Medicare drugs expansion under George W. Bush). I tried an equation edgy in statistical terms that directly weighted 1 to 4 each of the 114 entries of the win–loss variable.

[98] The term is from Jacob S. Hacker and Paul Pierson, *Off Center: The Republican Revolution and the Erosion of American Democracy* (New Haven: Yale University Press, 2006).

Table 2.4.
High-Weighted Presidential Proposals Tied to Core Party Ideologies

President	Legislative proposal	Weight	Win	Loss	Later?
Truman	Omnibus civil rights	2		loss	
Truman	Repeal of Taft–Hartley	2		loss	
Truman	Federal aid to education	2		loss	
Truman	National health insurance	2		loss	
Truman	Agriculture (Brannan Plan)	2		loss	
Truman	Omnibus housing	2	win		
Ike (1)	Tidelands oil to states	2	win		
Ike (1)	Revision of tax code	2	win		
Ike (1)	Flexible crop prices	2	win		
Ike (1)	Revision of Taft–Hartley	2		loss	
Kennedy	Aid to depressed areas	2	win		
Kennedy	Federal aid to education	2		loss	
Kennedy	Medicare	2		loss	
Kennedy	Minimum wage hike	2	win		
Kennedy	Omnibus housing	2	win		
Johnson	Federal aid to education (ESEA)	3	win		
Johnson	Medicare/Medicaid	3	win		
Johnson	Model Cities	2	win		
Johnson	Open housing (civil rights)	2		loss	yes
Nixon (1)	Revenue sharing with states	2		loss	yes
Nixon (2)	Budget-cutting poverty programs	2		loss	
Carter	Omnibus energy plan	4		loss	
Carter	Tax reform	2		loss	
Reagan (1)	Tax cuts (ERTA)	4	win		
Reagan (1)	Expenditure cuts (OBRA)	3	win		
Reagan (2)	Tax Reform Act (TRA)	3	win		
Clinton (1)	Omnibus budget package	4	win		
Clinton (1)	Health-care reform	4		loss	

TABLE 2.4. (*Continued*)

President	Legislative proposal	Weight	Win	Loss	Later?
Bush 43(1)	Tax cuts	3	win		
Bush 43(1)	USA Patriot Act after 9/11	2	win		
Bush 43(2)	Privatization of Social Security	3		loss	
Bush 43(2)	Military tribunals for terrorists	2	win		

seeing a real imbalance. Possibly the prying-apart idea works. Possibly the small House and Senate tilts have emanated in a Baucus effect and made it harder for the Democratic presidents to perform on their campaign promises.

Yet two comments seem in order. First, the skew emerging in the data here may exist, but is it *seen* to exist? The answer may be yes for a class of elite commentators, yet it seems doubtful that the skew idea has much resonance or grounding in the perceptions of the general American public. Supplementing, or bearing out, the ambiguous statistical results shown here, the drama of American politics supplies too much in the way of countermanding impressions. In the surface arithmetic of elections and governing—the Democrats control 257 House seats, the Republicans 178, and so on—the Democrats have obviously done pretty well over the years. In Congress, it is obvious that Democrats as well as Republicans can win great legislative victories. The New Deal and the Great Society carved the high notches. The Democrats won their health-care plan in 2010. It is obvious that a president of either party can suffer a spectacular loss in a major legislative drive. Clinton's drive for health-care reform was a complete loss, but so was George W. Bush's drive to partly privative Social Security. In another aspect, voters seem to react symmetrically to liberal and conservative policy drives that actually end in laws. In general, the enactment of conservative laws spurs a liberal reaction in voter mood. Liberal laws spur a conservative reaction. As the government drifts from one party to the other, there seems to be a homeostatic pattern of symmetric voter response to ideological overreach.[99] If the Democrats were not achieving their legislative aims, they might not be spurring a reaction.

Second, the prying-apart dynamic is not the only conceivable cause of the imbalance suggested by the equation. Here is one alternative line of speculation (there might be others). In the analysis so far, voters are posited to send messages in presidential elections, but, in reality, they can also send message *between* elections. The dynamics of the public sphere go on continuously. If a president sends up a legislative proposal that wins major attention, its ensuing stock in public opinion polls or other manifestations may bleed back into Capitol Hill processes. It is not good for a proposal to sink in the polls. For example, negative public opinion capped by the shock election of Massachusetts Senator Scott Brown nearly derailed Obama's health-care reform in early 2010.[100] "The longer it was debated, the more skeptical people became," President Obama commented in his State of the Union address of January 2010.[101] Similarly, Clinton's plan for health-care reform and George W. Bush's for part-privatization Social Security did not play well with the public once they were unpacked. In general, here is a variable that could use some systematic comparative work. Opinion surveys would need to be probed for usable questions across several decades. Yet good studies exist: Roosevelt's

[99] Robert S. Erikson, Michael B. MacKuen, and James A. Stimson, *The Macropolity* (New York: Cambridge University Press, 2002), ch. 9. In this study, which covers 1953 through 1996, the enactments in question were not necessarily ones promoted by presidents.

[100] On January 14, 2010, a RealClearPolitics average of ten recent polling firms' results on the Democrats' health-care legislation had it down by 11.3 points—39.2 percent in favor, 50.5 percent against. http://www.realclearpolitics.com/epolls/other/obama_and_democrats _health_care_plan-ll. Wording on surveys like these during the fall and winter of 2009–10 pointed to the legislation under consideration on Capitol Hill yet varied. In general, the antis turned up more intense than the pros, a nontrivial aspect in political terms. A report on Massachusetts election day went: "A new [nationwide] Washington Post–ABC News poll found that 44 percent of Americans support the proposed changes in the health-care system being debated in Congress, while 51 percent oppose them. Opposition is more intense than support, with 39 percent saying they strongly oppose the legislation and 22 percent saying they strongly favor it." Dan Balz and Chris Cillizza, "Senate Election in Massachusetts Could Be Harbinger for Health-Care Reform," *Washington Post*, January 19, 2010, online.

[101] Quoted in Robert Pear and David M. Herszenhorn, "Health Care Gives Way to Economy and Jobs," *New York Times*, January 28, 2010, p. A18.

Court-packing plan of 1937, for example, did not go over well with the public;[102] George W. Bush's tax cut of 2001 did.[103]

What are the implications? A public that won't buy can hurt. The public marketability of proposals—not during presidential election campaigns when they tend to be vague, but later on when they become concrete—is another factor that might trump everything else in the fates of White House requests. Is another party asymmetry lurking here? Is it possible that, on average over time, the Democratic presidents' first-order proposals once vetted have proven to be *less popular* than the Republican proposals? Consider the entries in table 2.4. Grist for at least one pattern seems to appear. One Democratic bent, to draw on an earlier idea, has been grand, comprehensive rationalizing schemes to regulate large sectors of the economy—from Truman's health-insurance program and his Brannan Plan for agriculture through Carter's omnibus energy program, Clinton's health-care program, and, beyond table 2.4, Obama's drives for cap-and-trade and health-care reform. The *kind* of ambition in these enterprises is a party signature: you can't do anything without doing everything.[104] They have proven a hard sell. Once laid out in clear specifics, they have been picked apart and drawn suspicion and opposition.[105]

Why do the Democrats keep doing this? There are the obvious policy reasons. Goals such as insuring the uninsured and preserving

[102] Gregory A. Caldeira, "Public Opinion and the U.S. Supreme Court: FDR's Court-Packing Plan," *American Political Science Review* 81:4 (December 1987), 1139–53. This Roosevelt initiative had not been a campaign promise in 1936. It was a surprise unveiled after the election.

[103] Larry M. Bartels, *Unequal Democracy: The Political Economy of the New Gilded Age* (New York: Russell Sage, 2008), ch. 6.

[104] For a discussion of this theme, see William Schambra, "Obama and the Policy Approach," *National Affairs*, no. 1 (Fall 2009), 127–44.

[105] On cap-and-trade in calendar 2009: "Speaker Nancy Pelosi . . . is paying a price for the arm-twisting she did on the climate change bill last month. Democratic House members were rankled by how the climate bill passed—and stunned by the criticism they got at home." Mike Soraghan and Jared Allen, "Pelosi Paying a Price for Climate Bill," *The Hill*, July 16, 2009, online. "Moderate House Democrats who voted in favor of the cap-and-trade bill just before the July 4th recess came under fire back home, and Republicans have vowed to make the issue a key line of attack during next year's elections." Lisa Lerer, "Dems to W. H.: Drop Cap-and-Trade," *Politico*, December 27, 2009, online.

the environment seem to require it. There is an ideological reason. Planning is trusted over markets. There is a kind of interest-group reason. Intellectuals, a party constituency, are at ease with large doses of smart complexity. With health care, there has been a heritage reason. Elaine Kamarck writes, "Because universal health care is the last stone in the social safety net edifice created by Franklin Roosevelt, it has been, for decades, an obsession of the Democratic Party's elite. Unfortunately for them, this obsession has never been shared by the public."[106]

At any rate, a popularity differential between the proposals of the two parties might be seeping into the win–loss patterns of table 2.4 and its associated equations. This is speculation. Note that failure to enact unpopular proposals does not supply a solid platform for blaming the system.

Yet all said and done, the prying-apart idea as pursued in this chapter hangs out there, too. Perhaps a general Baucus effect exists and is consequential.

ADDENDUM

I use multivariate probit regression to explore whether the presidents of one party have done better than those of the other party in getting their legislative proposals enacted. There are 114 observations ranging from 1949–50 through 2005–06. These are the boldface entries from table 2.1. The dependent variable is a binary formulation indexing whether a proposal made by a president was enacted during his first two years in office. There are two independent variables: the party of the president (coded 1 for Democrats, 0 for Republicans), and party control (coded 1 if one party simultaneously controlled the House, Senate, and presidency, 0 if control was divided).

In addition, I coded proposals according to the priority placed on them by the presidents. The 82 proposals weighted as 1 in

[106] Elaine Kamarck, "The Opposition's Opening Remarks," http://www.economist.com/debate/days/view/457/print, February 3, 2010.

TABLE 2.5.
Enactment Success as a Function of Party Control

	All 114 proposals	The lower-priority 82	The high-priority 32
Unified party control	0.591**	0.788**	0.135
	(0.292)	(0.332)	(0.730)
Democratic president	−0.073	0.212	−0.765
	(0.280)	(0.329)	(0.580)
Constant	−0.152	−0.351	0.431
	(0.218)	(0.250)	(0.529)
N	114	82	32
Pseudo R2	0.0314	0.0871	0.0533

$^*p < .10, ^{**}p < .05, ^{***}p < .01$. Standard errors in parentheses.

table 2.1 appear here as lower priority. The 32 proposals weighted as 2, 3, or 4 in table 2.1 (and listed again in table 2.4) appear as high priority. The result is three regressions: one for all 114 observations, one for the 82 lower-priority items, one for the 32 high-priority items. The tests are two-tailed.

One strong result appears. In two of the three regressions, there is a statistically significant positive relationship (p-value <0.05) between unified party control and enactment success. In the 114-item equation, for the case of a Republican president, unified control raises the predicted probability of enactment success from 44.0 percent to 67.0 percent. For a Democratic president, unified control raises this probability from 41.1 percent to 64.3 percent. Further, although not statistically significant, the results nevertheless suggest that, all else equal, unified party control is more likely to predict enactment success when the proposals are lower priority.

No statistically significant relationship appears between presidential party and enactment success in any of the regressions. However, there is suggestive evidence that Democratic presidents might have more difficulty enacting high-priority proposals (those with weights of 2, 3, or 4) than do Republicans. Under unified party control, Republican presidents appear to have a 71.4 percent probability of success with high-priority proposals, compared with the Democrats' 42.1 percent. When party control is divided, Republican presidents have a 66.7 percent predicted probability of winning on high-priority proposals compared with the Democrats' 36.9 percent. These results should be interpreted with caution, given the very large standard errors and small dataset associated with this regression.

CHAPTER 3

House and Senate I

How has Congress positioned itself vis-à-vis the presidency? That was the subject of chapter 2. How have the House and Senate *differed* in positioning themselves vis-à-vis the presidency? That is the subject of this chapter and the next, once again relying on chapter 2's list of presidential requests as an analytic lens. This time, I rely chiefly, although not exclusively, on a subset of those requests that have seen the House respond one way, the Senate another. In the background of the discussion again are the questions of balance and strain in the American system.

In chapter 1, using presidential popular-vote share as a yardstick, it emerged that the House and Senate medians in that vote share have on average diverged, respectively, 1.1 and 1.3 percent in a pro-Republican direction from the national popular vote-share taken straight. A difference of 0.2 percent is very small. What should it predict? If partisanship were the sole force in American public life, and if, beyond the 1.1 versus 1.3 disparity, no other general sources of dissonant behavior existed between House and Senate, we would expect the two chambers not to diverge in their responses to presidential requests, except trivially. At least, we would not expect their response *rates* to differ. On average, a near symmetry across the chambers would prevail. That would be the default.

Over the long haul, I argue in this chapter and the next, the historical record has not departed all that far from the posited default. Alas for the White House, either the House or the Senate is free to balk all by itself. The Senate, for example, said no to Truman on civil rights, shredded Carter's energy program, and blocked George W. Bush on drilling for oil in Alaska. Yet the House thwarted Kennedy on federal aid to education, buried Carter's plan for hospital cost containment, and damagingly derailed George H. W. Bush's otherwise agreed-on (the Senate was in favor, too) omnibus deal for deficit reduction in 1990.

In probing for asymmetric policy results, I consider two measures. The first casts a broad net. Have presidents, regardless of party, encountered what might be called a "general outlier disparity" in pressing their requests on Capitol Hill? That is, has either of the two houses notably outpaced the other in giving the White House, regardless of which party has held it, trouble? In general, has either the House or the Senate played the role of dominant naysayer? Probably most of us would nominate the Senate for that role, yet has the Senate actually performed it? The argument here is: not really. The Senate does have an edge, owing no doubt chiefly to its internal procedures, but over the long haul that edge has been limited.

The second measure sorts the data specifically by party. Have either Democratic or Republican presidents enjoyed disproportionate success in the Senate as opposed to the House in pressing their requests? Has either chamber disproportionately favored the presidents of either particular party? Has there been a "partisan outlier disparity"? The answer here is: no. Over the long haul, on the evidence, no such differential tilt has existed.

These two measures yield patterns that are similar albeit not identical. In probing for "general outlier disparities," I depart from the strict partisan focus of this work. Institutions as such come into play. But I do not depart very far, and the direct institutional analysis places the strict partisan patterns in relief and offers its own kind of illumination.

These null, or nearly null, results are for the long haul. For it, an implication is that the plain language of the Constitution may still be an unsurpassed guide to U.S. legislative behavior. Generic processes tend to prevail. But also of relevance is the short, or perhaps the local, haul. By that I mean congressional policy behavior in particular eras, in particular policy areas during eras, or by particular Capitol Hill institutions during eras. At this level, professional political science has been very good. That is perhaps its singular merit. In general, in addressing topics of either the electoral underpinnings or the internal procedures of Congress, political scientists studying that institution have tended to focus on wrinkles, singularities, or distortions. What is wrong with the American system? Why don't the institutions do what the public wants them to do? Certainly, plenty of relevant wrinkles, singularities, and distortions have been worth attending to during the last six decades. Yet as it happens—I will take pains to demonstrate this—the singularities or distortions of relevance in the congressional sphere have tended to be short haul or local in the sense employed above. Thus also the political science theorizing, which has tended to center on circumstances in a current time frame and to be validly explanatory—when it reaches that standing—for those, and often just those, existent circumstances. Apart from everything else, one of my objectives in this chapter and the next is to comment on the tradition of theorizing that we have witnessed since the 1940s regarding congressional singularities or distortions. Several theories or accounts are explored.

In general, over the last sixty years taken as a whole, the case for near House versus Senate policy symmetry looks pretty good. The long-term policy record is *consistent with* an interpretation that the small 1.1 versus 1.3 vote-shares dissonance between the two chambers has underpinned a rendition of near symmetry across them in policy terms. That is the best that can be said. A direct demonstration of any such cause and effect is not possible.

Yet it is possible to peer through a haze of several other potential sources of policy dissonance between House and Senate during the sixty years to envision *why* the overall near policy symmetry predicted by the 1.1 versus 1.3 dissonance has likely been more
or less realized. It is a matter of plausible reasoning and marshal-
ling of evidence. The argument goes as follows. In general, there
has been a canceling-out effect. Certain structural causes, procedural and otherwise, that have might have tilted one chamber or
the other toward policy outlier behavior during the sixty years
either have favored the White House and each of its two presidential parties impartially or have had their day and fallen away,
yielding the way to other structural causes that have cut the politics differently.

There is an ancillary feature. In analyzing the record, I kept
reflecting that certain structural singularities have been more
limited in their policy effects than is commonly believed. In particular, at the level of real empirical activity in both chambers,
obstruction to textbook rule by floor majorities has had limits.
Whatever their customs, their formal procedures, or their parties'
pretensions, both chambers have, on balance, steered closer than
one might suppose to a default framework of majority rule when
operating at the level of high-priority White House requests.[1] At
this level, certain well-known congressional processes of the last
sixty years do not seem to have brought the stubborn assertion of
antimajoritarianism that a variety of political scientists writing
across three generations of scholarship have theorized them to
do. Pushed to their limits, certain of these processes might have
thrown the system decisively out of whack. It is difficult to know.
The counterfactuals are difficult to plumb. In the cases of any such
processes taken alone or in the aggregate, to push things routinely to the antimajoritarian wall might have brought a politically
intolerable overall imbalance to the success rates of presidents or
presidential parties, or, at a more workaday level, an intolerable

[1] For the idea of a "majoritarian postulate," see Krehbiel, *Information and Legislative Organization*, 16.

spectacle of issue-by-issue deadlock on Capitol Hill. But, in general, the pushing has fallen short of the wall.

To sum up, over the long haul the canceling out of the various, and often quite perishable, structural singularities associated with the two congressional chambers has arguably helped confine the system to an envelope of policy symmetry consistent with the prediction of the small underlying 1.1 versus 1.3 vote-shares dissonance—which, after all, had it been something like 1.1 versus 4.3, could have been wreaking real havoc. An ancillary feature, which will be probed in detail, is the apparently limited thrust, in actual practice, of a variety of nonmajoritarian processes on Capitol Hill.

I use a truncated two-part dataset to ground this chapter and the next. Of the 184 presidential requests listed in table 2.1, using binary judgments as earlier, the White House got its way on 110 but not on 74. Except where noted, I do not weight the proposals in this chapter or the next. What can be said about the 74? In which cases did one chamber vote to approve a measure but the other chamber not do so, resulting in nothing at all being passed? There are 27 such instances. This is the first part of the dataset. It is reasonably hard evidence. Given the 74 losses as a starting point, any replication of the search should yield the same list. We can see with certainty whether or not a chamber actually passed something.[2]

Still, it is well to realize that a list like this might owe its membership, at least in part, to certain twists of strategic behavior by parties or politicians. A president who foresees success for a

[2] There is one asterisked case. I coded Clinton's request for fast-track trade authority in 1997–98 as approved by the Senate (the House balked), although that is not exactly what happened. In fact, however, the Senate fully made up its mind on the matter. The account in *CQA 1997* (pp. 2–87) reads: "On November 4 [1997], the Senate easily invoked cloture on the motion to proceed to the fast-track bill. The margin was surprisingly large, 69–31, and despite its procedural nature was taken as a definitive sign that the Senate would be able to pass the legislation. . . . On November 5, the Senate agreed by a similar margin to proceed to floor consideration of the bill. The vote was 68–31. . . . Then the Senate stopped and waited for the House to act." But the House did not act. See also Benjamin Allen, "The Derailment of Fast-Track Trade Legislation," presented at the annual conference of the American Political Science Association, Atlanta, September 2–5, 1999; Kedron Bardwell, "The Puzzling Decline in House Support for Free Trade: Was Fast Track a Referendum on NAFTA?" *Legislative Studies Quarterly* 25:4 (November 2000), 591–610.

request in one chamber yet failure in the other might make no request at all. Why waste the time and energy? Also, one chamber bent on approving a request might hold off action if it sees the other chamber stalling. Again, why waste the time and energy? Through anticipations like these, the list of twenty-seven formal dissonances might have been, so to speak, trimmed down. Yet happily, at the level of the politics of presidential requesting, a striking feature of the American system is its immense transparency. Neither the strategies nor the issue stances of politicians are all that difficult to figure out. On the congressional side, we are told every day what they are. Little is more transparent than the manipulations of a Harry Reid. On the White House side it can take longer, but an unending traffic in journalistic coverage, memoirs, insider accounts, and scholarship performs the same role in the long run.[3] On the basis of casual inspection of the elaborate sixty-year record, I would guess that strategic behavior of the kinds adumbrated above has not trimmed down the eventual list of twenty-seven House versus Senate instances very much. Presidents can indeed fold their aims as suggested. It is amply documented, for example, that presidents Franklin D. Roosevelt and John Kennedy shied away from championing civil rights bills in anticipation of Senate, although not House, obstruction.[4] It is easy to *see* these two presidents' calculations.[5] Strategies, like issue

[3] As in the skilled interviews conducted for Light, *The President's Agenda*; and Peterson, *Legislating Together*.

[4] See, for example, Fred Greenbaum, "The Anti-Lynching Bill of 1935: The Irony of 'Equal Justice—Under Law,'" *Journal of Human Relations* 15:3 (1967), 72–85, at 75–76; William E. Leuchtenburg, *Franklin D. Roosevelt and the New Deal, 1932–1940* (New York: Harper and Row, 1963), 186; Sorensen, *Kennedy*, 342; Sundquist, *Politics and Policy*, 256–57; Light, *The President's Agenda*, 104–5. Also, it is easy to document that presidents Truman and Johnson were no less aware of the filibuster barrier on civil rights. See, for example, William Frank Zornow, *America at Mid-Century: The Truman Administration* (Cleveland: Howard Allen, 1959), 114; Rowland Evans and Robert Novak, *Lyndon B. Johnson: The Exercise of Power* (New York: New American Library, 1966), 378–79.

[5] Another instance involves the Clinton administration and health-care reform in early 1993. The White House planners thought they could sell their initiative to the public and the House (which turned out not to be true), but that even if they did, a Senate filibuster might loom. For that reason, they toyed with the idea of folding health care into a budget reconciliation measure to shield it against a filibuster. For plausible complicated reasons, they rejected that course. The point here is that the White House strategizing on this

stances, can be approached as empirical matters—not just as deposits of theoretical imputation. On presidential requests, has chamber-specific calculation of this Roosevelt or Kennedy sort played much of a role during the last sixty years? So far as I can tell, it has not. Similarly, the incidence of one action-prone chamber holding off as it eyes the other one stall has probably been low, albeit not zero.[6] For one thing, members of Congress, as well as presidents, like to express themselves, or to move ideas or measures along, even in the face of adversity or immediate inconsequence.

There is an additional wrinkle regarding the list. On money bills, the House enjoys the constitutional role of first mover. In other policy areas, two houses have equal entry and they tend to exercise it. Yet in the money realm, the Senate gets a shot at rejecting House-passed bills but the House does not get a shot (in principle at any rate; the practice can deviate) at rejecting Senate-passed bills.[7] For the dataset here, what is the implication? Is the

---

matter is easy to see. Accounts appear in Johnson and Broder, *The System*, 118–27; Bill Clinton, *My Life* (New York: Vintage, 2004), 492–93.

[6] Forty-seven of the seventy-four White House losses were *not* straight-up instances where one chamber formally voted approval but the other did not. Of the forty-seven instances, eighteen involved money bills, which are considered below. In twenty of the remaining twenty-nine instances, compelling evidence exists via preferences expressed in formal processes or otherwise that one chamber was *not* action-prone yet inert because the other chamber was stalling. In a further instance (statehood for Hawaii in 1958), as a practical matter it was too late in a session for either chamber to act. In two instances (the Columbia Valley plan in 1949–50 and the Colorado Valley plan in 1953–54), little action occurred in either chamber; there seems to be no good reason to suppose that one chamber was ready to act yet the other not. In two instances under Eisenhower (postal reform and national health insurance), the House formally turned thumbs down and it is not clear what the Senate would have done otherwise, but positive Senate action does not seem to have been a good bet. That leaves four instances. On promanagement revision of the Taft–Hartley Act in 1953–54, it is possible that the House would have acted if the Senate had not said no. It is possible that the Senate would have approved a Consumer Protection Agency in 1977–78 if the House had not said no. It is possible that the Senate would have approved Eisenhower's federal aid to education plan in 1957–58 if the House had not said no. These are of course cloudy judgments dependent on counterfactuals. There is only one surefire bet for counterfactual behavior: the House would very likely have enacted a Kennedy-backed civil rights bill in 1961–62 if a Senate filibuster had not loomed. In these last four instances, the House was the possible "waiting to see" chamber twice, the Senate twice.

[7] For classical accounts, see Richard F. Fenno, Jr., *The Power of the Purse: Appropriations Politics in Congress* (Boston: Little, Brown, 1966); Richard F. Fenno, Jr., *Congressmen in Com-*

Senate's actual naysaying role, compared with that of the House, thus artifactually, in a sense, boosted? I would guess not—or at least very much—in the dataset here. Again, the marked transparency of, in this case, issue stances in the politics of White House requesting makes possible a plausible assessment. I doubt that the chamber balance in the dataset of twenty-seven House versus Senate results has much rooting in first-mover considerations.[8]

Now for the second part of the truncated dataset. Here I consider certain instances of the 184 requests in which, even though a statute did end up getting passed and signed, one of the two houses showed itself to be a distinctly more hostile to a White

---

mittees (Boston: Little, Brown, 1973); John F. Manley, *The Politics of Finance: The House Committee on Ways and Means* (Boston: Little, Brown, 1970). Congress's post-1974 budget process has apparently allowed the Senate somewhat more of an initiating role. See Strahan, *New Ways and Means*, 51.

[8] At stake is a counterfactual. Might equal-mover rights on money bills have inflated, in violation of the pattern arrived at here, the incidence of White House requests passed by the Senate yet rejected by the House? Of the seventy-four White House losses, twenty-six involved requests that fell at least partly within the jurisdiction of the House Ways and Means, Appropriations, or Budget committee. That includes trade and entitlements proposals and also Carter's 1977 energy plan. Of these twenty-six, eight resulted in straight-out formal House-versus-Senate dissonance—we know what the up versus down chamber preferences were—thus largely foreclosing counterfactual speculation. Another six emanated in final enactments that along the way revealed floor preferences in both houses, thus also largely foreclosing counterfactual speculation. In two other cases, Reagan's ideas for a "new federalism" and tuition tax credits do not seem to have lit much of a fire in either house. In another three instances, great inspiration would be needed to envision scenarios in which the Senate, although not the House, might have approved Truman's request for an upper-income-bracket tax hike, Clinton's for his health-care plan, or George W. Bush's for part-privatization of social security. In another four cases—trade under Eisenhower, Medicare under Kennedy, welfare reform under Carter, and child care under Clinton—the Senate held at least one roll-call vote *defeating* a White House request even though the House had not officially acted. The moves in these cases are suggestive although not dispositive. Some were fly-by-night amending moves. And circumstances can vary. In the case of Medicare, which the Senate rejected by 52–48 in a high-publicity, showdown vote in 1962, Sundquist (*Politics and Policy*, 477) speculates that the measure might have attracted the needed increment of Senate votes if the House had approved it previously rather than bottling it up in the Ways and Means Committee. That leaves three instances. It is conceivable that an equal-mover Senate would have approved Nixon's revenue-sharing plan in 1969–70, or Clinton's welfare reform in 1993–94, although I do not see any reason to declare these eventualities good bets. Perhaps the most intriguing counterfactual is that the Senate as equal-mover might have bought into Nixon's national health insurance plan in 1973–74, although that too does not look likely. In all, there is a shortage, albeit not a complete vacuum, of promising counterfactuals on this front. Of course, all this discussion is necessarily speculation.

House request than the other as an enactment was being thrashed out. In instances like these, too, an important kind of difference between House and Senate can emerge. In such cases, of which I identified twelve,[9] the evidence is necessarily less than clipped and sure. It lacks the laydown ingredient of whether or not this or that chamber actually passed something at all. It is normal for White House requests, after all, to run into complicated gradations of hospitality or hostility between House and Senate as they are addressed on Capitol Hill. I had to make my own judgments here about whether an apt interchamber dissonance was pronounced enough to warrant attention. Yet it would be a mistake to ignore certain instances of starkly contrasting, even if not ultimately yielding a clean no versus yes, hostility to the White House. Neither policy historians nor contemporary commentators have ignored them. Shocked by the Senate's singular hostility toward Carter's energy plan, for example, an energy lawyer from that administration later wove a case in the *New Republic* for a reconstruction of the upper chamber. Constitutional revision was needed. The Senate's all-states-are-equal design, viewed as the difficulty, would have to go.[10] As backing for the judgments that generated these twelve instances, I relied on the sources listed in the appendix as well as, in all cases, the relevant accounts in *Congressional Quarterly Almanac* or *Congressional Quarterly Weekly*.

The twenty-seven instances of formal yes versus no chamber behavior appear in table 3.1. The twelve instances of dissonance that fell short of ultimate formal yes versus no behavior appear in table 3.2. I recommend an examination of these tables. Vexed as the now thirty-nine instances may be by considerations of, in the case of the twenty-seven, strategic behavior or House first-mover rights, or, in the case of the twelve, decisions about which instances to include, the thirty-nine cases cohere into an interesting and usable, I hope, exhibit of dissonant behavior wending through

[9] In table 2.1, I coded ten of these twelve as eventual White House wins, two as losses. The latter two were Nixon's tax plan in 1969 and Carter's energy plan in 1977–78.
[10] Tom Geoghegan, "The Infernal Senate: The Real Source of Gridlock," *New Republic*, November 21, 1994, 17–23.

TABLE 3.1.
Presidential Requests Approved by One Chamber but Not the Other

Congress	President	Blocking chamber	Request	Comment
81st	Truman	Senate	civil rights	House votes anti–poll tax and fair employment practices; Senate blocks all via filibustering.
81st	Truman	House	education	Senate passes federal aid to education; House deadlocks in Education and Labor committee.
83rd	Eisenhower	Senate	Hawaii	House votes Hawaii statehood straight up; Senate won't admit Hawaii without Alaska.
87th	Kennedy	House	education	Senate passes federal aid to education; House Rules Committee blocks it; House floor then rejects it in Calendar Wednesday process.
89th	Johnson	House	DC home rule	Senate votes it; House bogs down in messy squabble.
89th	Johnson	Senate	14b repeal	House votes repeal of antiunion Taft–Hartley provision, but Senate filibuster kills the move.
89th	Johnson	Senate	open housing	House passes this civil rights proposal; Senate blocks it via filibuster.
91st	Nixon	Senate	family assistance	House passes Family Assistance Plan; Senate Finance Committee won't buy it.
91st	Nixon	Senate	SST	House approves funding for Supersonic Transport; Senate blocks it in floor fight.

TABLE 3.1. (*Continued*)

Congress	President	Blocking chamber	Request	Comment
93rd	Nixon	House	emergency energy authority	Senate votes Nixon largely the emergency energy authority he asked for; House insists on windfall profits tax; Nixon and Senate balk; no bill passes that Nixon will sign.
95th	Carter	House	hospital costs	Senate approves hospital cost containment plan, but it doesn't reach the floor of House.
95th	Carter	House	education department	Senate approves new Department of Education; House kills it in late-session filibuster move.
97th	Reagan	House	balanced budget	Senate approves balanced budget amendment to the Constitution, but House can't get the needed 2/3 vote.
97th	Reagan	House	school busing	Senate passes measure outlawing school busing for racial balance, but House Judiciary Committee buries it.
101st	Bush 41	Senate	capital gains	House votes capital gains tax cut; Senate filibusters it.
103rd	Clinton	Senate	economic stimulus	House votes economic stimulus plan; Senate filibusters it.
103rd	Clinton	Senate	campaign finance	House votes for campaign finance reform; Senate filibusters it.
103rd	Clinton	Senate	lobbying	House vote for lobbying reform; Senate filibusters it.
105th	Clinton	House	fast track	Senate, in effect, approves fast-track trade authority to president; House doesn't have the needed votes.

TABLE 3.1. (*Continued*)

Congress	President	Blocking chamber	Request	Comment
105th	Clinton	Senate	campaign finance	House votes campaign finance reform; Senate can't get the votes for cloture.
107th	Bush 43	Senate	faith based	Houses approves faith-based initiative, but it doesn't reach the Senate floor.
107th	Bush 43	Senate	energy	House votes Bush plan; Senate won't agree to it.
107th	Bush 43	Senate	Medicare	House approves Bush plan to add prescription drugs to Medicare, but it lacks a majority in the Senate.
109th	Bush 43	Senate	estate tax	House votes repeal of estate tax, but Senate can't vote cloture.
109th	Bush 43	Senate	drilling in Alaska	House votes for oil drilling in Alaska, but Senate can't vote cloture.
109th	Bush 43	Senate	medical malpractice	House votes to curb medical malpractice suits, but Senate can't vote cloture.
109th	Bush 43	House	immigration	Senate approves comprehensive plan pressed by Bush, but House won't act; holds countrywide hearings instead.

Sources: The references listed in the appendix as well as relevant accounts in *Congressional Quarterly Weekly* or *Congressional Quarter Almanac* underpin this table. In certain cases, additional sources proved helpful: Frank J. Munger and Richard F. Fenno, Jr., *National Politics and Federal Aid to Education* (Syracuse: Syracuse University Press, 1962), 10–11, 16, 124–36, 138–44, 155–69, on federal aid to education in 1949 and 1961; James L. Sundquist, *Politics and Policy: The Eisenhower, Kennedy, and Johnson Years* (Washington, D.C.: Brookings Institution Press, 1968), 180–95, on federal aid to education in 1961; 275–82, on open housing in 1965–66; Daniel P. Moynihan, *The Politics of a Guaranteed Income: The Nixon Administration and the Family Assistance Plan* (New York: Random House, 1973), chs. 5–7.

Table 3.2.
Presidential Requests That Emanated in Enactments yet Were Treated Considerably More Hostilely by One Chamber than the Other in at Least Certain Major Provisions

Congress	President	Hostile Chamber	Request	Comment
83rd	Eisenhower	House	housing	Senate approves 35,000 public housing units per year for four years; House won't approve any at all; final act provides for one year.
85th	Eisenhower	Senate	civil rights	Under filibuster threat, Senate insists on "jury trial amendment" that weakens voting rights bill passed by House.
85th	Eisenhower	House	scholarships	Senate votes new federal scholarship program as part of National Defense Education Act; House says no scholarships, only loans; no scholarships are voted.
87th	Kennedy	House	minimum wage	Major confrontation over coverage of laundry and other categories of workers; Senate says yes, House says no; compromise ensues.
91st	Nixon	Senate	taxes	Senate version seen as worse by the White House on ground of fiscal unsoundness.
93rd	Nixon	Senate	trade	White House gets its plan but at the cost of an amendment levering Jewish immigration from the USSR insisted on by the Senate (and a year's delay regarding it).
95th	Carter	Senate	energy	House approves Carter's omnibus plan; Senate dismantles it and shifts emphasis from regulation to deregulation.

TABLE 3.2. (*Continued*)

Congress	President	Hostile Chamber	Request	Comment
101st	Bush 41	House	S&Ls bailout	Senate buys Bush's plan; House doesn't; compromise ensues.
101st	Bush 41	House	deficit reduction	Summit omnibus deal agreed on by White House plus House and Senate leaders derailed by House insurgency led by Newt Gingrich; ensuing remake of deal tilts more to Democrats.
103rd	Clinton	Senate	motor voter	Under filibuster threat, Senate won't agree to require voter registration sites at unemployment offices; the provision is dropped.
103rd	Clinton	Senate	budget	Energy state senators, notably Democrats, force dropping of energy taxes from Clinton's House-passed omnibus plan.
105th	Clinton	House	Social Security funding	Senate backs Clinton's plan to run a budget surplus to "save Social Security first"; House votes a tax cut instead; White House wins in final settlement.

Sources: Generally relied on were the accounts cited in the appendix, as well as those in *Congressional Quarterly Almanac* or *Congressional Quarterly Weekly*. Certain other sources were useful. On housing under Eisenhower: Nathaniel S. Keith, *Politics and the Housing Crisis since 1930* (New York: Universe Books, 1973), ch. 7; D. Bradford Hunt, "How Did Public Housing Survive the 1950s?" *Journal of Policy History* 17:2 (2005), 193–216, at 206–8. On, respectively, scholarships and civil rights under Eisenhower: James L. Sundquist, *Politics and Policy: The Eisenhower, Kennedy, and Johnson Years* (Washington, D.C.: Brookings Institution Press, 1968), 173–80, 221–38. On energy under Carter: Charles O. Jones, *The Trusteeship Presidency: Jimmy Carter and the United States Congress* (Baton Rouge: Louisiana State University Press, 1988), 135–43. Several volumes of *Congressional Quarterly Almanac* were especially helpful: on scholarships under Eisenhower, 1958, 213–16; on manpower retraining under Kennedy, 1962, 513; on taxes under Nixon, 1969, p. 589; On trade under Nixon, 1974, 553–68; on S&Ls under G.H.W. Bush, 1989, 117–18; on Social Security funding under Clinton, 1998, 21:14–18.

the six decades. Strategy and the rest aside, this record of chamber versus chamber dissonance is what the public has seen. Again, the legitimacy of a system probably hinges to a considerable degree on what is *seen* to happen—not on what might have happened in any chancy or shielded counterfactual universe. Also, as will become plain, there are intelligible patterns in the House versus Senate dissonance brought to light here. Certain patterns have existed, they have been important, they have survived or transcended whatever instrumental strategizing might have been going on in the background, and they have been reckoned with by political actors.

The requests listed in the two tables are sorted into summary numbers in table 3.3. Here I faced a problem of presentation. Too little detail or too much detail? On the one hand, the lists of twenty-seven and twelve requests differ in provenance, and also a bit (although probably not importantly) in the patterns of balance they exhibit, and accordingly it makes sense to keep an eye on their intricacies. On the other hand, too much detail can cloud the mind. Perhaps table 3.3 has too much detail. But I try to get around that problem by suggesting which results to key on. In the table, summary results are given in one pair of columns for the subset of twenty-seven up-or-down instances, then separately in another pair for the full set of thirty-nine instances.

Three noteworthy patterns—or nonpatterns—appear. See first the cluster of numbers in the upper right-hand corner of table 3.3. When the two chambers have diverged, how often has the House in particular, or the Senate in particular, brought grief to the White House regardless of which party was holding it? The answer is: the House sixteen times and the Senate twenty-three times. (Note by reading across to the left that the twenty-seven clean yes rather than no instances emanate in a 10–17 disparity; an undifferentiating 6–6 record in the second subset of twelve, not directly visible in the table, promotes the overall balance to 16–23.) Here in this 16–23 pattern, in alignment with conventional wisdom, we see the Senate in a role of outlier naysayer. Yet this Senate edge is really very small. Put it this way. In the various

TABLE 3.3.

Number of Presidential Requests on Which One Chamber Responded with Distinctive Hostility

	Of the 27 formal yes-versus-no responses		Of all 39 dissonant responses	
	House hostile	Senate hostile	House hostile	Senate hostile
Requests counted equally				
Democratic presidents	6	7	8	10
Republican presidents	4	10	8	13
All presidents	10	17	16	23
Requests weighted as in table 2.1:				
Democratic presidents	8	9	11	18
Republican presidents	4	11	11	15
All presidents	12	20	22	33
Requests pre-1988 counted equally				
Democratic presidents	5	3	6	4
Republican presidents	3	3	5	6
All presidents	8	6	11	10
Requests pre-1988 weighted				
Democratic presidents	7	5	9	9
Republican presidents	3	4	6	8
All presidents	10	9	15	17
Requests post-1988 counted equally				
Democratic presidents	1	4	2	6
Republican presidents	1	7	3	7
All presidents	2	11	5	13

TABLE 3.3. (*Continued*)

	Of the 27 formal yes-versus-no responses		Of all 39 dissonant responses	
	House hostile	Senate hostile	House hostile	Senate hostile
Requests post-1988 weighted				
Democratic presidents	1	4	2	9
Republican presidents	1	7	5	7
All presidents	2	11	7	16

responses to the presidents' 184 requests during the sixty years, the *gross* of distinctive revealed hostility—that is, *either* chamber proved more hostile than the other—was 39, or 21 percent of the total. The *net* of distinctive hostility—the Senate's edge over the House—was 7, or 4 percent of the total. This latter edge does not look like the kind that would call a system into question. For the record, see also in table 3.3 the cluster of numbers just below the upper right-hand corner. There, the balance of 16–23 becomes a not very different 22–33 if the presidential requests are weighted by their importance as was done in table 2.1.[11]

Evident also in the upper right-hand corner of table 3.3 is the second noteworthy pattern. Taking the parties separately, have Democratic and Republican presidents fared differently in the politics of House-versus-Senate dissonance? The answer is a clear no. Over the long haul, there is no evidence of disproportionate treatment. The Senate has kept its small naysayer edge as the two chambers have addressed the requests of each party's presidents. For Democratic presidents, the summary House–Senate balance

[11] In percentage terms, with weighting, using a suitable overall weighted denominator, the Senate edge grows from 3.8 percent to 4.5 percent. The increase here from seven to eleven, or from 3.8 percent to 4.5 percent, is small and at any rate somewhat impeachable. It relies heavily on a four-count for Clinton's 1993 budget, the core of which did after all win enactment even though the Senate balked on energy taxes.

is 8–10 and, with weighting, 11–18.[12] For Republican presidents, the summary record is 8–13 and, with weighting, 11–15.

The bottom two-thirds of table 3.3 shows a third pattern. Possibly there are too many numbers, but the gist of them can serve as an introduction to the more fine-grained discussion ensuing in this chapter and the next. As it happens, the Senate's entire edge in naysaying has inhered in the request politics of recent times during the presidencies of Clinton and the two Bushes. See the rightmost columns of numbers in the table. Before 1988, during the presidencies of Truman, Eisenhower, Kennedy, Johnson, Nixon, Carter, and Reagan taken collectively, neither of the two chambers dominated in revealed naysaying. For the presidents back then, with party held blind, the House–Senate balance was 11–10 and, with weighting, 15–17. After 1988, however, the presidents regardless of party, and with grand impartiality the presidents of each party, encountered a good deal more difficulty on the Senate side than on the House side. See the clusters in the bottom right-hand corner of the table. After 1988 a marked disparity came into play, yet it has been, in a sense employed earlier with the long haul in mind, a local one.

That is the general picture. Now for the wrinkles, singularities, or distortions that have figured, or have been thought to do so, during the sixty years. When or in what policy areas has the House or Senate brought special trouble to the White House or to the individual presidential parties? And why has any such trouble been brought on? These questions invite a scrutiny of certain historical situations as well as of certain theories or accounts that analysts during recent generations have offered as they have puzzled about the situations. In general on these matters, a side of historical experience has twinned with a side of theorizing, although some situations have perhaps been undertheorized and others overtheorized. I follow a practical course in the remainder of this chapter and the next. I divide the history in a particular way. I take up one by one a series of six well-known couplings of experience

---

[12] The four-coding of Clinton's 1993 budget plan figures again in the eighteen.

and theory, emphasizing in each case where it seems sensible to do so the relevant empirical and theoretical aspects. In general, my treatment is chronological although it is not neatly that. Occasionally, I extend the analysis beyond the datsasets of tables 3.1 through 3.3 by drawing on additional historical information.

CIVIL RIGHTS AND SENATE FILIBUSTERS

One range of experience can be taken off the top. In outlier chamber behavior, nothing in American history has topped in prominence or importance the Senate's defeating or watering down, by way of filibusters staged or threatened by southerners, of civil rights bills aimed at guaranteeing the rights of African Americans. Three of the early instances in tables 3.1 and 3.2 qualify. That is, in each case the House approved a White House proposal in the civil rights area that ran into filibuster trouble in the Senate—Truman's omnibus program in 1949–50 (defeated), Eisenhower's voting rights plan in 1957 (watered down), and Johnson's open-housing proposal in 1966 (defeated).[13] Nearly half the Senate's outlier edge during the sixty years—that is, three of the edge of seven—traces to these civil rights instances. Of course, these three cases index a larger universe of historical experience. All told, it extended episodically from 1890 through 1968. During those years, a trademark dissonance between the chambers kept appearing even though the presidents before Truman, taken by themselves, tended to bypass civil rights.[14] Yet Congress could take the initiative. Senate filibusters or cloture failures doomed House-passed civil rights bills in 1890–91 (voting rights), 1922

---

[13] A revised version of Johnson's open-housing request won enactment two years later in the fresh political context of 1968.

[14] President Benjamin Harrison had a hand in the 1890–91 drive and Truman played a role in 1945–48, yet these requests occurred too early to appear in this chapter's dataset. On Harrison: Anne Cheiko Moore, *Benjamin Harrison: Centennial President* (New York: Nova Science, 2006), 114–15. On Truman: Robert J. Donovan, *Conflict and Crisis: The Presidency of Harry S. Truman, 1945–1948* (Columbia.: University of Missouri Press, 1996), 32, 114, 173, 333, 352.

(antilynching), 1938 (antilynching), 1940 (antilynching), 1942 (anti–poll tax), 1944 (anti–poll tax), and 1946 (fair employment practices), as well as Truman's plan in 1949–50 and Johnson's open-housing drive in 1966.[15] In addition, a Republican-controlled House passed an anti–poll tax measure that went nowhere in the Senate in 1948 (it was late in the session); an Eisenhower request for voting rights brought House passage yet no Senate action in 1956 (it was again too late in the session; no filibuster was needed); and a House-passed voting rights bill won enactment after a Senate filibuster watered it down—as in the 1957 process—in 1960.[16] In all, that makes for thirteen instances of cleanly revealed interchamber dissonance on civil rights across those many decades—all involving the Senate as the negative voice.

Three comments seem in order. First, conflict over civil rights during those several generations was constantly regional, yet only sometimes partisan. Starting in the 1930s, most northern Democrats were pro–civil rights whenever issue cleavages arose. From the 1890s, Republicans tended to back voting rights, anti–poll tax, and antilynching legislation yet balk at government intrusions into the labor market (as in 1949–50) or the housing market (as in 1966).[17] Given this nuanced pattern, it is easy to see that civil

[15] For the record from the 1920s through World War II, see Harvard Sitkoff, *A New Deal for Blacks: The Emergence of Civil Rights as a National Issue, vol. 1, The Depression Decade* (New York: Oxford University Press, 1978), 27, 136, 289–96; Edward Peeks, *The Long Struggle for Black Power* (New York: Charles Scribner's Sons, 1971), 229–30; Kevin J. McMahon, *Reconsidering Roosevelt on Race: How the Presidency Paved the Road to Brown* (Chicago: University of Chicago Press, 2004), 158; Steven F. Lawson, *Black Ballots: Voting Rights in the South, 1944–1969* (Lanham, Md.: Lexington Books), 1999), 73–74, regarding 1944; Keith M. Finley, *Delaying the Dream: Southern Senators and the Fight against Civil Rights, 1938–1965* (Baton Rouge: Louisiana State University Press, 2008), 60–61, regarding 1942; 70, 77, regarding 1944.

[16] Finley, *Delaying the Dream*, 99–102, regarding 1948; 153–56, regarding 1956. Sundquist, *Politics and Policy*, 226–29, regarding 1956; 238–50, regarding 1960. On the 1960 measure, Robert Mann, *When Freedom Would Triumph: The Civil Rights Struggle in Congress, 1954–1968* (Baton Rouge: Louisiana State University Press, 2007), ch. 8. The 1956 and 1960 instances do not appear in tables 3.1 or 3.2 because, following the decision rule of chapter 2, they came during the second half of a presidential term.

[17] For an analysis of the evolution of civil rights stances among Republican and Democratic politicians and voter coalitions before midcentury, see Eric Schickler, "Public Opinion, the Congressional Policy Agenda, and the Limits of New Deal Liberalism, 1936–1945," paper

rights could contribute a bit more to a general—that is, blind to party—outlier status for the Senate in regard to this study's presidential requests than to any disproportions in chamber outlier status specific to the presidential parties taken separately. To the point, Eisenhower, like the Democratic presidents, was a civil rights requester.

Second, there is ample theoretical as well as practical ground to cordon off civil rights in a category by itself in the treatment here. With no cloture rule at all in the Senate before 1917, and a two-thirds rule operative thereafter until 1975, a long-running perfect storm of opportunity existed for any large Senate minority that intensely opposed a measure to defeat a majority that weakly favored it. As such intensity gaps go in American history, possibly none has matched in magnitude that of civil rights until the mid-1960s. For Democratic senators representing the white South, the issue was fundamental. For most northern senators, it was marginal.[18] In the circumstances, the southerners could put their feet down, exhaust and roil the chamber, threaten every other legislative cause, and prevail. Partly this seems to have been a matter of agenda space. After enduring southern obstruction for awhile, northern senators whose support of civil rights often extended little beyond the pro forma were ready to move on to other legislative causes they cared more about. Civil rights could thus be, in effect, traded away on the spot. Down, without a straight-out vote, would go another bill.[19]

Third, without trivializing the Senate's record, it is an interesting sideline question how much the chamber's nonmajoritarian

presented at the annual conference of the American Political Science Association, Toronto, 2009.
[18] A comment on the Senate's failure to vote cloture on antilynching in 1938: "The cloture vote [37 aye, 51 nay] reveals much regarding the piecemeal importance of racial equality outside the South. [Northern] members of both parties demonstrated a marked disinterest in civil rights." Finley, *Delaying the Dream*, 49.
[19] For elaborations of the theoretical case regarding intensity, see David R. Mayhew, "Supermajority Rule in the U.S. Senate," *PS: Political Science and Politics* 36:1 (January 2003), 31–36; Kathleen Bawn and Gregory Koger, "Effort, Intensity and Position Taking: Reconsidering Obstruction in the Pre-Cloture Senate," *Journal of Theoretical Politics* 20:1 (2008), 67–92.

practices during those many generations *indexed* the U.S. system of racial domination as opposed to *causing* it—or at least helping along its continuation. I would opt for chiefly indexing. There is a certain dreaminess to a counterfactual scenario that has a majority-rule Senate administer a major setback to the South's entrenched caste system by adding its acquiescence to civil rights bills. The sectional intensity gap was rooted in on-the-ground violence in the South. So far as one can tell, from the 1870s when President Grant wrestled with insurgencies in the Deep South, through 1957 when President Eisenhower sent the national guard to Little Rock, it would likely have taken military occupation to make a major dent. The northern will for that was lacking, and it does not seem plausible that majority-vote victories in a coun- terfactual Senate would have supplied it. To be sure, civil rights issues have varied. Possibly an antilynching measure enacted by majority-rule processes would have been enforceable in normal terms as early as the mid-1930s. The South might have been ready for that.[20] But voting rights, housing, the schools, and the labor market were tougher nuts to crack.

HOUSE CONSERVATISM AND CHAMBER STRUCTURE

In a kind of counterpoint to civil rights, a second pattern appears in tables 3.1 and 3.2 also centered on the early decades after World War II. Five of the thirty-nine presidential requests figure in it. Two of them brought flat-out defeats—Truman's and Ken- nedy's plans for federal aid to education in 1949 and 1961. Three,

[20] The idea of national policing in general was catching on in the United States during the 1920s and 1930s. More specifically, in a Gallup poll conducted in 1936, majorities of both southerners and northerners favored an antilynching law. Christopher Waldrep, "Na- tional Policing, Lynching, and Constitutional Change," *Journal of Southern History* 74:3 (August 2008), 590–626, 606 regarding the survey. But polling sentiment of this sort was an uncertain guide to southern white intensities or what they might wreak. There is a tell- ing anecdote. In 1938 Senator Claude Pepper of Florida, a standout liberal then as later among southern Democrats, faced the question of whether to join a filibuster against that year's antilynching bill at the same time he faced an upcoming election. He joined the fili- buster. Finley, *Delaying the Dream*, 47–48.

although bills were enacted, brought nontrivial interchamber dissonance—regarding public housing and college scholarships under Eisenhower and minimum wage provisions under Kennedy. Here is the pattern. In all five cases, the House performed as an outlier vis-à-vis both the Senate and the White House. And in all five cases, in customary terminology, the House took a more conservative stance than either of the other branches.

Five of the thirty-nine is a healthy share. Yet as in civil rights, a larger universe seems to loom beyond the dataset at hand. Additional ingredients of it are not available here from anything as systematic as the designs for tables 3.1 and 3.2 but rather, more loosely, from a resort to standard policy histories. With an eye for instances that jumped out and seemed to belong together in a set, I proceeded as follows: Begin the time span earlier so that it includes the entire Truman (from 1945 onward), Eisenhower, and Kennedy administrations. This bracketing seems to be true to the history. Allow instances during the second halves of presidential terms, not just the first halves. Allow instances whether or not they derived from White House requests. As before, accommodate both up versus down interchamber dissonance (the motif of table 3.1) as well as nontrivial interchamber dissonance where measures did pass (the motif of table 3.2). As a central criterion, search for major legislative projects on which the House took a decisively more conservative stance than the Senate— notwithstanding, for the analytic side-exercise here, what the stance of the White House might have been. This is House-versus-Senate dissonance—a category that the instances in tables 3.1 and 3.2 fit into but do not exhaust.

I spotted five additional legislative enterprises that seem to satisfy these standards. They are all reasonably well-known. They appear in table 3.4, each annotated and referenced, interleaved chronologically among the five relevant instances carried over from tables 3.1 and 3.2. They are as follows. In the passage of the important Employment Act of 1946, the Senate pressed for a considerably stronger dose of government planning than the House would buy. In the context of a major post–World War II housing

TABLE 3.4.
Cases Where House Behavior Was More Conservative than Senate's under Truman, Eisenhower, and Kennedy

Congress	President	Measure	Comment
79th	Truman	employment	The Employment Act of 1946 draws from substantially different House and Senate versions. Liberals win in Senate. House version "rejected the fundamental principles of the Senate bill. It eliminated the declaration of the right to employment opportunity, of federal responsibility for full employment, the pledge of all the federal resources, including financial means to that end, and the safeguard against international economic warfare." A "national budget" gave way to an "economic report." In general, a Senate bent for government planning lost out to a cooler House commitment.
79th	Truman	housing	Senate approves in April 1946 the Wagner–Ellender–Taft housing bill, an omnibus measure offering among other things a "giant public housing program" of 125,000 units a year for four years. But then the bill is "literally ripped apart by the private-housing lobby" in the House Banking Committee, where filibuster tactics foreclose any chamber action as the session draws to a close.
80th	Truman	housing	Taft–Ellender–Wagner housing bill (now the project's tag-name in the Republican 80th Congress) clears Senate again in 1948 yet dies in House again via footdragging in Banking Committee then interment in Rules Committee.

Table 3.4. (*Continued*)

Congress	President	Measure	Comment
80th	Truman	labor–management relations	House version of Taft–Hartley Act is decisively more hostile to unions than Senate version. House bill contains "just about every restriction on union power which management lobbyists could think of. Mass picketing and industry-wide bargaining were outlawed. Unions could not bargain for pension plans, group insurance, and hospitalization insurance . . . . Unions would be made subject to the antitrust laws . . . . Unions could have no part in the administration of pension and welfare funds. None of these provisions, however, emerged in Taft's bill"—that is, the Senate version shepherded by Senator Robert Taft.
81st	Truman	education	Senate passes federal aid to education. House deadlocks in Education and Labor Committee.
83rd	Eisenhower	housing	Senate approves 35,000 public housing units per year for four years; House won't approve any at all; final act provides for one year.
85th	Eisenhower	scholarships	Senate votes new federal scholarship program as part of National Defense Education Act; House says no scholarships, only loans; no scholarships are voted.
86th	Eisenhower	labor–management relations	New Landrum–Griffin Act contains, at behest of the House (and Eisenhower) yet over the opposition of the Senate, tough antiunion provisions regarding secondary boycotts, hot cargo contracts, no man's land jurisdiction, picketing. Major defeat for organized labor in a House of 283 Democrats.

TABLE 3.4. (*Continued*)

Congress	President	Measure	Comment
87th	Kennedy	education	Senate passes federal aid to education; House Rules Committee blocks it; House floor then rejects it in Calendar Wednesday process.
87th	Kennedy	minimum wage	Major confrontation over coverage of laundry and other categories of workers; Senate says yes, House says no; compromise ensues.

Sources:

—On employment: Stephen K. Bailey, *Congress Makes a Law: The Story Behind the Employment Act of 1946* (New York: Columbia University Press, 1950), chs. 6, 8, quotations at 166–67.

—On housing in the 79th: Michael Barone, *Our Country: The Shaping of America from Roosevelt to Reagan* (New York: Free Press, 1990), quotations at 90; Nathaniel Keith, *Politics and the Housing Crisis since 1930* (New York: Universe Books, 1973), 62–63; J. J. Huthmacher, *Senator Robert F. Wagner and the Rise of Urban Liberalism* (New York: Atheneum, 1971), 322–25; Alexander von Hoffman, "A Study in Contradictions: The Origins and Legacy of the Housing Act of 1949," *Housing Policy Debate* 11:2 (2000), 299–326, at 306–7.

—On housing in the 80th: Keith, *Politics and the Housing Crisis*, ch. 4; von Hoffman, "A Study in Contradictions," 307–8.

—On Taft–Hartley: Barone, *Our Country*, 192–93; quotation at 192; R. Alton Lee, *Truman and Taft–Hartley: A Question of Mandate* (Lexington: University of Kentucky Press, 1966), ch. 3.

—On Landrum–Griffin: R. Alton Lee, *Eisenhower and Landrum–Griffin: A Study in Labor–Management Relations* (Lexington: University of Kentucky Press, 1990), chs. 5–7; Barone, *Our America*, 305.

shortage, during the spans of both the Democratic-controlled Congress of 1945–46 and the Republican-controlled Congress of 1947–48, the Senate voted for ambitious housing initiatives—authorizing, among other things, hundreds of thousands of new public housing units. The House of Representatives buried the measures both times. And in the passage of the Taft–Hartley Act of 1947 and the Landrum–Griffin Act of 1959—the promanagement rollbacks of the Wagner Act of 1935 that still stand as Congress's most significant initiatives in the area of labor–management relations since the New Deal—the House voted for versions that were decisively more antiunion than the Senate's.

Employment, housing, education, labor–management relations—that is the content of table 3.4, taking into account all ten of its cases. Represented is much of the early postwar domestic agenda pursued by liberal reformers. Civil rights aside, during the three presidencies in question, I have not spotted any otherwise comparable domestic initiative where the Senate, as opposed to the House, tilted to the conservative side when the two chambers diverged. To bring the White House back in, accommodating again all three institutions, the House of Representatives acted as conservative outlier in nine of the ten instances, including two Eisenhower instances—all except that of the Landrum–Griffin Act in 1959 where Eisenhower also championed the conservative side. The partisanship is clouded in another interesting way. Senator Robert A. Taft, the domestic policy leader of the Senate Republican party during the Truman years, went out of his way to promote three of the major initiatives listed in table 3.4 that cleared the Senate but died in the House—the omnibus housing bills of 1945–46 and 1947–48 and federal aid to education in 1949.

My presentation here does not seem to be a fluke. "Why is the Senate more liberal than the House?" is a question that has been addressed in a line of respected literature, chiefly of interest today for its illumination of history, centering on the 1940s through the 1960s.[21] For political activists of those times, that question hung in the air. What was, or were, the answers? Given that the House tended to diverge in a conservative direction from both the Senate and the White House, one line of speculation centered, not surprisingly, on possible peculiarities of the lower chamber.

[21] See Stephen Kemp Bailey, *Congress Makes a Law: The Story Behind the Employment Act of 1946* (New York: Columbia University Press, 1950), 126; Louis W. Koenig, "Kennedy and the 87th Congress," in *American Government Annual, 1962–1963* (New York: Holt, Rinehart and Winston, 1962), 80–81; Lewis A. Froman, Jr., *Congressmen and Their Constituencies* (Chicago: Rand McNally, 1963), ch. 6 ("Why the Senate Is More Liberal than the House"); Frederic N. Cleaveland, "Legislating for Urban Areas: An Overview," 350–89 in Cleaveland (ed.), *Congress and Urban Problems* (Washington, D.C.: Brookings Institution Press, 1969), at 374; Sam Kernell, "Is the Senate More Liberal than the House?" *Journal of Politics* 35:2 (May 1973), 332–66; Bernard Grofman, Robert Griffin, and Amitai Glazer, "Is the Senate More Liberal than the House: Another Look," *Legislative Studies Quarterly* 16:2 (May 1991), 281–95.

I take up in this section the House peculiarity that was perhaps most widely thought to be culpable. In its own ways, it was argued, the House was a distinctively antimajoritarian institution. All too often, a floor majority couldn't get its way. That was the difficulty. At fault was a gestalt of pathology featuring the seniority system, powerful committee chairs, the chamber's hierarchy in general, veto-point processes, the obstructive Rules Committee in particular, and crafty conservative southerners whose long experience and connections allowed them, in a kind of weighted voting, to pull the wool over the eyes of northerners.[22] James MacGregor Burns wrote about one ingredient, for example, in 1949: "Yet the Rules committee has little responsibility to the House or to the majority party."[23] The general spirit of the antimajoritarian case appears nicely in *House Out of Order*, an influential work published by liberal reformer and House member Richard Bolling in 1964. In the lower chamber, Bolling argued, "power is divided among a few autocrats and unrepresentative groups." "Key committee posts have prestige and authority that enable them to obstruct legislation, make behind-the-scenes deals, reward political favors without regard to the public good, defy their party leadership and the House majority and the will of the voters at large."[24] This was a standard, widely shared assessment.

In retrospect, how good was this antimajoritarian explanation? More specifically, of relevance here, how good was it, or is it, in illuminating the ten instances of dissonant legislative behavior listed in table 3.4? Counterfactuals are always difficult, yet suggestive evidence does exist, and the answer seems to be: not all that good. In seven of the instances—the Employment Act and the Taft–Hartley Act under Truman; public housing, college scholarships, and the Landrum–Griffin Act under Eisenhower; and federal aid to education and the minimum wage provisions under

[22] Certain of these ideas are considered and weighed in, for example, Froman, *Congressmen and Their Constituencies*, 77–80; Kernell, "Is the Senate More Liberal than the House?" 336–38.

[23] James MacGregor Burns, *Congress on Trial: The Legislative Process and the Administrative State* (New York: Harper, 1949), 56.

[24] Richard Bolling, *House Out of Order* (New York: E. P. Dutton, 1965), 21.

Kennedy—the full House, whatever might have happened earlier in committee processes, got to make a direct choice by voice, teller, or roll-call vote between a conservative version or the status quo, on the one hand, and one or more liberal-leaning alternatives on the other, and the liberal-leaning proposals lost.[25] That, at the least, can be said.[26] Formal House majorities had their way. In three of these seven cases—college scholarships, Landrum–Griffin, and minimum wage—it is interesting to note that the losing, more liberal version was one that a standing committee had reported out. Of the seven instances, Kennedy's loss on aid to education in 1961 was a hybrid affair. Referred to above is the rejection of it (more accurately, a softened version of it) by a floor vote of 170–242 in a Calendar Wednesday process. Previous to that demise, the plan was famously blocked by the House Rules Committee.

In the cases of federal aid to education in both 1949 and 1961, the House's committees did footdrag and deadlock. The 1961 plan

[25] In the case of the Taft–Hartley Act, ten amendments were offered in the process open to the full House that would have softened the measure's antiunion stance. They all lost. See *CQA 1947*, 282. On public housing in 1954: *CQA 1954*, 201. On scholarships in 1958: *CQA 1958*, 215. On Landrum–Griffin: R. Alton Lee, *Eisenhower and Landrum–Griffin: A Study in Labor–Management Relations* (Lexington: University of Kentucky Press, 1990), 148. On minimum wage: Koenig, "Kennedy and the 87th Congress," 74–75.

[26] Some ambiguity attaches to the Employment Act of 1946. The House Expenditures Committee reported out a conservative version of the plan, whereupon the full House "rejected a motion to substitute the Administration-approved plan, doing this in the committee of the whole by a teller vote of 185 to 95." Frederick R. Barkley, "Changed Job Bill Passed by House," *New York Times*, December 5, 1945, 1. That seems clear enough. Yet there was a background story. At the outset, the Truman administration had "managed to extract a promise from [southern Democratic committee members Carter] Manasco and [William] Whittington that some sort of bill would be reported out in return for his assurance that he would not insist on the original bill, the Senate-passed bill, or even a bill with the words 'full employment' in it." Once the committee bill reached the House floor, the Truman administration stuck by its promise, helping to stave off the liberal substitute in the Committee of the Whole. "When the chips were down, the House sponsors of the [liberal] bill did not have the cards, Manasco and Whittington, with the aid of [Republican committee member Clare] Hoffman, the Rules Committee, a conservative House majority, and the administration [sticking by its promise], held a royal flush." The situation was murky, but a counterfactual liberal House majority on the matter is hard to envision. See Bailey, *Congress Makes a Law*, ch. 8, quotations at pp. 162, 177. See also Frederick R. Barkley, "Revised Job Bill Debated in House," *New York Times*, December 14, 1945, 19; Felix Belair, Jr., "Truman Battles for Full-Job Bill: Asks Congressional Conferees to Adopt Stronger Version Passed by Senate," *New York Times*, December 21, 1945, 14.

did not reach the floor by ordinary processes; the 1949 plan—
instance number eight here—did not reach the floor at all. Yet in
either case, it is hard to discern a thwarted floor majority in the
background. There was multidimensional conflict. Both times,
the question of extending aid to parochial schools meshed with
other concerns to disable the relevant committees, and, given
the oppositional stances of several Roman Catholic committee
members—for example, second-term congressman John F. Kennedy in 1949—it seems a realistic judgment, ratifying the formal
Calendar Wednesday outcome in the 1961 case, that floor majorities were not available for either of these education initiatives.[27]
Decades later, in 2009–10, Church views on abortion entered into
health-care deliberations in a similar crosscutting way.

That is eight of the instances. Of the other two, the best case—
and it seems a quite good one—for an antimajoritarian result is the
demise of the Wagner–Ellender–Taft housing initiative in 1946.
Conservatives on the House Banking and Currency Committee
staged a full-dress slowdown as the session neared a close. Two
sources use the term "filibuster." No bill was reported out. Wari-
ness of a loss on the floor is indicated by the committee's tactics.[28]
It seems probable that a floor majority was available. Somewhat
cloudier is the fate of the follow-up Taft–Ellender–Wagner housing bill in 1948. Again, the Senate acted and the House Banking
and Currency Committee footdragged, yet this time the House

[27] See Frank J. Munger and Richard F. Fenno, Jr., *National Politics and Federal Aid to Education* (Syracuse.: Syracuse University Press, 1962), 124–27, 132–36, 166–69. These authors
concluded in 1962: "It is doubtful . . . whether any firm federal aid majority has ever existed in the House of Representatives" (p. 169). Secretary of Health, Education, and Welfare Abraham Ribicoff is quoted in the wake of the 1961 defeat: "It was impossible to bring
together a majority for a bill when most members didn't want one" (p. 169). See also Sundquist, *Politics and Policy*, regarding the Rules Committee's stall on the 1961 bill: "The
Rules Committee, by the time the religious feud had boiled up, was not an unrepresentative sample of the full House" (p. 193). On the 1961 process in general, see Hugh Douglas
Price, "The Congress: Race, Religion, and the Rules Committee: The Kennedy Aid-to-
Education Bills," ch. 1 in Alan F. Westin (ed.), *The Uses of Power* (New York: Harcourt,
Brace and World, 1962), at 59–67, and in particular on the Calendar Wednesday move
("The Administration Tries Again"), 64–67.
[28] Nathaniel S. Keith, *Politics and the Housing Crisis since 1930* (New York: Universe Books,
1973), 62–63; J. J. Huthmacher, *Senator Robert F. Wagner and the Rise of Urban Liberalism*
(New York: Atheneum, 1971), 325.

was Republican-controlled and more conservative. In the end, a petition to discharge the bill from the Rules Committee fell nearly fifty signatures short. The measure never reached the floor. Even so, a floor majority for it might have existed. In a surprise move in mid-1948, antecedent to the Rules Committee stall, the Banking and Currency voted 14–13 to approve the measure. Given the normal ideologies of the members of the House, an extrapolation of that 14–13 split to the full House points to a likely floor majority. In particular, the favorable votes of certain Republicans on the Banking and Currency Committee from metropolitan areas might have predicted the floor votes, given a chance, of the party's full complement from such areas, rendering a victory. Thwarted floor success in this case seems at least a tenable argument.[29]

Nonetheless, the summary result for the ten measures is eight no, one probable yes, one a good chance yes. That does not add up to a good case for any overall antimajoritarian explanation for those decades based on chamber structure. Missing entirely is any supportive instance for the idea after 1948. In chapter 4 I take up the idea of House antimajoritarianism in a more general way.

[29] On the fortunes of this measure, see Keith, *Politics and the Housing Crisis*, 83–85; Susan M. Hartmann, *Truman and the 80th Congress* (Columbia: University of Missouri Press, 1971), 150; Lee E. Cooper, "Housing Measure Facing Showdown Soon in Congress," *New York Times*, May 9, 1948, R1; "Housing Bill Stays in House Committee," *New York Times*, June 6, 1948, 21; "Housing Bill Test Won by Democrats, *New York Times*, June 11, 1948, 19; "Housing Measure Blocked in House," *New York Times*, June 17, 1948, 3; Felix Belair, Jr., "New Housing Bill Signed, but Truman Denounces It," *New York Times*, August 11, 1948, 1. After 1948, credible expert testimony is ordinarily available regarding the likely fortunes of measures on Capitol Hill. For earlier years such testimony is spotty, but inferences from general roll-call patterns are sometimes possible. Here, for the housing measures, I used first-dimension DW-NOMINATE scores to extrapolate the 1948 House committee vote to a floor split. In 1945–46 no comparable committee vote was taken. Yet an inference is available backwards using the votes of the 14–13 committee split of 1948. Many House members served on the same committee during both Congresses. An assumption of constant member positioning in those cases, combined with a speculative extrapolation to a floor split in the considerably more Democratic Congress of 1945–46, strengthens the case that the Wagner–Ellender–Taft bill would probably have attracted a House floor majority in that previous Congress. Source for the DW-NOMINATE scores: the website of Keith T. Poole, http://www.voteview.com. Source for committee memberships: the website of Charles Stewart, http://web.mit.edu/17–251/www/data_page.html.

HOUSE CONSERVATISM AND CONSTITUENCY DEMOGRAPHY

What else might explain the House's conservative outlier stance from Truman through Kennedy? There is a second familiar account, and I would estimate that it does a better job, although this judgment rests on speculation rather than any direct proof. It is the rural versus urban account. Back in those times, the House was more rural in texture than the country as a whole, the argument goes. That was at least because the state legislatures had notoriously neglected to redraw their congressional districts to accommodate a major population shift from the countryside to the cities during the twentieth century.[30] That bias made for a conservative House tilt. In one account that alleges this growing demographic skew, the House's conservative outlier policy status is associated with it as early as the late 1930s.[31]

That is the theory. At least on the demographic side, what are the facts? I have not calculated whether any such demographic skew was growing in the 1930s, 1940s, and 1950s. Yet it is possible to explore whether one existed in the 1950s and 1960s, and to see what happened after that. As in chapter 1, the question can be addressed through a logic of medians—but this time centering on demographic data rather than the presidential vote. For at least some decades, the U.S. Census has reported a percent rural (or, conversely, percent urban) value for the total U.S. population as well as for each of the country's relevant subunits. For any decade following a census, data permitting, the rural percent (I use that value here) of the population of the country as a whole can be compared with the rural percent in the median House district once districts are lined up according to their ruralness, and in the median Senate district (that is, state).

---

[30] See Bailey, *Congress Makes a Law*, 126–27, 184–86; Burns, *Congress on Trial*, 49–54; Koenig, "Kennedy and the 87th Congress," 80; Froman, *Congressmen and Their Constituencies*, 80–83.

[31] Bailey, *Congress Makes a Law*, 126–27.

See the patterns in figure 3.1.[32] They track the relevant values through the 1950s, 1960s, and 1970s as well as, after a gap, the 1990s and 2000s.[33] Obviously, the country taken as a whole has been growing more urban, but that is not in question. For a start, focus on the values in figure 3.1 for the median House district (the filled-in diamonds) and total USA (the filled-in squares). Ignore for a moment the Senate values. For purposes at hand, a merit of the 1950s-through-1970s sector of figure 3.1 is that it captures the redistricting revolution of the 1960s. Scarcely a U.S. House district anywhere in the country stayed untouched by the Supreme Court's rigid new standards for population equality laid down during that decade. For awhile, redistricting took place nonstop.

[32] I calculated the medians myself. Source for House districts of the 1950s (that is, the districts in place after the reapportionment and in some cases redistricting levered by the 1950 census): U.S. Department of Commerce, Bureau of the Census, *County and City Data Book, 1956* (Washington, D.C.: U.S. Government Printing Office, 1957), appendix G, Selected Data for Congressional Districts. Source for House districts of the 1960s (that is, the ones used at least in the 1962 election, although a great deal of redistricting took place between 1962 and 1970): U.S. Department of Commerce, Bureau of the census, *Congressional District Data Book, Districts of the 88th Congress* (Washington, D.C.: U.S. Government Printing Office, 1963). Source for House districts of the 1970s (that is, the ones levered for 1972 by the data of the 1970 census): U.S. Department of Commerce, Bureau of the Census, *Congressional District Data Book, Districts of the 93rd Congress* (Washington, D.C.: U.S. Government Printing Office, 1973). Source for House districts of the 1990s: Michael Barone and Grant Ujifusa, *The Almanac of American Politics 1996* (Washington, D.C.: National Journal, 1995). Source for House districts of the 2000s (including the Texas districts drawn between 2002 and 2004): Michael Barone with Richard E. Cohen and Grant Ujifusa, *The Almanac of Politics 2006* (Washington, D.C.: National Journal, 2005). For all but one of these decades the calculation of the House medians was straightforward. The 1950s posed a problem. The House districts back then that did not follow county lines—roughly a third of them—lacked data on rural versus urban. But the problem turned out to be minor. The great majority of these missing-data districts were obviously high-urban in texture, so it was easy to place them on the urban side of the median. In instances where that recourse did not work (as, for example, for certain districts in New England), I consulted demographic statistics for the same (or similar: in general, the districts did not change much between censuses before the 1960s), districts as reported in the succeeding 1960 census. Ordinarily, that comparison supplied what seemed a safe inference for placement of a district on one side or the other of the median. Failing all else, in a few cases, I made what seemed to be a sensible judgment. Given a yardstick of perfect information, I doubt that the median House value I came up with for the 1950s would be off reality by as much as 1 percent.

[33] The District of Columbia contributes to the "total USA" value starting in the 1960s, in recognition of the District's enfranchisement for presidential elections beginning in 1964. As a statistical matter, this addition makes only a tiny difference.

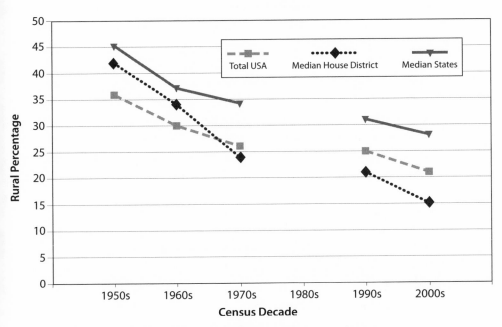

3.1. Rural population percentage in three constituency universes

Virtually all the old maps were torn up. Earlier, note in figure 3.1, the House of the 1950s and 1960s—which means in the latter case the districts drawn for the 1962 election before the Court started handing down its decisions—really did have, compared with the country as a whole, the flavor of a pitchfork. By 42 percent versus 36 percent in the 1950s, and by 34 percent versus 30 percent in the early 1960s, the House median out-tilted the country as a whole in a rural direction. Those margins do not seem trivial. Yet then the lines crossed. In the 1970s, after the redistricting revolution, and very likely because of it, the House median lurched to the urban side of the country as a whole and has stayed there since.

Again, figure 3.1 says nothing about any midcentury or so *growth* in a demographic gap. Yet the figure's revealed demographic gap of the 1950s and 1960s, whatever its genesis, is consistent with—to put it that way—that era's pattern of intermittent policy conflict between a relatively liberal-leaning White House and a conservative outlier House. The gap correlates with the manifestation of that policy dissonance even when Eisenhower was president, as happened in certain respects on housing and education—not only when Democrats held the White House. Note that public housing, which figured importantly in the policy disputes of the 1940s into the 1960s, was an especially urban-centered issue. In addition, afterwards, the disappearance of the relative rural tilt of the House in the 1970s matches the disappearance then of any notable conservative policy positioning by the House vis-à-vis the Senate—at least in the records of dissonant behavior supplied in tables 3.1 and 3.2.

How good is the case for a causal relation? How would we find out? As a first cut, I sought clues in one data exploration that unfortunately came up dry. I looked into House showdown votes on certain of the legislative drives listed in table 3.4 to see if the districts of the members on the conservative winning side had, on average, smaller populations than those of the members on the losing liberal side. This is a roundabout move; it does not get at the question directly. Yet in a strict arithmetic sense, ignoring any direct component of rural versus rural, were the overrepresented members of the House defeating the underrepresented members in these ideological showdowns back then? The answer is, perhaps surprisingly, no. I came away convinced that this size hunch goes nowhere.

Where does that leave the speculation? If the rural tinge to the House was leaving a policy imprint in the 1940s through the 1960s, the *contours* of the districts rather than their *sizes* might have been doing the work.[34] For generations, state legislatures in

[34] Recent scholarship centering on the preexisting inequalities in the *population sizes* of legislative districts has given new life to the idea that the redistricting revolution of the 1960s brought significant changes in public policy. At the level of the individual states, at least in those governments' supply of dollars-and-cents benefits, the revolution in districting seems to have brought a comparable revolution in the behavior of the state legislatures. The urban share of state spending rose, and the absolute level of urban-centered benefits rose. See Stephen Ansolabehere, Alan Gerber, and James M. Snyder, Jr., "Equal Votes, Equal Money: Court-Ordered Redistricting and Public Expenditures in the American States," *American Political Science Review* 96:4 (December 2002), 767–77; Ansolabehere and Snyder, *The End of Inequality*, chs. 9, 10.

all the regions of the country, regardless of which party controlled
them, had favored rural areas, and they had drawn typically congressional districts that favored rural areas, too, even in an absence
of disparities in district population size. Ordinarily, the district
lines stayed intact decade after decade. Vitiated in the redistricting
shakeup of the 1960s, to follow this line of thinking, was an in-
grained nationwide pattern of prorural *gerrymandering* beyond
any arithmetic population disparities.

This interpretation seems plausible. In our own day, when legislative districting in all settings is held to strict standards of population equality, the parties carry out their gerrymandering schemes
with finesse anyway. Witness the remap of the U.S. House districts in Texas led by Tom DeLay in 2003–04. Gerrymandering is
the art of prying medians away from means. That can be done by
causing the other side to "waste votes," producing small victory
margins for one's own districts and large margins for the other
side's districts, even in a context of district population equality.
In the present study, the argument would have to be that pitchfork gerrymandering, so to speak, pursued at the state level by
either party or both parties or neither party, was the likely long-
time perpetrator of the skewed U.S. House representation of the
1940s through the 1960s. In the 1960s, the whirlwind of new
line-drawing forced by the courts erased the pitchfork flavor.

That is the case. All in all, I would guess that the House's demographic skew offers a better wedge into the politics of the immediate postwar era than does the chamber's much-discussed procedural antimajoritarianism. The lines crossing in figure 3.1 seem to
tell a story.

Still, an obvious embarrassment to any account of this sort is the
behavior of the Senate. See the top line in figure 3.1 (the triangles).
Since World War II, in ordinal terms, the Senate has always tilted
more rural than *either* the House or the country as a whole.[35] What
could have been going on during the 1950s and 1960s? How could
the Senate have outpaced the House in liberalism back then if it

---

[35] For a discussion of this disparity in recent times, see G. Ross Stephens, "Urban Under-
representation in the U.S. Senate," *Urban Affairs Review* 31:3 (January 1996), 404–18.

was more rural? This is a puzzle. It is a puzzle to which the posers of the "Why is the Senate more liberal?" question have given thoughtful attention.[36] One line of speculation has accented the greater heterogeneity of the states as opposed to the House districts. To the point, most states back then had cities even if they were generally rural. Stephen Bailey wrote, for example, in 1950: "More fundamental perhaps is the fact that most Senators have at least one urban area in their constituency to worry about."[37] Louis Koenig wrote again in 1962: "The Senator, who is answerable to a state-wide constituency, is becoming increasingly dependent upon the great mass of urban voters for his election."[38] As for labor–management issues, it is analogously possible that unionized workers in the nonunion states tended to cluster in urban or mining enclaves—thus drawing the attention of senators but not most House members.[39]

These assessments reflect a pluralistic views of politics in which every squeaky wheel is likely to get some grease. As applied to the Senate's districts, the idea is at least plausible, yet I have not seen it given a serious evidence workout, and there is a theoretical objection. Politics is not always pluralistic. It can be zero-sum. It can pit taxpayers against government beneficiaries, liberals against conservatives, or, of considerable aptness to the postwar decades, labor against management. In a dominantly rural state, why would taxpayers have wanted to fund the cities? In any state, why would business interests have lain dormant? From instances in, for example, California in 1934 and Ohio in 1950, we know very well that state business communities of those times were open to creative mobilization, which could contribute to statewide polarization, in elections that placed their interests at stake.[40]

---

[36] See Bailey, *Congress Makes a Law*, 126–27; Koenig, "Kennedy and the 87th Congress," 80; Kernell, "Is the Senate More Liberal than the House?" 336; Grofman et al., "Is the Senate More Liberal Than the House: Another Look," 283–86.

[37] Bailey, *Congress Makes a Law*, 126.

[38] Koenig, "Kennedy and the 87th Congress," 80.

[39] I owe this idea to Lucas Thompson.

[40] On California in 1934, see Greg Mitchell, *The Campaign of the Century: Upton Sinclair's Race for Governor of California and the Birth of Media Politics* (New York: Random House,

There seems to be room for more explanation. One might be a kind of historical hangover account. Generally speaking, as it happens, progressive or left-wing causes had enjoyed considerable success during a previous stretch of American history in sparsely populated states. See table 3.5, which organizes the Populist percentage of the total presidential vote in 1892, and the Progressive percentage of the vote in 1924, according to state population size (as indexed by the states' numbers of U.S. House members). These third-party drives, featuring candidates James B. Weaver and Robert La Follette, set a standard for the historical Left and probably indexed its support base. The 20 percent mark is the cutoff in table 3.5. As can be seen in the table, being a small-population state was not a sufficient, but it was very nearly a necessary, condition for the Populist or Progressive causes doing well in those earlier days. In particular, the plains, mountain, and Pacific northwestern states had few people, but a lot of them voted for the Left. Very likely, this had something to do with the economies of those peripheral areas. Mining, timber, and agriculture, in a context of open spaces where organized railroad workers could supply key networking, seem to have added up to a powerful political cocktail.[41] In the mountain Southwest, union densities already high in such traditional industries got a boost in new sectors during World War II.[42] In the plains and mountain states in general, complicated farmer–labor coalitions, often abnormal by

---

1992). The relevant, quite fascinating material appears in chunks at 139–40, 184–85, 187–89, 200–3, 217–18, 225–27, 244–45, 273–75, 291–92, 297–98, 305–6, 327–28, 338–40, 369–72, 393–95, 415–17, 436–37, 499–501. On Ohio in 1950, which featured Senator Taft in a showdown reelection contest against a CIO-backed candidate: James T. Patterson, *Mr. Republican: A Biography of Robert A. Taft* (Boston: Houghton Mifflin, 1972), 462.

[41] See the accounts in Elizabeth Sanders, *Roots of Reform: Farmers, Workers, and the American State, 1877–1917* (Chicago: University of Chicago Press, 1999), 1, 5, 160, 413–16, and ch. 10; Erik Olssen, "The Making of a Political Machine: The Railroad Unions Enter Politics," *Labor History* 19 (1978), 373–96. Olssen addresses the upper Midwest, yet it seems a good bet that his interesting argument would apply farther west.

[42] Elizabeth Tandy Shermer, "Counter-Organizing the Sunbelt: Right-to-Work Campaigns and Anti-Union Conservatism, 1943–1958," *Pacific Historical Review* 78:1 (2009), 81–118, at 86–89. This study addresses California but also the inland states of the region whose small populations of the 1940s are suggested by the sizes of their U.S. House delegations then: Arizona 2, Colorado 4, Nevada 1, New Mexico 2, Utah 2.

TABLE 3.5.

Populist Vote in 1892 and Progressive Vote in 1924, in States
According to Their Population

N congressional districts	Populist percent 1892		Progressive percent 1924	
	Under 20%	Over 20%	Under 20%	Over 20%
1–5	CT	CO	CO	AZ
	DE	ID	CT	ID
	FL	NV	DE	MT
	ME	ND	FL	NV
	MT	OR	ME	ND
	NH	SD	NH	OR
	RI	WA	NM	SD
	VT	WY	RI	WA
	WV		VT	UT
				WY
6–10	AR	AL	AL	MN
	CA	KS	AR	NE
	LA	NE	KS	
	MD		LA	
	MN		MD	
	MS		MS	
	NJ		NC	
	NC		OK	
	SC		SC	
	TN		TN	
	VA		VA	
	WI		WV	
11–15	GA	TX	GA	CA
	IN		IN	IA
	IA		KY	WI
	KY		MI	
	MA		NJ	
	MI		TX	
	MO			

Table 3.5. (*Continued*)

N congressional districts	Populist percent 1892		Progressive percent 1924	
	Under 20%	Over 20%	Under 20%	Over 20%
16 and over	IL		IL	
	NY		MA	
	OH		MO	
	PA		NY	
			OH	
			PA	

the standards of national partisan politics, could grow and flourish in third-party campaigns and major-party primaries as well as in the conventional November vote.

Here is the relevance. As a result of that small-state slant, a certain rotten-borough radicalism probably came to invest the Senate, given its constituency underpinnings. It was a matter of intensity as well as direction. Senators like William Borah (R-ID), Burton K. Wheeler (D-MT), Edward Costigan (D-CO), Bronson Cutting (R-NM), and Gerald P. Nye (R-ND) supplied a generous helping of both qualities in the 1920s and 1930s. And the 1940s, 1950s, and 1960s? The argument would have to be that enough of that earlier tradition of farmer-laborism hung on in the coalitional bases of enough small-state senators—such as, for example, Glen Taylor (D-ID), Elbert Thomas (D-UT), William Langer (R-ND), and James Murray (D-MT)—to keep making a difference. Perhaps it did.

There is another possible argument, which would hold for the postwar decades and otherwise. One thing that differentiates senators from House members is that many senators aim for the White House.[43] To do that, they need to reckon with not just their

[43] See, for example, Joseph A. Schlesinger, *Ambition and Politics: Political Careers in the United States* (Chicago: Rand McNally, 1966), 34; Paul R. Abramson, John H. Aldrich, and David W. Rohde, "Progressive Ambition among United States Senators, 1972–1988," *Journal of Politics* 49:1 (February 1987), 3–35.

home constituencies but the median voter nationwide.[44] Note, for example, the issue positioning of Senator Taft on housing and education in the 1940s. On those domestic issues, Taft, who reached for the presidency in 1948 and 1952, seems to have rivaled Eisenhower in appealing to the national median voter.[45] Other examples could be cited.

Constituency diversity, a lingering small-state radicalism, and White House aspirations—those, at any rate, are a few reasons specific to the Senate why that rural-leaning chamber, except on civil rights, might have outflanked the House to the liberal side during the postwar decades. Yet the question is understudied and remains something of a puzzle.

This chapter has addressed a bygone era. It has highlighted dissonances of historical importance in the representation and policymaking of that era. Also on exhibit is a theoretical importance. For quite awhile, the stances of the Senate as the negative outlier on civil rights and the House as the conservative outlier on domestic policy in general were available for all to see. In each case, open, energetically contested dissonance ending in losses rose to the status of an equilibrium. This is far from a kind of equilibrium in which politicians deftly adjust their proposals to their audiences and thus avoid losing.

---

[44] An argument of this sort appears in Mayhew, *Divided We Govern*, 104–8.

[45] Twice in 1951–52, during the latter half of Truman's second term, Taft saved the public housing program from gutting by appropriations riders advanced by House conservatives. See D. Bradford Hunt, "How Did Public Housing Survive the 1950s?" *Journal of Policy History* 17:2 (2005), 193–216, at 195. Taft also seems to have mirrored the median voter in driving to curb labor unions. That was a winning position in the 1940s. See Schickler, "Public Opinion, the Congressional Policy Agenda, and the Limits of New Deal Liberalism."

CHAPTER 4

House and Senate II

Two generations ago, critics of American government dwelt on the civil rights filibuster in the Senate and the conservative waywardness of the House. Windy southern senators, hayseed bias, and a House Rules Committee chairman known to go home rather than legislate were cultural artifacts. Those now distant topics were taken up in chapter 3. This chapter continues the discussion but in a more general way. It takes up three additional couplings of theory and historical experience that have entailed, in principle at least, the entire post–World War II era.

HOUSE PROCEDURAL ANTIMAJORITARIANISM IN GENERAL

As discussed in chapter 3, House procedural antimajoritarianism was said to veer the chamber in a conservative direction from the 1940s through the 1960s. The case seems shaky. But, over the long term there is a more general possibility. It centers here on White House proposals. Ideological direction aside, has procedural antimajoritarianism plagued presidents in general as they have dealt with the House during the last six decades? Certainly, in political science as well as in common understandings, there is no shortage of arguments that the lower chamber has exhibited an inventive range of antimajoritarian bents of various kinds.

The answer seems to be: very little. At the level of White House requests, where, among other things, the maneuvers of politicians tend to have their own dynamics and the stakes and the publicity tend to be high, procedural antimajoritarianism does not seem to have played a major House role. This is notwithstanding what might have gone on in the lower chamber at other, for the most part less prominent, levels of legislative politics. There is a theoretical implication: Even if it makes sense for some purposes to cast the House as a self-contained legislative body, that kind of theorizing seems to run into limits in the realm where the White House intrudes.

Following is some evidence. It needs the customary caution that attends any trafficking in counterfactuals. Yet it is evidence. As was documented in table 2.1, the presidents lost out on 74 of their 184 legislative requests. Also, as documented in table 3.2, they ran into tougher sledding on the House than the Senate side in 6 instances where the White House eventually won. That makes for 80 instances about which the question can be posed: Did a House floor majority, formally revealed or otherwise counterfactually discernible, favor a White House request yet not get its way in the chamber?[1]

The eighty instances can be segmented into six categories. I list the categories in table 4.1 and discuss them here in turn. In nineteen of the instances, the first category, as can be seen in tables 3.1 and 3.2, the White House got what it wanted (more or less) from

[1] In 5 of the 80 instances, "House floor majority" needs to read "House constitutionally required supermajority." Those five involved constitutional amendments that were pressed by Reagan and George H. W. Bush.

TABLE 4.1.
In Instances Where the White House Lost or Ran into Trouble, Did a
House Floor Majority Favor a Presidential Request but Not Get Its
Way in the Chamber?

Number of instances	
19	No, the White House won in the House; the Senate was the problem
27	No, a House floor majority turned thumbs down in a formal decision
14	Very unlikely
12	Unlikely
4	Can't tell
4	Likely

the House; the Senate was the problem.[2] No House antimajoritarian impediments there.

In another twenty-seven instances, a formal decision on the House floor, taken by teller, voice, or roll-call vote, pitted a (more or less) White House version of a measure directly against an alternative option (a competing version or the status quo), and the White House version lost. In these cases, there seems to be no ground for an antimajoritarian interpretation of the results. For example, Eisenhower's plan for national health insurance and Carter's for a consumer protection agency were brought up and voted down on the House floor, respectively by 238–134 (a recommittal motion) and 189–227.[3] In another kind of example, a Carter-friendly version of tax reform, offered in the form of an amendment, lost out by 193–225 to a more conservative tax bill

[2] That includes the seventeen instances in table 3.1 where the Senate distinctively blocked measures, as well as the two instances in table 3.2—taxes under Nixon and energy under Carter—that are coded as White House losses and where the Senate was the problem.
[3] National health insurance under Eisenhower, *CQA, 1954*, 210, 444–46; Reichard, *The Reaffirmation of Republicanism*, 133–35. Consumer protection agency under Carter, *CQA 1978*, 473.

sent to the floor by the Ways and Means Committee.[4] In one
unusual turn of events, Kennedy asked for a cabinet department of
urban affairs and housing, yet support for that idea proved lukewarm on Capitol Hill, and the House Rules Committee stalled, so
Kennedy then resubmitted the proposal as an executive reorganization plan, and the House voted down that plan by 264–150.[5]

[4] Losing was the Corman–Fisher amendment, which brought "the major tax bill showdown," *CQA 1978*, 233. The twenty-seven instances include all six of the entries from table
3.2. The additional particulars are as follows. Taft–Hartley repeal under Truman: conservative Wood substitute defeats White House–backed version 210–196 and 217–03, *CQA
1949*, 444. Brannan Plan for agriculture under Truman: producer-backed high price-support Gore substitute beats White House–backed Pace bill, 239–170, *CQA 1949*, 132.
Housing coops under Truman: killed 218–155, *CQA 1950*, p. 161. Housing under Eisenhower: White House–friendly Bolling amendment calling for four years of public housing
units loses 176–211, *CQA 1954*, 201. The 1957 budget under Eisenhower: many floor
amendments cut into White House program, *CQA 1957*, e.g., 119–21. Federal aid for
school construction under Eisenhower: killer amendment wins 208–203, *CQA 1957*, 588.
College scholarships under Eisenhower: Judd amendment to strike scholarships wins by
109–78, Sundquist, *Politics and Policy*, 178. Federal aid to education under Kennedy: this
was discussed earlier; the measure's floor rejection in a Calendar Wednesday process is the
formal expression relied on here. Minimum wage under Kennedy: conservative Ayres–
Kitchin version wins by 216–203, *CQA 1961*, 481. D.C. home rule under Johnson: in a
"smashing defeat for the Administration," Sisk substitute wins by 227–174, *CQA 1965*, 618.
The 1973 Nixon budget to cut poverty programs: programs are protected against cuts by,
e.g., floor votes of 110–288 and 186–213, *CQA 1973*, 66-H. Emergency energy powers
under Nixon: Broyhill amendment to award powers loses by 152–256, *CQA 1973*, 691.
Energy R&D under Nixon: four White House–friendly Hosmer amendments voted down,
CQA 1974, 286, 746. Water projects under Carter: Conte amendment backing Carter's
plan loses 194–218, *CQA 1977*, 657. Agriculture under Carter: in two key floor tests, administration forces lose on a new sugar subsidy by 246–155, then decide to cave rather than
lose on higher wheat prices, *CQA 1977*, p. 427. The general context: "A lobbying campaign
by farmers, farm organizations, and farm state representatives had paid off, and the votes
obviously were there [in the House] for raising price supports to the [Carter-defying] levels
in the Senate bill" (p. 419). Balanced budget constitutional amendment under Reagan:
loses 236–187 (lacking the needed 2/3), *CQA 1982*, 391–94. Agriculture under Reagan: key
White House–friendly sugar and dairy amendments lose by 142–263 and 166–244, *CQA
1985*, 530. Anti-flag-burning constitutional amendment under G.H.W. Bush: loses by
254–177 (lacking the needed 2/3), *CQA 1990*, 524. S&Ls bailout under G.H.W. Bush: key
vote on funding plan, the source of later conference friction and Bush veto threat, brings
White House setback by 280–146, *CQA 1989*, 130–33. Summit deficit-reduction plan
agreed to by Bush plus Senate and House leaders of both parties is voted down by 179–254,
CQA 1990, 136–37. Fast-track trade authority under Clinton: voted down by 180–243,
CQA 1998, 23–3. Patients' bill of rights under Clinton: White House–friendly Dingell
substitute defeated 212–217, *CQA 1998*, 14–3. Save Social Security under Clinton: Rangel
substitute offering White House plan voted down by 197–227, *CQA 1998*, H-132.

[5] Judith Helmreich Parris, "Congress Rejects the President's Urban Department, 1961–
62," 177–223 in Frederic N. Cleaveland (ed.), *Congress and Urban Problems* (Washington,

That leaves thirty-four instances. On these, judgment is re-quired, since the House did not make direct floor decisions. Four-teen of these seem to belong in a third category meriting the label "very unlikely"—that is, the odds seem very poor that a White House–supportive floor majority would have manifested itself if given a suitable formal chance to do so. The fourteen are a mixed bag. Some White House proposals seem to have stirred little in-terest on Capitol Hill. That was the problem.[6] In certain other cases, it is a stretch to see the Democratic House of 1973–74, if suitably interrogated, awarding the then-beleaguered Nixon the natural gas deregulation or the cabinet energy department he asked for, or the Democratic Houses of 1981–82 and 1985–86 awarding Reagan the tuition tax credits and the constitutional amendments addressing abortion, school prayer, and budget balancing that he asked for.[7] Kennedy's design for agriculture, once it met public exposure in committee, seemed to face dismal prospects on the House floor and was not raised there.[8] Truman's proposal for a tax hike ran into prefloor barriers: "Congressional sentiment was strongly in opposition to tax increases, or any suggestion of them." "Practically no one was in favor of increasing taxes."[9] Truman's plan for national health insurance, and George W. Bush's for part-privatization of Social Security, ran into a fatal mix of hostil-ity and lukewarmness once they were unveiled and reacted to; un-derstandably, they never reached the House floor.[10] Regarding

D.C.: Brookings Institution Press, 1969). In this case, there is some chance that the House members were objecting to the White House's circuitous process as well as to substance.
[6] Reagan's sketchy plans for a "new federalism," and his odd request for a change in Inter-nal Revenue Service rules, went nowhere: *CQA 1982*, 18, 397. George W. Bush's request for an extension of "No Child Left Behind" to high schools faded quickly in a Republican-controlled Congress: *CQW 2005*, 305, 492–93; *CQW 2006*, 3168–69.
[7] Natural gas deregulation: *CQA 1974*, 800–2. Cabinet department of energy: *CQA 1973*, 697. Tuition tax credits: *CQA 1982*, 15. Abortion and school prayer: *CQA 1982*, 403. The balanced-budget reference is to 1985: *CQA 1985*, 233. This was a replay request. The House had already voted down a Reagan request for a balanced-budget amendment in 1982, by 236–187 (the necessary two-thirds was lacking).
[8] On Kennedy's supply-management plan: *CQA 1961*, 104–11.
[9] *CQA 1950*, 577–78.
[10] On the Truman plan: *CQA 1949*, 292–97. On the American Medical Association's cam-paign against the Democrats' national health insurance program in the late 1940s, see, for

Clinton's health-care plan, which generated a long-running legislative drama in 1994 yet never did reach the House floor, Speaker
Tom Foley later reflected, "There wasn't anything out there they
wanted to vote for. We weren't close to a majority on any specific
health care plan."[11]

Up a notch I see a category of "unlikely," which has twelve
entries. In several cases, the scantiness of information widens
the uncertainty. Floor majorities might have been available, yet
there is no particularly good reason to think so, and they probably were not. Perhaps a small share of these proposals could
have made it on the floor, but just which ones is unknowable.
That seems to be the story for Truman's plan for a Columbia Valley Authority (it was defeated on the Senate floor; the House
did nothing),[12] Nixon's plan for revenue sharing in 1969–70
(the Senate held hearings; the House did nothing),[13] Carter's
move for welfare reform (the Democrats could not agree on a
package),[14] Clinton's move for welfare reform in 1993–94 (the
Democrats were late, slow, lukewarm, irresolute, and otherwise
preoccupied),[15] and Clinton's requests for a minimum wage hike
and an expensive new child-care program in 1997–98 (these were
not the sorts of issues the House Republican leadership of those
days was eager to stage public votes on, although whether favorable floor majorities would have materialized is another matter;
probably not).[16]

---

example, Colin Gordon, "Why No National Health Insurance in the U.S.? The Limits of
Social Provision in War and Peace, 1941–1948," *Journal of Policy History* 9:3 (1997), 277–310,
at 292–95. On the Bush plan: *CQW 2005*, 550–53, 1238–39, 2888; *CQW 2006*, 14–17, 82.
[11] Quoted in Johnson and Broder, *The System*, p. 509. It is easy to understand the skittish-
ness of many Democratic House members, which has been documented. See chs. 14, 16.
In a national Gallup poll in April 1994, two-thirds of respondents thought that "quality of
care would decline and they would be worse off" if Clinton's plan passed (p. 371).
[12] *CQA 1950*, 607.
[13] *CQA 1969*, 961; *CQA 1970*, 923; Beer, "The Adoption of General Revenue sharing,"
174, 179–80. The next Congress approved a version of the idea.
[14] *CQA 1977*, 471; *CQA 1978*, 600–603.
[15] *CQA 1994*, 364.
[16] On minimum wage: The previous Congress had raised it, there was strong business re-
sistance this time, and the Senate voted it down by 55–44 this time. *CQA 1998*, 10–7. On
child care, *CQA 1998*, 6–12.

Still under "unlikely," Truman's proposal for federal aid to education that died in committee was discussed earlier. Carter's plan for hospital cost containment was a close-run thing; in the end, it died in committee—in fact, two committees—yet I do not see any ground that the full House would have treated it better.[17] George H. W. Bush's plan for education did not receive a clear test on the House floor in 1989–90, but, given one, it would probably have lost out to a more expensive version that the House actually did pass and that the White House found intolerable.[18] Eisenhower's proposal for three-year trade authority in 1953–54 is a close call. Certainly, the Ways and Means Committee footdragged. Yet it is also reported that the House Republican leadership was not eager to head into the 1954 election having just passed the measure. Why not wait until next year? It seems plausible that that stance echoed House Republicans in general, although the context is cloudy.[19] As for Eisenhower's plan for a Colorado River project, committees in both chambers approved it in mid-1954, but protests poured in to Capitol Hill, and the House leadership declared it "too controversial to consider at that late date [late 1954]."[20] Finally, Kennedy's proposal for Medicare died in committee in 1961–62. It was a major loss. But what are we to make of that? Here is James Sundquist's assessment: "The House Ways and Means Committee was therefore the measure's true burial place. But, like the Rules Committee, the Ways and Means Committee accurately reflected the makeup of the House itself. Chairman Wilbur Mills was representative not just of the second district of Arkansas but of his region; medicare had little backing anywhere in the South. And such vote counts as were taken indicated that the bill did not command majority support in the House in 1962."[21]

That leaves eight instances. Four seem to belong in a category I would label "can't tell one way or another." It is an open question

[17] *CQA 1978*, 619–25.
[18] *CQA 1990*, 614.
[19] *CQA 1954*, 265–69; Bauer, et al., *American Business and Public Policy*, 51–56; Reichard, *Reaffirmation of Republicanism*, 78–84. The next Congress approved the measure.
[20] *CQA 1954*, pp. 508–9. The next Congress approved the measure.
[21] Sundquist, *Politics and Policy*, 477.

whether a House majority in 1953–54 might have favored Eisenhower's probusiness revision of the Taft–Hartley Act. A House
committee was deliberating and waiting for the Senate to act. It
folded once the Senate acted negatively.[22] At certain times during
1974, a House floor majority might have favored Nixon's plan for
national health insurance. There was a roller coaster of delibera-
tion and calculation centering in the Ways and Means Committee.[23] It is an intriguing question whether a House majority in
1972, facing a floor vote, would have backed a measure approved
by 58–38 in the Senate to place tough restrictions on court-ordered school busing for racial balance. The House Judiciary
Committee buried the idea. A discharge petition came up short.[24]
But that failure might not be dispositive. The issue was toxic, notably in Michigan, in the runup to the 1972 election. Finally, it is
not clear whether a House floor majority existed for the comprehensive immigration plan fostered by the Senate and the George
W. Bush administration in 2006. Most Democrats were on board,
and some House Republicans were said to be favorable, but the
House Republican leadership, in effect, pocket-vetoed the measure late in the session.[25]

The final category, which includes four instances, is "likely."
That is, it is likely that a majority of House members favored a
White House request that the chamber did not enact. In a parliamentary tangle in 1954, a postal-reform package backed by Eisenhower commanded a 228–171 floor majority, but that was not
enough in a suspend-the-rules circumstance requiring two-thirds,
and the measure died.[26] In 1958 committees in both chambers
reported out statehood for Hawaii, but it had become too late in
the session to act. Probably a supportive House majority existed.[27]

[22] CQA 1954, 300–304; Reichard, Reaffirmation of Republicanism, 145–46.
[23] CQA 1974, pp. 386–91; Light, The President's Agenda, pp. 206–7; John B. Gilmour, Strategic Disagreement: Stalemate in American Politics (Pittsburgh: University of Pittsburgh
Press, 1995), 82–85; Randall Strahan, New Ways and Means: Reform and Change in a Congressional Committee (Chapel Hill: University of North Carolina Press, 1990), 33.
[24] CQA 1972, 385–86.
[25] CQA 2006, 1–5, 14:3–6; CQW 2006, 974–75, 1400–2, 1473, 2315, 2600, 2634, 3357.
[26] CQA 1954, 385–86, 448.
[27] CQA 1958, 285.

Success came easily in the next Congress. In 1962 the House Judiciary Committee would likely have approved a Kennedy-backed civil rights bill and gotten it passed if Senate obstruction had not loomed. Here is a case of why waste the effort.[28] In late 1978 Republican obstruction on the House floor killed a Senate-passed measure creating a cabinet department of education.[29] Success on that front came in the next Congress.

That is the end of the exhaustive discussion. Those are the eighty cases. To be sure, they do not include the two public housing failures during 1945–48 that I considered earlier. Those two casualties were good candidates for the antimajoritarian case. Committee blockades seem to have won out. Yet it seems that very seldom after 1948, during the six decades of this study's dataset, were presidents thwarted by the thwarting of House majorities. Placed in a larger context, the record seems even scantier. Consider the last three categories analyzed here—"unlikely," "can't tell," and "likely." Of the twenty requests in those categories, fifteen, for what it is worth, were not passed by the Senate either, and five (there is an overlap of four with the fifteen) were successfully enacted by the next Congress under the same president. Of the eight instances in the "can't tell" or "likely" categories, only two were House-blocked, Senate-passed items that did not make it in the next Congress either. That is, they are possibly the best cases, although neither is a particularly convincing one, for the thwarting of House majorities as a unique and enduring obstacle to enactment. Those are the Nixon-backed anti–school busing plan of 1972 and the Bush-backed comprehensive immigration plan of 2006. What a surprising yield for the sixty years.

But what about the various theories that have accented House antimajoritarianism? One line of argument has highlighted the House's standing committees, which, at least during much of the time since World War II, are said to have enjoyed property rights over issues, agenda power, informational advantages, and a general deference from the full House anchored in cross-committee

[28] CQA 1962, 371.
[29] CQA 1978, 571–74.

reciprocity. According to an influential 1988 interpretation, "Within their jurisdictions, committees possess the monopoly right to bring alternatives to the status quo before the legislature."[30] Payoff in policy leeway was the hypothesized result. Given any off-floor-median propensities among the memberships of committees, here is a recipe for the thwarting of House majorities and possibly for White House difficulties.

One might expect any such pattern to stand out in policy areas where the politics can be easily distributive and where committees friendly to particular sectors or interests have famously existed—highways, dam-building, the post office, agriculture, and the like. Those areas are not heavily represented in this study's dataset of 184 White House requests, except for agriculture, which figured in 7 requests. Yet it is interesting to see what happened in those 7 instances. There is virtually no support for the idea that the reputedly muscular House Agriculture Committee won its way over House floor majorities, or over White House wishes, through agenda control. In 1949 the Truman-backed Brannan Plan cleared the Agriculture Committee (at least for a trial run) but lost out on the House floor by 239–170 to a Farm Bureau–backed plan favored by Republicans and southern Democrats. This was an upside down result, so to speak.[31] In 1954 the Eisenhower administration joined with the House Republican leadership to crush a bill reported by the Agriculture Committee in a showdown 228–170 vote on the House floor.

[30] Barry R. Weingast and William J. Marshall, "The Industrial Organization of Congress, or, Why Legislatures, Like Firms, Are Not Organized as Markets," *Journal of Political Economy* 96:1 (February 1988), 132–63, quotation at 143. See also Kenneth A. Shepsle, "The Changing Textbook Congress," 238–66 in John E. Chubb and Paul E. Peterson (eds.), *Can the Government Govern?* (Washington, D.C.: Brookings Institution Press, 1989), at 238–48; Kenneth A. Shepsle and Barry R. Weingast, "Positive Theories of Congressional Institutions," *Legislative Studies Quarterly* 19:2 (May 1994), 149–79, at 154–56. For a presentation of the genre, see also Keith Krehbiel, *Information and Legislative Organization* (Ann Arbor: University of Michigan Press, 1992), 34–39, 43–44.

[31] *CQA 1949*, 132; John Mark Hansen, *Gaining Access: Congress and the Farm Lobby, 1919–1981* (Chicago: University of Chicago Press, 1991), 119–24; J. Roland Pennock, "Party and Constituency in Postwar Agricultural Price-Support Legislation," *Journal of Politics* 18 (May 1956), 167–210, at 173.

This was a victory for "flexible" over fixed high crop supports.[32] In 1958 the Eisenhower administration used veto threats and Senate leverage to defeat the Agriculture Committee's offerings twice on the House floor (by 171–214 on a rule to take up a bill, and later by 210–186 on a move to suspend the rules that lacked the necessary two-thirds to pass a bill), winning a signal victory in the end by voice vote.[33] In 1961, as discussed earlier, Kennedy's supply-management plan sank in committee. Then, the White House seems to have done a reality check and given up. Once that year's farm bill reached the House floor, there was plenty of amending activity, but the Kennedy plan did not figure in it.[34] In 1965 a Johnson package prevailed both in the Agriculture Committee and, amid ample amending activity, on the House floor.[35] In 1977 Carter sent up a plan that emerged from the Agriculture Committee a degree too producer-friendly for the taste of that budget-conscious administration. But then the House floor rendered the program even more producer-friendly in a flurry of amending action that brought, among other things, significant White House losses as a new sugar subsidy and costlier wheat supports were added on (in the sugar case, by 246–165; in the wheat case, the White House, facing defeat, elected to fold rather than fight).[36] In 1985 the House floor struck again in a

[32] *CQA 1954*, 100–9; Hansen, *Gaining Access*, 126–31; Reichard, *Reaffirmation of Republicanism*, 139–41. "The administration gave the Harrison amendment its full support [against the Committee bill] and 'used all possible pressures' on recalcitrant Republican House members, employing state political machines to put pressure on waverers and in some cases even threatening retaliation at the polls" (140–41). See also Pennock, "Party and Constituency in Postwar Agricultural Price-Support Legislation," 185–89.

[33] *CQA 1958*, 269–75; Charles O. Jones, "The Agriculture Committee and the Problem of Representation," ch. 8 in Robert L. Peabody and Nelson W. Polsby (eds.), *New Perspectives on the House of Representatives*, 2d ed. (Chicago: Rand McNally, 1969).

[34] *CQA 1961*, 104–14. "There was no effort made in either the House or Senate to reverse the setback suffered by the Administration when the Agricultural Committees turned down its proposed price support and production control programs" (p. 111). See also Robert Dallek, *An Unfinished Life: John F. Kennedy, 1917–1963* (Boston: Little, Brown, 2003), 110–12, 379.

[35] *CQA 1965*, 114–30.

[36] *CQA 1977*, 417–34. Strictly speaking, it was Congressman Tom Foley, the White House's agent on the spot, who chose to fold rather than fight: "It was apparent that the wheat-state congressmen had done their homework and had the votes in hand to pass the amendment

context of variegated amending activity as the free-market-oriented Reagan White House came nowhere near carrying its key sugar and dairy cuts (losing by 142–263 and 166–244).[37]

In agricultural politics, at least in these seven cases, and although parliamentary situations can of course be tricky, House floor sovereignty seems to have prevailed.[38] Sometimes it aided the presidents, sometimes it thwarted them.

How about the parties? The House's majority party, no less than its committee system, has been posited to constitute, at least sometimes, an antimajoritarian instrument. In the "party cartel" theory offered by Gary W. Cox and Mathew D. McCubbins, the chamber's majority party is said to be able to use agenda control and other devices to advance its own interests, even if those sometimes might conflict with the views of the House's median members—that is, with floor majorities.[39] At stake is a party's overall "public record," which might hinge partly on "major pieces of legislation passed."[40] Yet the authors are circumspect on the question of whether in any remarkable way a House majority party can serve as an instrument to actually enact laws—more specifically, to convert a party's central aims into floor victories even if doing so might require taming significant intraparty dissent.[41] House majority parties in the "party cartel" model, despite all their prerogatives, do not seem to act very much as offensive teams. That caution is perhaps surprising, given the customary role assigned to political parties by political theorists and society in general.

---

without him" (427). See also Burton I. Kaufman, *The Presidency of James Earl Carter, Jr.* (Lawrence: University Press of Kansas, 1993), 55–57.

[37] *CQA 1985*, 517–39, votes at 530–31. "Republican leaders conceded that the Reagan administration, as a result of the votes, lost considerable ground in its efforts to scale back price- and income-support benefits in the remaining sections of the bill" (530).

[38] The interpretation here accords with that in Krehbiel, *Information and Legislative Organization*, 9–14, 255.

[39] Gary W. Cox and Mathew D. McCubbins, *Legislative Leviathan: Party Government in the House* (Berkeley: University of California Press, 1993); Gary W. Cox and Mathew D. McCubbins, *Setting the Agenda: Responsible Party Government in the House of Representatives* (New York: Cambridge University Press, 2005).

[40] Cox and McCubbins, *Legislative Leviathan*, 110–11.

[41] Ibid., 269, 271; Cox and McCubbins, *Setting the Agenda*, 5, 7, 34, 101, 223.

Parties are supposed to be able to carry their programs. Possibly that is their number one purpose.

This is a complicated subject. The majority parties of the House obviously do take the offensive in some ways. By means of bill design plus a followup bargaining that might feature exclusions and side payments, they can aim to build winning party-centered coalitions that *please* a floor majority. That is one way to enact proposals—from the tariff bills of the nineteenth century through cap-and-trade and health-care reform in 2009–10.[42] Also, majority party leaders occasionally do call on loyalty or engage in strong-arming to attract the pivotal floor member at the 218-vote point, even without making policy concessions. Examples would include the passage of Clinton's budget package in 1993 and the Republicans' expansion of Medicare into prescription drugs in 2003.[43]

Yet beyond these terrains, a realism seems to inhere in the Cox and McCubbins caution. For a House majority party, the median floor member can be a tough nut to crack. This study's sixty-year dataset of White House requests bears on the subject. An interesting circumstance is the one where a president and a majority of the House are of the same party and the president sends up legislative requests. In fact, in that configuration during the sixty years, albeit chiefly during the earlier part of that time span when the Democratic party suffered particular unity problems,[44] presidents often did win the backing of a majority of their House copartisans—a plausible indicator of party stance—yet fail to win chamber

[42] For example, to reach the needed 218 votes on health-care reform in 2009, the Democratic leadership of the House accommodated the Stupak amendment pressed by prolife interests. See Lisa Wangsness and Susan Milligan, "House Passes Sweeping Health Care Bill: Impassioned Obama Pep Talk, Hours of Acid Debate Precede 220–215 Vote; Concession on Abortion Roils Liberals, but Seals Margin for $1 Trillion Plan," *Boston Globe*, November 8, 2009, A1, A14.

[43] On the Clinton budget: Richard E. Cohen, *Changing Course in Washington: Clinton and the New Congress* (New York: Macmillan, 1994), 111–15, 210–11. On Medicare expansion: *CQA 2003*, 11–7; Cox and McCubbins, *Setting the Agenda*, 201–2.

[44] It is also true that the balance of party control shifted. From Truman in 1949–50 through Carter in 1977–78, five out of eight of the initial two-year spans of the presidencies featured same-party control of the House and White House. From Reagan in 1981–82 through George W. Bush in 2005–6, the balance was three out of seven.

TABLE 4.2.

Cases Where Same Party Controlled Presidency and House, White House Request Commanded a Majority of the House Majority Party, but House as a Whole Did Not Act Favorably

Congress	President	Weighted value of request	Presidential request
81st	Truman	2	repeal of Taft–Hartley Act
81st	Truman	2	federal aid to education
81st	Truman	2	Brannan Plan for agriculture
81st	Truman	1	middle-income housing coops
83rd	Eisenhower	1	national health insurance
83rd	Eisenhower	2	amend Taft–Hartley Act
83rd	Eisenhower	1	postal reform
87th	Kennedy	2	federal aid to education
87th	Kennedy	1	cabinet department of housing
87th	Kennedy	2	Medicare
89th	Johnson	1	D.C. home rule
95th	Carter	2	tax reform
95th	Carter	1	consumer protection agency
95th	Carter	1	hospital cost containment
95th	Carter	1	cabinet department of education
103rd	Clinton	4	health-care reform

approval for their requests. The losses were many.[45] See table 4.2 for a list of sixteen instances in which this disparity was evident or, I would estimate, solidly likely. In ten of the instances, the revealed positions of House members on roll-call votes demonstrate it. In 1954, for example, the House recommitted Eisenhower's plan for national health insurance by 238 to 134, yet the Republican members opposed that recommittal by 75–120. In

[45] At least during the early phase of the sixty years under analysis here, the House Democratic leadership had to compete with a conservative-flavored Rules Committee for agenda-setting power in the chamber. See Eric Schickler and Kathryn Pearson, "Agenda Control, Majority Party Power, and the House Committee on Rules, 1937–1952," *Legislative Studies Quarterly* 34:4 (November 2009), 455–91.

1978 the Carter-backed plan for a consumer protection agency lost by 189–227, yet the Democratic members backed it by 172–101.[46] In the other six instances, which did not emanate in floor votes, extrapolation from other evidence strongly suggests such a disparity. Examples are federal aid to education in 1949, Medicare in 1961–62, and health-care reform in 1993–94.[47] In none of these sixteen cases, notwithstanding the unambiguous go-ahead central tendencies within the majority-party caucuses, did a party cartel materialize and enact.

These sixteen failures were not trivial. Much theorizing and angst have gone into especially the Democrats' nonachievements appearing in table 4.2. Bedrock party aspirations were often at stake—education, labor, housing, health care, progressive taxation. Note in the table the weightings of the sixteen requests according to their importance.[48] In nearly all the sixteen instances a House enactment success would have been, in the terminology

[46] The source for the ten instances is *CQA* published in the years specified as follows. Repeal of Taft–Hartley under Truman: the Wood substitute 217–203, Democrats alone 71–180, *1949*, 444. Brannan Plan under Truman: Gore substitute 239–170, Democrats alone 79–165, *1949*, 133. Middle-income housing under Truman: the motion to kill coops 218–155, Democrats alone 81–141, *1950*, 160–61. National health insurance under Eisenhower: votes as above, *1954*, 216. Postal reform under Eisenhower: House passage vote 228–171 (which fails under suspension-of-rules procedure), Republicans alone 207–2, *1954*, 385. Federal aid to education under Kennedy: the Calendar Wednesday passage vote 170–242, Democrats alone 164–82, *1961*, 225. Cabinet department of housing under Kennedy: the vote to kill the idea as an executive reorganization plan 264–150, Democrats alone 111–137, *1962*, 383. D.C. home rule under Johnson: the Sisk substitute 227–174, Democrats alone 122–151, *1965*, 618. Tax reform under Carter: the Carter-friendly Corman–Fisher amendment loses 193–225, Democrats alone 185–91, *1978*, 233, 170H. Consumer protection agency under Carter: votes as above, *1978*, 473, 12-H.
[47] The six instances that did not end in House floor votes were discussed earlier—federal aid to education under Truman, amending the Taft–Hartley Act under Eisenhower, Medicare under Kennedy, hospital cost containment under Carter, the cabinet department of education under Carter, and health-care reform under Clinton. An additional ingredient of evidence exists regarding Eisenhower's generally probusiness plan to amend Taft–Hartley. The Senate voted 50–42 to recommit (kill) a version of the White House request, but the Republican senators taken alone voted 3–42—that is, not to recommit. Given this pattern, it seems exceedingly likely that a majority of House Republicans would have backed the plan on the chamber floor if given the opportunity. See *CQA 1954*, 302; Reichard, *Reaffirmation of Republicanism*, 145–46.
[48] As documented in table 2.1.

employed here, antimajoritarian. A party majority favored action, but a floor majority did not.[49]

All this having been said, it is wise to step back for a moment. From a broader perspective, how much better off would the presidents have been if friendly majority-party cartels in the House had been able to spirit White House proposals to floor victories? For the presidents, particularly the Democratic ones of the earlier decades, would minority rule, in effect, by majority party cartels in the House have solved a lot of problems? Well, possibly just a few. In general, taking the sixteen instances in table 4.2, it is not a political fluke that House floor majorities were lacking. The Senate had a representative policy voice, too. Of only *four* of the sixteen cases is it simultaneously true that majorities of the House majority party were available, that House floor majorities were apparently lacking, *and* that the Senate on its side voted to enact. Those were the proposals for federal education under Truman and Kennedy, D.C. home rule under Johnson, and hospital cost containment under Carter. The appearance here of the two education initiatives is interesting: it places in relief the House's distinctive openness back then, possibly owing to the textures of its geographic constituencies, to the Roman Catholic Church as a veto group. These four instances were important,[50] but there are limits to the idea that history would have been greatly different if House majority-party cartels had operated frictionlessly during the sixty years.

[49] Among the sixteen, there are at least two exceptions to this particular generalization. In the two instances, the actual outcome was antimajoritarian. Both Eisenhower's postal reform and Carter's department of education enjoyed the apparent support of House floor majorities, but they fell victim to floor-level procedural entanglements. A possible third exception is the attempted probusiness revision of Taft–Hartley under Eisenhower. We know that the Senate rejected that move by 50–42, and we can be nearly certain that a majority of House Republicans would have favored it, given a chance, but we do not know what the House floor balance would have been. Perhaps a disparity would have existed between the House Republican median and the House floor median on that measure, perhaps not. All sixteen of the instances, however, are embarrassments for a strong, offensive-team version of party cartel theory.

[50] Federal education had to wait sixteen years beyond Truman's request in 1949, and four years beyond Kennedy's in 1961, for enactment. D.C. home rule was delayed nearly a decade.

In the Cox and McCubbins argument, it is as defensive teams, not offensive ones, that House majority parties are said to excel. To the point, they are said to be able, chiefly through control of procedure, to prevent minority rumps of their own party from joining with the opposition party to win floor victories.[51] The result is antimajoritarian. Measures favored by House floor majorities are not taken up. They do not pass. In general, as the authors themselves say, the defensive side of the theory seems to have solider grounding than does an offensive argument. Such a defensive instance here might be immigration reform in the House during 2005–6 under George W. Bush. That is, it is possible that an agenda stall by the House Republican leadership warded off a Democratic-centered floor victory for this White House–backed measure. Otherwise, not much in the sixty-year dataset of White House requests leaps out. No doubt strategy and counterfactuality are in play. Why, notably under conditions of divided party control, would presidents waste their time and energy sending up proposals that might command such cross-party floor majorities should they reach the House floor but probably wouldn't reach it? Also, for that matter, from the standpoint of voter choice, a perspective might be: Why would an electorate wish or expect a president to keep making legislative proposals in this gratuitous fashion when it has decided, more or less, by generating divided government, to award the House as well as the White House a large share of agenda control? Consider the diminished role of George W. Bush as agenda-setter during 2007–08 as Nancy Pelosi's role grew.

This having been said, the record of cross-party floor victories that violated the party cartel model during the sixty years is not meager. From the dataset of White House requests, see the instances listed in table 4.3 (all except the last entry). The record *looks* meager. There are not many entries. But it encompasses the Reagan revolution of 1981—the taxes cuts, ERTA, weighted 4[52];

[51] Cox and McCubbins, *Setting the Agenda*, 2–3, 12, 92, 101, 223.
[52] The decisive vote on ERTA in 1981 was not a final-passage vote. It came on a Barber Conable substitute that the Reagan forces won by 238–195, the majority-party Democrats

TABLE 4.3.
Cases Where White House Requests Won Enactment on House Floor
in Odd Configurations of Party Support

Congress	President	Weighted value of request	Presidential request
Same party controlled presidency and House—requests won on House floor backed by majority of minority party, but by only minority of majority party:			
103rd	Clinton	2	NAFTA
Different parties controlled presidency and House—requests won on House floor backed by majority of minority (the president's) party, but by only minority of majority party:			
97th	Reagan	4	tax cuts (ERTA)
97th	Reagan	3	expenditure cuts (OBRA)
105th	Clinton	1	campaign finance reform
Different parties controlled presidency and House—Requests won on House floor backed by majority of majority party, but by only minority of minority (the president's) party:			
101st	Bush 41	3	deficit reduction package

and the expenditure cuts, OBRA, weighted 3. It is hard to imagine the domestic legislative history of the last half of the twentieth century absent the Reagan revolution, which possibly ranked second to the Great Society of the 1960s in significance. To enact ERTA and OBRA, minorities of Democrats joined with Republi-

---

voting 48–194, the Republicans 190–1. A later final-passage vote was 323–107, with Democrats voting 133–106, Republicans 190–1. Politicians shy away from going on record against tax cuts. Yet it is clear that the ERTA showdown came on the Conable substitute. Much tension and attention accompanied the vote. Without much doubt, this 238–194 result was one of the most important roll-call outcomes of the last half century. For many years, this cross-party victory over the O'Neill-led Democrats helped shaped the terms of contestation between the parties on questions of political economy. For one account of the House action in 1981, see Steven F. Hayward, *The Age of Reagan: The Conservative Counter-revolution, 1980–1989* (New York: Crown Forum, 2009), 156–66.

cans to defeat the majority Democratic party of the House led at that time by Thomas P. O'Neill.[53] Also appearing in table 4.3 is the North American Free Trade Agreement (NAFTA). Clinton won approval of that major measure in 1993 by participating in a defeat of *his own* House majority party. Most Democrats in the House voted against NAFTA (102–156), whereas most Republicans voted for it (132–43).[54]

If this study's canvass of White House requests were extended to the second halves of presidential terms, it would pick up more such instances. One would be the Landrum–Griffin Act of 1959—a model cross-party victory. In this legislative drive targeting unions, Eisenhower resorted to radio and television: "For the first time in his presidency, the most popular incumbent president in history made a public appeal for legislation he wanted and specified the bill by name." It is said that a "deluge of mail" ensued, and that "the overwhelming response and pressure on wavering congressmen brought [the measure] through Congress."[55] The showdown House floor vote was 229–201, the majority-party Democrats voting 95–184, the Republicans 134–17.[56] Another instance would be the FISA fix of 2008—that is, the overhaul of foreign

[53] The third instance in the triplet in table 4.3, campaign finance reform in 1997–98, did not end in a statute. Clinton sent up a request. In the House, controlled by the Republicans, a minority of Republicans joined a majority of Democrats to enact a bill opposed by a majority of Republicans. The House final passage vote was 252–179; Republicans taken alone, 61–164; Democrats taken alone, 190–15. Then the measure failed in the Senate absent sufficient votes for cloture. See *CQA 1998*, p. H-114. Cox and McCubbins downplay this event on the ground that the House Republican leadership anticipated the Senate nonaction and perhaps for that reason did not bother to block the bill in the House. *Setting the Agenda*, 109–10. Yet soon afterwards in 2001–2, a similar cross-party majority defeated the House Republican party to approve campaign finance reform *after* the Senate had already passed it during that Congress. George W. Bush did not request this latter measure, yet he signed it, reluctantly. Here in this latter case was a prime opportunity for the House Republican leadership to block a measure if they could. They did not. See *CQA 2002*, 14–7; Dean McSweeney, "Reform in a Cold Climate: Change in US Campaign Finance Law," *Government and Opposition* 40:4 (Augumn 2005), 492–514. Generally speaking, the Republicans on Capitol Hill have detested the idea of campaign finance reform.
[54] See David R. Mayhew, "Clinton, the 103rd Congress, and Unified Party Control: What Are the Lessons?" ch. 10 in John G. Geer (ed.), *Politicians and Party Politics* (Baltimore: Johns Hopkins University Press, 1998), 280–81.
[55] Lee, *Eisenhower and Landrum–Griffin*, 136.
[56] *CQA 1959*, 167, 382.

intelligence surveillance law requested by George W. Bush. On this high-priority White House measure, the House floor vote was 293–129, the majority-party Democrats voting 105–128, the Republicans 188–1.[57]

Other kinds of off-script coalitions can play a role. See the last entry in table 4.3. George H. W. Bush, although the ultimate version of his deficit-reduction package of 1990 was shaped as much by the Senate and the Democrats as the White House, won his make-or-break victory on that measure on a House voting pattern of 250–164—the majority-party Democrats voting 218–28, the Republicans 32–136.[58] Bush's own party in the House performed as the system outlier.[59] This result did not bring a majority-party

---

[57] See Siobhan Gorman, "Many Democrats Object as House Passes Spying Bill: Near Unanimity among Republicans Gives Bush Victory," *Wall Street Journal*, June 21–22, 2008, A3; *CQW 2008*, 1771, 1790. This study's dataset is confined to domestic requests. Not reached, therefore, by extending it to the second halves of presidential terms, would be the measures funding the Iraq War voted by the Democratic-controlled House in 2007 and 2008 at the behest of the George W. Bush administration, cross-party victories both. In 2007 the House floor vote was 280–142; the majority-party Democrats taken alone, 86–140; the Republicans, 194–2. *CQA 2007*, 6–10, H-140. In 2008 the House floor vote was 268–155; the majority-party Democrats taken alone, 80–151; the Republicans, 188–4. *CQW 2008*, 1728–29. Regarding the 2007 case, there is a revealing comment by House Speaker Nancy Pelosi, who arranged the procedure that yielded the result: "I'm the Speaker of the House. . . . I have to take into consideration something broader than the majority of the majority in the Democratic Caucus." Susan Davis, "Pelosi Brings End to 'Hastert Rule,'" *Roll Call*, May 29, 2007, 1. In the area of foreign policy, another key cross-party victory during the sixty years was the Gulf War resolution of 1991 favored by George H. W. Bush, which cleared the Democratic-controlled House on a vote of 250–183, with Democrats voting 86–179 and Republicans 164–3. *CQA 1991*, 437, 2-H.

[58] *CQA 1990*, 140-H; Dan Balz and Ronald Brownstein, *Storming the Gates: Protest Politics and the Republican Revival* (Boston: Little, Brown, 1996), 135–40; David M. Herszenhorn, "House Approves Sweeping Effort to Help Housing," *New York Times*, July 24, 2008, 1; *CQW*, July 29, 2008, 2068–69; Steven T. Dennis, "Bush Undercuts GOP on Housing," *Roll Call*, July 24, 2008, 3.

[59] Following later in his father's footsteps, George W. Bush relied on coalitions of this shape in two premium enactments near the end of his second term in 2008 as the U.S. economy was crumbling. That is, the White House joined with majorities of Senate Democrats, Senate Republicans, and House Democrats against majorities of House Republicans. On the $300 billion mortgage guarantee of July 2008, the House voted 272–152, with Democrats breaking 227–3 and Republicans 45–149. David M. Herszenhorn, "House Approves Sweeping Effort to Help Housing," *New York Times*, July 24, 2008, 1; *CQW*, July 29, 2008, 2068–69; Steven T. Dennis, "Bush Undercuts GOP on Housing," *Roll Call*, July 24, 2008, 3. On the $700 billion bailout of the bank nexus in October 2008,

loss, but it exhibited majority rule in action and a resourceful, if somewhat desperate, president.[60]

Presidents enjoy prerogatives and influence and they can be inventive. That is one lesson from all the above. They do not need to bow to the standard customs and procedures of the House of Representatives, at least not always. If a potential floor majority is there, they can seek a way to liberate it or crystallize it. Thus the Eisenhower administration, in cooperation with Republican House leaders, quite ruthlessly used discharge threats to spring an excess profits tax extension from the Ways and Means Committee in 1953.[61] Eisenhower's routing of the House Agriculture Committee in 1957–58, discussed earlier, remains a model of legislative finesse. In a surprise move, the Reagan administration colonized, or perhaps seized, Congress's then seven-year-old and still evolving budget reconciliation process as a mechanism to advance its budget revolution in 1981.[62] Reagan acting as public pitchman for that budget, like Eisenhower promoting Landrum–Griffin, supplies a good example of a president as public mobilizer.[63] On trade policy, Clinton cooperated across the aisle with

the House voted 263–171, with Democrats breaking 172–63 and Republicans 91–108. *CQW*, December 15, 2008, 3351, 3362.

[60] John W. Carey comments on chief executives in presidential systems in general, "Presidential elections allow the possibility that politicians whose political careers and fortunes are built outside the legislative party system occupy the chief executive office, and they may use their influence and authority toward ends at odds with legislative voting discipline, even within their own parties." Carey, "Competing Principals, Political Institutions, and Party Unity in Legislative Voting," *American Journal of Political Science* 51:1 (January 2007), 92–107, quotation at 94.

[61] Reichard, *Reaffirmation of Republicanism*, 103–7.

[62] *CQA 1981*, 245–46. "By packaging the budget cuts together, then forcing the House and Senate to vote on a single measure, Republicans hoped to prevent congressional committees and interest groups from chipping away at the president's budget plan. The strategy worked, far better than many dismayed Democrats could have imagined" (245). See also Lance T. LeLoup, "After the Blitz: Reagan and the U.S. Congressional Budget Process," *Legislative Studies Quarterly* 7:3 (August 1982), 321–39.

[63] On Reagan as mobilizer of the public in 1981, see, for example, John Ehrman, *The Eighties: America in the Age of Reagan* (New Haven.: Yale University Press, 2006), 54–55; Hayward, *The Age of Reagan*, 163–65. On the general point, see Cox and McCubbins, *Setting the Agenda*, 106. In a circumstance of such publicity, "the cost of blocking the president's proposal may increase to such an extent that [for a House majority party] it is no longer worth blocking the bill." The idea of changing the result by enlarging or intensifying the

Newt Gingrich.[64] George W. Bush kept pressing publicly for his FISA fix until he won it.

I would emphasize the policy importance of the various off-script winning coalitions. After scanning the domestic policy history of the late twentieth century, for example, a committed free-trade, small-government neoliberal might conclude: give me ERTA, OBRA, and NAFTA, and you can have the rest.

Generally speaking, although there are ambiguities and exceptions, the picture that emerges from the above considerations of committee power and party cartels is one of House floor sovereignty. From Truman through George W. Bush, in the realm of White House requests, the views of the House floor majorities for the most part matched the chamber outcomes. In general, procedural antimajoritarianism seems to have played a limited role. Among other things, one political fact of life and two deep structural norms might be on exhibit here: presidents can be tough and inventive. A president who asks should get an answer. Generally speaking, majority rule is the right way to go.

THE SENATE FILIBUSTER IN GENERAL

So much for the House. The leader in antimajoritarian behavior has been, after all, the Senate. The filibustering bent of the Senate deserves a full sixty-year examination.

What is the pattern? As earlier, on offer is this study's list of White House requests sent up during the first halves of presidential terms. Certain of those requests met a special fate. See table 4.4, which draws on earlier tables 3.1 and 3.2. That fate was: The president asked, the House said yes, and then the Senate, because

---

audience is an old political science chestnut. However, it does present a theoretical difficulty. What may happen in instances like this is that some House members veer from their personal or party-induced ideal points toward constituency-induced ideal points. In such a migration, it is not clear what the true House median should be thought to be.

[64] See, for example, Nigel Hamilton, *Bill Clinton: Mastering the Presidency* (New York: Public Affairs, 2007), 228–29; Steven M. Gillon, *The Pact: Bill Clinton, Newt Gingrich, and the Rivalry That Defined a Generation* (New York: Oxford University Press, 2008), pp. xiii, 116.

TABLE 4.4.

Instances in Which Senate Blocked or Significantly Weakened
House-Approved Version of a Presidential Request, Notwithstanding
Availability of Apparent Floor Majority There, by Actual or
Threatened Filibuster Activity

Congress	President	Presidential request
81st	Truman	omnibus civil rights
85th	Eisenhower	voting rights (weakened)
89th	Johnson	repeal of 14b of Taft–Hartley Act
89th	Johnson	open housing (approved in next Congress)
101st	Bush 41	capital gains tax cut
103rd	Clinton	economic stimulus
103rd	Clinton	motor voter (weakened)
103rd	Clinton	campaign finance reform
103rd	Clinton	lobbying reform
105th	Clinton	campaign finance reform
109th	Bush 43	repeal of estate tax
109th	Bush 43	oil drilling in Alaska
109th	Bush 43	curb medical malpractice suits

a floor majority there could not get its way, said no (eleven cases)
or else significantly weakened the House's version (two cases).
Actual or threatened filibustering made the difference. As a practical matter, since the other two institutions had already declared,
the Senate's thumbs-down (or partly down) was determinative.

At the top of table 4.4, capturing the eye are the civil rights
initiatives sent up by Truman (omnibus plan), Eisenhower (voting
rights), and Johnson (open housing). As noted earlier, these cases
index a much larger universe of civil rights initiatives blocked
or watered down by Senate obstruction across many decades.[65]
As argued earlier, a vast and possibly unique gap in preference

[65] Missed in table 4.4, although it appears in the dataset of 184 presidential requests, is
the Kennedy initiative filibustered by the Senate that had *not* already been passed by the
House.

intensities that separated northerners and (white) southerners and, as a consequence, their Capitol Hill representatives probably underpinned that effective Senate obstruction. For a long time, civil rights was the signature venue of the killer filibuster. A leading analysis concludes: "During a forty year period from the late 1920s until the late 1960s, the filibuster became almost entirely associated with the battle over civil rights."[66]

No less quick to the eye in table 4.4 is the Senate's behavior since the late 1980s. The presidencies of the two Bushes and Clinton—starting with the stretched-out defeat of George H. W. Bush's capital gains tax cut maneuvered by Democratic Majority Leader George Mitchell in 1989–90[67]—brought nine of the thirteen entries in table 4.4. Beyond the capital gains tax cut, blocked or trimmed were Clinton's requests for an economic stimulus, motor voter (trimmed), campaign finance reform (twice), and lobbying reform,[68] and George W. Bush's requests for repeal of the estate tax, oil drilling in Alaska, and a curb on medical malpractice suits.[69] Importantly, the top-priority budget instruments and trade

[66] Catherine Fisk and Erwin Chemerinsky, "The Filibuster," *Stanford Law Review* 49:2 (January 1997), 181–254, at 199.

[67] On the capital gains tax cut, a more complicated parliamentary situation is scarcely imaginable. As part of the story a budget reconciliation measure, always a mind-clouder, played a role, as did the Senate's Byrd rule—a barrier independent of the chamber's cloture rule yet similarly requiring, as a guard against threats to budget integrity, sixty votes to enact. Yet it seems clear that a majority of the senators favored the tax cut (as had a majority of House members), and that a conventional inability to invoke cloture at a critical juncture on a free-standing Packwood–Roth initiative made the difference. Available were fifty votes but not sixty. See *CQA 1989*, 113–16; *CQA 1990*, 168; Michael J. Graetz, *The U.S. Income Tax: What It Is, How It Got That Way, and Where We Go from Here* (New York: W.W. Norton, 1999), 141–42.

[68] In 1993–94 another bill of significance that cleared the House yet foundered in the Senate for filibuster reasons was one to ban the hiring of permanent replacement workers for striking employees. See *CQA 1994*, 402. This initiative was a labor-union priority, but on the evidence reported here in the appendix it was not a White House priority. Sometimes it is claimed that Clinton's health-care drive owed its demise—more specifically, its failure in the House—to the background threat of a subsequent Senate filibuster. Why would Democratic House members choose to "walk the plank" for nothing? This interpretation seems doubtful. A great many causes fail in the House because they are unpopular back home, as had become the extravagantly aired and vetted Clinton health-care plan by the spring of 1994.

[69] On the failure of estate tax repeal in 2006, see Larry M. Bartels, *Unequal Democracy: The Political Economy of the New Gilded Age* (Princeton: Princeton University Press, 2008), 219–21.

agreements of these last three presidents were procedurally protected against Senate minority obstruction,[70] but, otherwise, a good deal of rain fell on White House plans, and it fell more or less impartially. Here, as in the post–World War II patterns discussed in chapter 3, we see an equilibrium of publicly played-out dissonance among the elective branches.

Starting in the 1980s, a conventional wisdom has with good reason accumulated: the real key to passing a bill in the Senate is the sixty votes needed for cloture, so as to shut down debate, rather than the fifty-one votes for a floor majority. On the theoretical side, accommodating the era's politics, possibly nothing in the history of congressional studies has supplied a more elegant and telling fit to a state of affairs than has Keith Krehbiel's *Pivotal Politics* model, featuring its Senate "pivot" at the three-fifths mark, as a fit to the upper chamber's supermajority politics of these recent decades.[71] Clinton and both Bushes suffered from the exercise of that pivot.

Yet that is recent times. Civil rights aside, the pre-1989 territory of table 4.4 is nearly a blank. Of this study's non–civil rights requests, only one during the forty years from 1949 through 1988—Johnson's drive to repeal section 14b of the Taft–Hartley Act—suffered the outlined filibuster fate. Something in the process or practices changed. By the mid-1990s a judgment went: "The contemporary filibuster is an entirely different—and generally more powerful—weapon than the filibuster of the past." At hand now was "simply a minority veto, and a powerful one at that."[72] Of relevance here, the Senate filibuster, actual or looming, came to hit White House requests harder. It is not easy to date the upgrading of that propensity. For one thing, during his second term, Reagan largely steered clear of legislative requests (except for tax reform in 1985–86, which ended in a consensual

[70] On the budget instruments, see Fisk and Chemerinsky, "The Filibuster," 215–17.
[71] Keith Krehbiel, *Pivotal Politics: A Theory of U.S. Lawmaking* (Chicago: University of Chicago Press, 1998).
[72] Fisk and Chemerinsky, "The Filibuster," 184. "The modern filibuster is powerful in a way that filibusters even forty years ago were not: It offers minorities a stronger veto, and is used with less political accountability" (186).

enactment).[73] But then came the hit. "For the first time ever," John B. Gilmour has written regarding the coming of the Clinton administration in 1993—although his categorization misses George H. W. Bush's capital gains tax defeat in 1989–90—"the minority party seeks to block important elements of a president's program through filibuster. . . . Never before has the minority party used the filibuster against a president of the other party to block important initiatives."[74] The cramped era of Clinton and the Bushes was under way.

Why did Senate filibustering played so weak a role in the preceding decades? This is a puzzle of both historical and theoretical interest. The two-thirds and then (starting in 1975) three-fifths cloture rule was in place. Of use in a suitable investigation of the matter would be an empirical curiosity not overshadowed by theories of rules. A kind of reality seems to have triumphed over rules. Senate minorities did not block even when, apparently, they could.[75] Of relevance here, this counterfactual result is significantly represented in the realm of actual White House requests. See table 4.5, which lists the White House requests of Truman through George W. Bush that the Senate approved below the cloture barrier.[76] That is, the chamber voted approval even though

[73] It is interesting to note, however, the level of hostility among many senators that greeted Reagan's nomination of Robert Bork to the Supreme Court in 1987.

[74] John B. Gilmour, "Senate Democrats Should Curb the Filibuster," *Public Affairs Report*, Institution of Governmental Affairs (March 1994), 10. Quoted in Sarah A. Binder and Steven S. Smith, *Politics or Principle? Filibustering in the United States Senate* (Washington, D.C.: Brookings Institution Press, 1997), 84. In the case of Bush's capital gains tax defeat, it was the dominant sector of the Senate *majority* party, although that group comprised a minority of the Senate as a whole, that did the filibustering.

[75] Given the cross-party coalitional patterns of those times, it would be an unwise exercise of deduction to posit anything like a clean relation between the size of a Senate's minority party and the likelihood of successful filibuster obstruction in the chamber. But, for the record, here are the times when the chamber's minority party—always the Republicans— fell below an arithmetic strength needed to block cloture cohesively by itself against a cohesive majority party: 1963–66 (when the cloture rule was 2/3) and 1975–78 (when it became 3/5).

[76] Not considered here are the budget measures insulated procedurally from minority obstruction. Outside this study's dataset are the earlier discussed housing measures that cleared the Senate yet foundered in the House during 1945–46 and 1947–48. Of those, the "why didn't the Senate block?" question arises at least in the case of the Taft–Ellender– Wagner measure of 1947–48. In a showdown vote in 1948, albeit not a final passage vote,

TABLE 4.5.
White House Requests Approved by Senate by Margins Under
Cloture Barrier

Congress	President	Presidential request	Vote
83rd	Eisenhower	tidelands oil	56–35
83rd	Eisenhower	St. Lawrence Seaway	51–33
87th	Kennedy	federal aid to education	49–34
87th	Kennedy	Housing Act of 1961	53–38
89th	Johnson	creation of HUD	57–33
89th	Johnson	Housing Act of 1965	54–30
91st	Nixon	D.C crime control	54–33

its winning majorities for final passage fell short of the two-thirds needed for cloture (all seven of the table's instances preceded the shift of the rule to three-fifths in 1975). There were instances under Eisenhower, Kennedy, Johnson, and Nixon on matters ranging from housing and education through energy, transportation, and crime. These were not minor issues. In all seven cases, an opposition was spirited and alert. The losing Senate minorities were large. But they did not block.

In these seven instances, were filibuster blockades attempted or even contemplated? To a certain degree, one can look and see. As remarked earlier, on Capitol Hill not only behavior but the contemplation of it tend to be transparent. For some relevant comparative data, see table 4.6, starting with the middle panel, which documents the Senate's vast obstructive activity on White House civil rights requests during the first halves of presidential terms in

---

the Senate defeated by 49–35 an amendment to kill the public housing provisions. Opposition to public housing in those days was fierce. But the Senate let through this ambitious plan in 1948 under, so it appears, the cloture barrier. See Nathaniel S. Keith, *Politics and the Housing Crisis since 1930* (New York: Universe Books, 1973), 83. It was not a sure thing that the House would subsequently block, although it did. Note the prominence of housing issues in table 4.5. Three of the seven measures, including the creation of HUD in 1965, centered on urban housing.

earlier times—FEPC in 1949–50 and the rest. That notorious activity is easy to document. *Congressional Quarterly Almanac* is the source. For each of the civil rights requests, entered in table 4.6 are the total number of *CQA* pages devoted to Congress's consideration of the legislation; the number of *CQA* lines of print discussing or documenting any threat, prediction, or anticipation of Senate filibuster activity; the number of lines documenting or discussing any filibuster activity actually taking place; a residual number of lines sizing up or discussing in any other way any filibuster activity that was happening or had happened in the legislative drive in question; and, finally, the total number of lines that addressed filibustering in one way or another. In these five civil rights instances, the "anticipation of filibuster" column is always populated, and the "actual filibuster activity" column tells a generous continuing story. This is a history we remember well.

Nor was it unknown for Senate members to get fired up on other issues in previous times. See the bottom panel of table 4.6, which records three additional instances of serious filibuster activity that greeted requests sent up by Eisenhower, Kennedy, and Nixon. These instances are meant to be illustrative, not exhaustive. They figure prominently in the historical accounts. Yet they are interesting for the legislative measures they targeted—ones aiming to create a private atomic energy industry, authorize a privately owned communications satellite, and fund plans for a supersonic transport to be built by private companies. Here we see another intensity nexus. It was the "antimonopoly" tradition—a bottomless suspicion of large-scale private capital that could induce certain senators on the progressive or liberal Left to talk on for hours, largely regardless, it seems, of the odds of actually blocking a legislative drive. A slumbering public had to be stirred up. The relevant columns in table 4.6 are amply filled in. In the event, the atomic energy measure cleared the Senate by 57–28, COMSAT by 66–11. The SST measure did die in the Senate thanks to the filibustering documented here that, in an odd twist, served to protect the chamber's earlier-revealed anti-SST

TABLE 4.6.

Congressional Quarterly Almanac Coverage of Certain Filibuster and Nonfilibuster Activity in Senate

Congress	Measure	Number of pages of coverage of measure	Number of lines of filibuster coverage centering on:			
			Anticipation of filibuster	Actual filibuster activity	Other discussion	Total lines
Seven instances where White House requests cleared Senate under cloture barrier						
83rd	tidelands oil	9.0	none	57	9	66
83rd	St. Lawrence	6.0	none	none	none	none
87th	education	13.3	none	none	none	none
87th	housing	17.2	none	none	none	none
89th	HUD creation	6.0	none	none	none	none
89th	housing	24.0	none	none	none	none
91st	D.C. crime	12.7	none	none	none	none
Five first-half-of-term White House requests for civil rights legislation (including 1961–62, on which the House took no action):						
81st	FEPC etc.	17.7	85	161	48	294
85th	voting rights	18.5	53	43	21	117
87th	voting rights	9.5	22	152	35	209
89th	VRA	31.3	43	96	none	139
89th	open housing	22.4	12	67	47	126
Certain instances otherwise where Senate filibuster activity jumps out of standard policy history:						
83rd	atomic energy	16.2	none	128	none	128
87th	COMSAT	16.7	13	222	12	247
91st	SST	14.0	8	57	19	84

majority view against tampering late in the session by a conference committee.[77]

Yet precious little trace of obstructive Senate activity or the
contemplation of it appears in the top panel of table 4.6. There,
again, appear the seven presidential requests enacted under the
cloture barrier. Only one of them, the move to award submerged
ocean tidelands to the state governments in 1953, exhibits any
nonblank entries. Opposition to that measure, which ultimately
cleared the Senate by 56–35, bore a kinship to the antimonopoly
expressions discussed above—most of them losing exercises, too.
A "giveaway" of the public domain the tidelands bill was said to
be, and oil companies were out there ready to drill. The cast of
filibusterers overlapped. Senator Wayne Morse of Oregon deliv-
ered a twenty-two-hour speech against the tidelands bill in 1953,
a twelve-hour speech against the atomic energy bill in 1954, and
at one point "provided the most heat" during the filibuster against
COMSAT in 1962.[78]

Yet in the other six instances at the top of table 4.6, nothing.[79]
In *Congressional Quarterly Almanac*'s saturation coverage of these

[77] On the atomic energy measure: *CQA 1953*, 434–36; *CQA 1954*, 534–48. On COMSAT:
CQA 1961, 1019–22; *CQA 1962*, 546–58. On the SST: *CQA 1970*, 776–89. By a vote of
52–41, the Senate had zeroed out funding for the SST. But then a conference committee
aided by pro-SST senators brought it back again in an appropriations measure. Whereupon, SST opponents led by Senator William Proxmire of Wisconsin successfully obstructed approval of the conference report until the SST funding was deleted. Thus, this
unusual exercise of the Senate filibuster was not an antimajoritarian move. That is why the
SST defeat does not appear as an entry in table 4.4. Regarding this sequence of SST
events, it is of theoretical interest that Senate floor majorities do not need to truckle to the
maneuvers of conference committees; they can rebel. On COMSAT, the Senate voted
cloture in 1962 for the first time since 1927. See Tom Wicker, "Senate Curbs Debate on
Satellite Bill; Votes 63–27 for First Closure Since '27; Majority Includes Many Who Have
Defended Unlimited Speech," *New York Times*, August 15, 1962, 1.

[78] On tidelands: *CQA 1953*, 393–94. On atomic energy: *CQA 1954*, 542, 547. On COM-
SAT: *CQA 1962*, 553.

[79] Under the "why not" question, two additional White House requests might merit consideration. In 1961 Kennedy's manpower-retraining proposal cleared the Senate by 60–31.
In 1966 Johnson's model-cities proposal cleared the Senate by 38–22. Both these margins
fell short of two-thirds, the cloture requirement in the 1960s. However, my impression in
each case is that two-thirds support would have been available for final passage if all the
senators had been present and voting. Yet there is another consideration. In one or both
cases, the envisioned final vote-shares might have been cloudy enough to invite obstruction

cases, there is no hint that it even occurred to the sizable, vanquished, and unhappy Senate minorities that they might play a killer role through obstruction.[80] Why that oversight?

After the 1960s, as noted earlier, something in the process or practices changed. It is not clearly exactly what. The question has been wrestled with.[81] Accelerating workloads and fund-raising demands put pressure on the senators' time, making them less willing to spend time breaking filibusters. Changes in Senate process ushered in "holds," "two-track" lawmaking, and "costless" filibustering. Yet an additional factor might have played a role, possibly in interaction with the process changes.

Here is the argument. In general on the filibuster question, the long-running civil rights record is there. The old antimonopoly expressiveness is there. The blockade record of the last twenty years is there. Can we see a pattern? Perhaps the Senate's cloture process is best thought of as an intensity net. It is deft at netting various kinds of intensity gaps. As in the case of pre-1970s civil rights, those can include gaps that are asymmetric—ones where the politicians at the opposing positional nodes differ greatly according to how much they care. Thus also the antimonopoly assertions. But how about the last twenty years? There is another

---

strategies, or at least the contemplation of them, by determined opponents eyeing the cloture rule. In the accounts presented in *Congressional Quarterly Almanac*, there is no hint of any such obstruction or contemplation. On manpower retraining: *CQA 1961*, 492–95; *CQA 1962*, 513–18. On model cities: *CQA 1966*, 210–19, 221–30.

[80] A clue to the strategic mindset of the mid-1960s appeared in a recently related anecdote. In December 1964 President Johnson's aide Mike Manatos wrote a memo "to update his bosses on Medicare's chances in the aftermath of the 1964 election. Surveying the incoming crop of senators, Manatos counted a solid majority in favor of the president's effort. 'If all our supporters are present and voting we would win by a vote of 55 to 45,' he predicted." Ezra Klein, "After Health Care, We Need Senate Reform," *Washington Post*, December 27, 2009, p. B1. In the event, Medicare passed the Senate over the cloture barrier, but note Manatos's calculation. It says nothing about needing sixty-seven votes. This is not surprising. I have not found anything in the ample coverage of Medicare politics in the 1960s that suggests a need for sixty-seven Senate votes to enact. Medicare was a heated and closely contested issue in the early 1960s.

[81] Illuminating discussions appear in Fisk and Chemerinsky, "The Filibuster," 200–9; Binder and Smith, *Politics or Principle?*, 6–19; Gregory J. Wawro and Eric Schickler, *Filibuster: Obstruction and Lawmaking in the U.S. Senate* (Princeton: Princeton University Press, 2006), ch. 11.

possible pattern. The cloture process may also net certain intensity gaps in which the opposing positional nodes, although symmetric in their intensity calibrations, either are especially far apart or, to look at it another way, the politicians poised at both of them care especially extremely. In either of these latter circumstances, a minority of senators—a requisite forty-one of them in recent times—might be especially inclined to put their feet down.[82]

To pose these speculations is to raise very tough questions of cardinal differentiation. What kind of yardstick can gauge such differences? Of particular relevance here, what kind of yardstick can show that such differences are greater at one time than at another? Congressional roll-call scales, which, for one thing, tilt toward ordinal or interval differentiation, seem to offer limited help.[83] Yet American history of recent decades, resistant as it may be to precise tracking, does offer the specter of rising polarization—of a growing, basic, symmetric intensity gap of the sort or sorts specified above. At least at the elite level, ideological polarization is said to have soared. These days, the activist elites on both sides are extreme, fierce, and vocal.[84] Sometimes, the years around 1990 are offered as a juncture.[85] Here is the implication: an accentuation of

[82] Increasing polarization enters the picture in the interpretations offered by Binder and Smith, *Politics or Principle?*, 15–17; Wawro and Schickler, *Filibuster*, 264, 280.
[83] On this point, see Krehbiel, *Pivotal Politics*, 74n28.
[84] See Morris P. Fiorina with Samuel J. Abrams, *Disconnect: The Breakdown of Representation in American Politics* (Norman: University of Oklahoma Press, 2009).
[85] In a search for change over time, the measurement difficulty is severe. There are at least two problems. One involves comparisons of cardinal as opposed to ordinal or interval differentiation. The other is that both the elite and nonelite sectors of the American public have apparently been sorting themselves better in recent times, in the sense that ideological positions have come to correspond better to party allegiances. It is possible for such sorting to take place without the occurrence of cardinal widening in any dimension of interest here. People might just be rearranging themselves. Both of these difficulties arise with both roll-call data and survey data. Yet survey data can be probed for patterns of longitudinal change that offer at least a suggestion of cardinal widening, either among the general public or in the elite realm, or both. Here are some promising examples: First, Alan I. Abramowitz, "Disconnected, or Joined at the Hip," 72–85 in Pietro S. Nivola and David W. Brady (eds.), *Red and Blue Nation*, vol. 1, *Characteristics and Causes of America's Polarized Politics* (Washington, D.C.: Brookings Institution Press, 2006), at p. 76, table 2–3, "Polarization on Seven-Item Policy Scale in Political Engagement, 1984–2004." Independently among voters, active citizens, and campaign activists, and blind to party, the standard deviations of positionings on a seven-point ideological scale have been rising. There

the basic ideological cleavage of American politics might have created a context in which large Senate minorities could wish to engage in, could get away with, and indeed might get electorally rewarded for, such exercises as the killing of George H. W. Bush's capital gains tax cut as well as the arrays of requests sent up by Clinton and George W. Bush. Indeed, such obstructive behavior might constitute all by itself an unobtrusive—or perhaps all too obtrusive—*indicator* of a growing basic intensity gap. All this is a new thing, the argument would go.[86]

---

is no obvious jump-up point during these two decades; the change looks gradual. Second, James E. Campbell, "Polarization Runs Deep, Even by Yesterday's Standards," 152–62 in Nivola and Brady (eds.), *Red and Blue Nation*, at 158, fig. 3–5, "The Shrinking Political Middle, 1972–2004." The share of the general public denominating themselves "moderates" or "don't knows," as opposed to conservatives or liberals, has been shrinking. The early 1990s seems to have been a breakpoint. Third, Gary C. Jacobson, *A Divider, Not a Uniter: George W. Bush and the American People* (New York: Pearson Longman, 2006), at 202, fig. 7.10, "First Post-election Approval Ratings of Presidents Elected to Second Terms." There is a monotonic downslope in this public-opinion series that extends from Eisenhower in 1957 through George W. Bush in 2005. The readings are reasonably high for Eisenhower, Johnson, and Nixon, middling for Reagan, and dismal for Clinton and George W. Bush. This plummet does not seem to be attributable to sorting. Possibly it is an indicator of cardinal widening among the public.

[86] The U.S. Congress is not the only institution that can be examined in a search for a growing ideological cleavage in recent times. There is, for example, the Supreme Court (which, to be sure, poses the same task of trying to peer past ordinal or interval differentiation into a less tractable cardinal differentiation). In tandem with Capitol Hill, one late-1990s study of the Supreme Court has the late 1980s jump out as a juncture of ideological polarization. The Court of the October Term of 1988 is said to have brought "the virtual disappearance of a meaningful center in favor of two sharply divided wings . . . , and the perpetuation of a Court culture that suffers from the same accusatory and uncompromising spirit of faction that now poisons American political society at large." At that time, the Court's young clerks broke into two ideological factions that ate lunch and dinner separately and fouled each other on the basketball court. Among the Justices making decisions, "the Court in October Term '88 and after possessed an altogether different depth and character." Edward Lazarus, *Closed Chambers: The First Eyewitness Account of the Epic Struggles Inside the Supreme Court* (New York: Penguin, 1998), 251–87, particulars, including quotations, at 262, 274, 281. Also around 1990, the clerks of the two persuasions began pursuing different career lines after Court service. See William E. Nelson et al., "The Supreme Court Clerkship and the Polarization of the Court," *Green Bag* 13:2D (Autumn 2009), 59–71. Note also the state legislatures. According to a mid-1990s study, the once harmonious Minnesota legislature, for example, had come to exhibit "growing partisan hostilities" in a context of take-no-prisoners partisan leadership. "By last fall, all sense of collegiality had vanished from the Minnesota House." "A liberal, labor-dominated Democratic conference collides with a Republican conference of anti-tax zealots. . . . The two parties are no longer merely at odds, they are now diametrically opposed to one another."

Where does this leave us? In the annals of White House defeats, pre-1970s civil rights and the last twenty years seem to be special cases. These exhibits of Senate obstruction have apparently been exceptional, and they can be analyzed as exceptions, notwithstanding their prominence and importance. Otherwise the Senate, most of the time, or perhaps one might say in its default mode, during the last sixty years, at least in saying yes or no to White House requests, has performed in a surprisingly majoritarian pattern. As for the recent two-decade bout of obstructiveness, is it a durable ingredient of American politics? The life expectancy of it will be taken up in chapter 5.

BLAME THE SENATE!

On the direct question of institutions as policy outliers, there is an additional literature. As with the preceding accounts, it is a genre of commentary anchored in historical experience. It has proceeded chiefly in journalistic outlets. Its claims are well-known and influential and should be addressed. In this genre, the Senate is the villain. That chamber, the case goes, owing to its small-states constituency base as well as its internal procedures, has compiled a long, sad record of being distinctively anti–civil rights, anticity, anti–welfare state, antilabor, probusiness, and in general antiprogress and pro–status quo. This is an indictment of a partisan or ideological variety. A selection of critiques includes:

- Robert A. Caro in a statement centered in 1957: "For decade after decade, the Senate had been not only a joke, but a cruel joke. For almost a century, it had not merely embroidered but had empowered, with an immense power, the forces of conservatism and reaction in America, had stood as an impregnable stronghold against which, decade after de-

---

Charles Mahtesian, "The Sick Legislature Syndrome, and How to Avoid It," *Governing* (February 1997), 16–20, quotations at 16, 18, 19.

cade, successive waves of demand for social change, for governmental action to promote justice and to ease the burdens of impoverished and disadvantaged Americans, had dashed themselves in vain."[87]

- Tom Geoghegan in 1994: "We can't raise our wages. We can't get health insurance. No aid to the cities. And why? The Senate votes it down. By a weighted vote, for small-state whites in pickup trucks with gun racks all out there shooting these things down. We have a Louisiana Purchase of Rotten Boroughs, full of Senators who are horse doctors, or in rifle clubs, targeting our bills." "The energy deadlock? It would have been impossible without the Senate." "Falling wages? Blame the Senate. We would've had labor-law reform twice. There would still be a union movement. We could have kept, in real terms, our minimum wage." As for the New Deal: "By Roosevelt's second term, he was being treated in the Senate as if he were Jimmy Carter. Senators like Carter Glass took apart his banking bill. They made a mockery of his minimum wage bill."[88]

- Michael Lind in 1995–96: "Public-spending programs that would benefit nonwhites and whites alike in the populous states are routinely killed by small-state senators in the Senate, after being passed by the more responsive House."[89]

- Hendrik Hertzberg in 2002: "The Senate is essentially a graveyard. Its record, especially over the past century and a half, makes disheartening reading. A partial list of the measures that—despite being favored by the sitting President, an apparent majority of the people, and, in most cases, the

[87] Robert A. Caro, *Master of the Senate: The Years of Lyndon Johnson* (New York: Alfred A. Knopf, 2002), xxiii. Caro's chief interest in this work is civil rights, but it is clear from the context—notably on page 105—that he intends a generalization that extends well beyond civil rights.
[88] Tom Geoghegan, "The Infernal Senate," *New Republic*, November 21, 1994, 17–23, quotations at 17, 22.
[89] Michael Lind, "Prescriptions for a New National Democracy," *Political Science Quarterly* 110:4 (Winter 1995–96), 563–86, quotation at 573–74.

House of Representatives to boot—have been done to death in the Senate would include bills to authorize federal action against the disenfranchisement of blacks, to ban violence against strikers by private police forces, to punish lynching, to lower tariffs, to extend relief to the unemployed, to outlaw the poll tax, to provide aid to education, and (under Presidents Truman, Nixon, and Carter as well as Clinton) to provide something like the kind of health coverage that is standard in the rest of the developed world."[90]

- A medley in 2009: The Senate has become "ominously dysfunctional."[91] It is "the chamber designed to thwart popular will,"[92] a "dysfunctional and undemocratic partisan hothouse,"[93] "a body that shuns debate, avoids legislative give-and-take, proceeds glacially and produces next to nothing."[94] "Democrats are especially susceptible to the dysfunction of the Senate."[95] Thanks to the Senate (plus the Republicans), "the great progressive dawn of the Obama era has ground to a near halt."[96]

What are we to make of these claims? Unquestionably valid is the classical civil rights history. Yet beyond that, questions arise. There is a tendency to extend the civil rights argument into other policy areas without warrant or else to generalize from one or two instances. There are distortions—Hertzberg's idea that the

[90] Hendrik Hertzberg, "Framed Up: What the Constitution Gets Wrong," *New Yorker*, July 29, 2002, 85–90, quotation at 88.
[91] Paul Krugman, "A Dangerous Dysfunction," *New York Times*, December 31, 2009, A29.
[92] Alec MacGillis, "The Gang on the Hill: In the Senate, Small States Wield Outsize Power: Is This What the Founders Had in Mind?" *Washington Post National Weekly Edition*, August 17–23, 2009, 26.
[93] E. J. Dionne, "The Democrats' Bush Nostalgia," *RealClearPolitics*, December 17, 2009, online.
[94] Harold Meyerson, "The Do-Nothing Senate," *Washington Post National Weekly Edition*, November 16–22, 2009.
[95] Jonathan Chait, "Why the Democrats Can't Govern," *New Republic*, March 30, 2009, online.
[96] Michael Tomasky, "Don't Blame Obama. The US Political System Is Broken," *Guardian*, December 14, 2009, online.

Senate was uniquely hostile to federal aid to education (consider 1949 and 1961), Geoghegan's that the chamber was distinctively stingy to the cities (consider the record on housing legislation in 1946, 1948, and 1954), Caro's general picture of the Senate, from the vantage point of 1957, as the system's "force of conservative and reaction" (in fact, analysts back then were speculating why the Senate, aside from civil rights, was more liberal than the House).

Otherwise, on the evidence of the sixty years, I do not see any respectable case that the Senate proved distinctively hostile to national health insurance.[97] Most recently in 2009–10, the mammoth enactment in that area clear both the House and the Senate in a form agreeable to the Obama White House. For the postwar era, I have not seen evidence that the Senate has taken any importantly distinctive position on tariff policy. I am not aware of a basis for Lind's statement regarding "public-spending programs." From Truman through Kennedy, at least, the Senate had a well-documented habit of *raising* domestic spending beyond House levels, not cutting it.[98]

In the energy area, it is true that the Senate gave special trouble to Carter's plan for a new regulatory regime in 1977–78 and to Clinton's request for a BTU tax in 1993. Yet it is also true that the upper chamber, diverging from the House, rejected George W. Bush's omnibus business-friendly energy plan in 2001–02 and his request for Alaska drilling in 2005–06. Senate liberals did the blocking in these latter cases.

In the civil rights area as it entails African American rights, I do not see any credible case that the Senate kept up its distinctively hostile stance past the 1960s—notably, past the enfranchisement

[97] On this subject, Hertzberg omits Eisenhower's legislative drive yet surprisingly brings up Carter. Yet no Carter plan for national health insurance ever reached Congress, and the significant contending forces on that issue in the late 1970s were not the Senate versus the other institutions, but rather Senator Edward Kennedy speaking for liberals and unions on the one hand and the cost-conscious Carter White House on the other. Those two sides deadlocked. See, for example, Gilmour, *Strategic Disagreement*, 85–89; Peter G. Bourne, *Jimmy Carter: A Comprehensive Biography from Plains to Postpresidency* (New York: Scribner, 1997), 432–35.

[98] Richard F. Fenno, Jr., *The Power of the Purse: Appropriations Politics in Congress* (Boston: Little, Brown, 1966), chs. 11, 12.

at that time of the South's African Americans. It is true that the Senate passed an anti–school busing measure (backed by the Nixon White House) in 1971–72 and that the House did not. But the Senate seems to have rivaled the House in advancing the successive renewals—expansions, really—of the Voting Rights Act in 1970, 1975, and 1982.[99] In fact, the Senate went one better in 1970: "A measure that had gone into the Senate weakened severely by House reverses emerged as a dramatically more powerful bill [in the view of civil rights activists] than anyone had expected."[100] Also, in this instance the Senate ended up prevailing over both the House and the White House.

Race as it plays through the national institutions is not a finished topic. It is an evolving one.[101] On this topic, another examination of medians is possible. In the U.S. Census, respondents may check the box "white" when asked about race. In 2000, 69.1 percent of the population checked that box. But how about percentage "white" as a dimension extending across each of the country's universes of electoral units? Also using the 2000 census, the figures for the first decade of the current century are as follows. In the median Electoral College unit, the "white" percentage was 70.1 percent; in the median House district, 75.6 percent; and in the median Senate district (that is, state), 78.8 percent.[102] There is variety. Note that, in spatial terms, the chief distance lay

[99] See Abigail M. Thernstrom, *Whose Votes Count? Affirmative Action and Minority Voting Rights* (Cambridge: Harvard University Press, 1987), chs. 2–6.

[100] Gary Orfield, *Congressional Power: Congress and Social Change* (New York: Harcourt Brace Jovanovich, 1975), 96–103, quotation at 101. In this account, Orfield notes the attenuation of the southern senators' opposition to the VRA brought about by black enfranchisement in the region. "'Don't ask me to go out there and filibuster,' said Senator Ernest Hollings of South Carolina [in the Senate cloakroom in 1970], who had been elected by black votes. 'I'm not going back to my state and explain a filibuster against the black voters'" (102). Among the southern senators, the old intensity was largely gone by 1970, and in some cases so was the oppositional stance, period.

[101] See, for example, John D. Griffin, "Senate Apportionment as a Source of Political Inequality," paper presented at the annual conference of the American Political Science Association, Chicago, 2004; Neil Malhotra and Connor Raso, "Racial Representation and U.S. Senate Apportionment, *Social Science Quarterly* 88:4 (December 2007), 1038–48.

[102] The figures going into these calculations were drawn from Michael Barone with Richard E. Cohen, *The Almanac of American Politics 2008* (Washington, D.C.: National Journal Group, 2007). The House districts are the ones in existence during 2007–08.

between the presidency and the other two institutions, not between the Senate and the other two. Certainly, this is a demographic dissonance to be watched. So far, however, it does not seem to have corresponded to any prominent and durable differences in policy positioning.

That leaves labor–management relations. This area has drawn the attention of Senate filibuster watchers, and for good reason: By threatening or conducting filibusters, Senate minorities defeated high-priority labor union aims four times during the sixty years: in 1965, a repeal of section 14b of the Taft–Hartley Act—the provision that authorizes state right-to-work laws; in 1978, a complicated package of alterations to collective bargaining; in 1994, a ban on the hiring of permanent replacement workers for striking employees; in 2007, an authorization of card-check unionization. In the first three of these drives, both the House and the White House were on board; in the last case, the House although not the White House.[103]

These four instances might seem enough. Yet there is more to the story. The labor movement's historic charter, the Wagner Act of 1935, itself emerged from the Senate.[104] During World War II, when the unions brought toxic unpopularity on themselves through strikes, "the anti-labor bills passed by the House often found themselves buried in the Senate Labor Committee, which had a strong pro-union majority."[105] As discussed earlier, the two

[103] The first three cases are deftly addressed in Tracy Roof, "Stalemate: The Senate, the Labor Law, and the Low Rates of Unionization in the United States," paper presented to the annual conference of the Midwest Political Science Association, Chicago, 2005. On repeal of 14b: *CQA 1965*, 818–20. On the 1978 package: *CQA 1978*, 284–87. On striker replacement: *CQA 1994*, 402. On card-check unionization: *CQW 2007*, 2044.
[104] See Kenneth Finegold and Theda Skocpol, "State, Party, and Industry: From Business Recovery to the Wagner Act in America's New Deal," in Charles Bright and Susan Harding (eds.), *Statemaking and Social Movements: Essays in History and Theory* (Ann Arbor: University of Michigan Press, 1984); Theda Skocpol, "Political Response to Capitalist Crisis: Neo-Marxist Theories of the State and the Case of the New Deal," *Politics and Society* 10:2 (1980), 155–201; Arthur M. Schlesinger, Jr., *The Coming of the New Deal* (Cambridge, Mass.: Houghton Mifflin, 1959), 400–6.
[105] Eric Schickler, "Public Opinion, the Congressional Policy Agenda, and the Limits of New Deal Liberalism, 1935–1945," paper presented at the Congress and History Conference, University of Virginia, May 13, 2009, 20.

classic rollbacks of the Wagner Act—the Taft–Hartley Act of 1947 and the Landrum–Griffin Act of 1959—were written a good deal more harshly on the House side than on the Senate side. It was the Senate that blocked Eisenhower's nudge of Taft–Hartley in a probusiness direction in 1954. In 1977 it was a House containing 292 Democrats, not the Senate, that voted down a union measure to legalize common-site picketing in the construction industry. This loss was "a crushing disappointment for organized labor," which had sought the reform for twenty-five years. (Both houses had approved such legislation in the previous Congress, but President Ford vetoed it.)[106] As for the minimum wage, perhaps a credible argument exists somewhere that the Senate has occupied an outlier stance, but I have not come across it. In this study's dataset, the only relevant differentiating case that emerged was the House's, not the Senate's, distinctive hostility toward the Kennedy minimum wage initiative in 1961. Regarding the Fair Labor Standards Act of 1938, the country's foundational minimum wage statute, I do not see a credible case that that measure had a harder time clearing the Senate than the House. If anything, the reverse seems to be true.[107]

---

[106] *CQA 1977*, 122–26, quotation at 122.

[107] A full, sensitive account of the enactment of the FLSA appears in James MacGregor Burns, *Congress on Trial: The Legislative Process and the Administrative State* (New York: Harper and Brothers, 1949), 68–82. See also Robert K. Fleck, "Democratic Opposition to the Fair Labor Standards Act of 1938," *Journal of Economic History* 62:1 (March 2002), 25–54. Otherwise in the 1930s, as Geoghegan claims, it was the Senate, courtesy of Carter Glass of Virginia, that gave the FDR White House special headaches on a major banking measure. That was during FDR's first term (not his second) in 1935. See Kenneth S. Davis, *FDR: The New Deal Years, 1933–1937: A History* (New York: Random House, 1986), 537–41; Arthur M. Schlesinger, Jr., *The Politics of Upheaval* (Cambridge, Mass.: Houghton Mifflin, 1960), ch. 16. Yet the Roosevelt years were a mixed case. Also involving the Senate as an impediment (this, to be sure, is a vantage point that favors the White House of those times; other vantage points are possible), it was the Senate, not the House, that advanced the damaging, albeit ultimately abandoned, Clark amendment to the Social Security Act in 1935. However, it was the House that gutted the White House's public utilities holding company measure in 1935 and voted down FDR's executive reorganization plan in 1938—in both cases after the Senate had voted favorably. On social security: Davis, *FDR: The New Deal Years, 1933–1937*, 459–62, 523; Jacob S. Hacker, *The Divided Welfare State* (New York: Cambridge University Press, 2002), 101. On public utilities reform: Davis, *FDR: The New*

All this having been said, a drift is discernible. In general, re-garding the ground rules of labor–management relations (not minimum wage hikes), the unions seem to have fared worse in the Senate as opposed to the House *recently*. For one thing, we may be witnessing here another instance of an intensity gap caught up in Senate cloture procedures. The union movement has been de-clining since the 1950s. Business interests are as strong as ever. In this evolving environment, it is no surprise to see Senate Demo-crats exhibiting a somewhat relaxed behavior on labor–manage-ment issues, which they seem to do, even as Republicans keep pressing hard. Perhaps the "blame the Senate" indictment has force in this issue area in recent decades. Still, it is not clear how the centrist Democrats of a "Blue Dog" type in the House of Representatives would position themselves on issues like repeal of 14b and card-check unionization if they had to face the full pressure of business mobilization back home. As it is, they can go along nominally with the unions in a low-pressure mode as they shield behind a veto-prone Senate. The thumbs-down by the House on common-site picketing reform in 1977, when a Senate veto could not be presumed, is thought-provoking.

Classical civil rights offers a clear story; labor–management re-lations a complicated one. Yet on a variety of other causes favored by liberals or progressives—housing, the cities, education, health insurance, welfare-state spending, the environment, post-1960s civil rights, and the rest—the "blame the Senate" critique seems to lack grounding. In general, the case for the Senate as an anti-progressive outlier is weak.

Still, change of some sort has occurred, and here is what it seems to be. In this chapter's domain of White House requests

Deal Years, 1933–1937, 529–37; Schlesinger, *The Politics of Upheaval*, ch. 17. On executive reorganization: Kenneth S. Davis, *FDR: Into the Storm, 1937–1940: A History* (New York: Random House, 1995), 220–23. An overall assessment of chamber balance during the New Deal years would take more work. One wrinkle is that, during 1933–35, the Senate often spurred major controversy by pressing FDR from the left. On this point see, for example, Ronald A. Mulder, "Reluctant New Dealers: The Progressive Insurgents in the United States Senate, 1933–1934," *Capitol Studies* 2:2 (Winter 1974), 5–22.

reacted to differently by the two congressional chambers, the Senate used to tilt to the liberal side (except on civil rights). It does not do that any more. But it does not tilt to the conservative side, either. It seems to tilt to the status quo side, which is not the same thing as the conservative side. Consider table 4.7, which repeats from tables 3.1 and 3.2 the eighteen proposals sent up by the two Bushes and Clinton that one chamber passed and the other chamber blocked or significantly watered down. Of the two chambers, the Senate was slightly more frequently the liberal, rather than the conservative, outlier. But the Senate was very dominantly the status quo outlier—that is, the blocker of a proposed move away from policy stability, regardless of whether the proposal came from the Left or the Right. Down went drives like campaign finance reform, a Clinton favorite, as well as curbs on medical malpractice suits, a George W. Bush favorite. Of the eighteen instances in table 4.7, the Senate took the change stance three times, the status quo stance thirteen times (the other two cases do not clearly code). As it happens, *nine* of the thirteen status quo instances owed to threatened or staged filibusters (see the details in table 4.4). It does not require filibuster arithmetic for the Senate to mount a negative outlier stance: it may simply be that a majority of senators is against something—for example, George W. Bush's faith-based initiative in 2001–02. But the Senate's pro-status quo *edge* in table 4.7 clearly owes to the cloture rule and the filibuster. Policy stability is what we would expect the Senate's supermajority practices of the last two decades to protect, and, with apparent grand impartiality across parties and ideologies, that is what happens.

It is into this context that the new Obama administration with its Democratic congressional majorities sailed in 2009. Soon loomed an unsurprising party frustration with the Senate—as seen in the medley of critiques cited earlier. An array of initiatives favored by the White House and the House ran into trouble on the Senate side. Out went the "public option" from heath-care reform. This is a complicated area. Sometimes, as on health care, the House Democrats of 2009 pressed a liberal stance that the

TABLE 4.7.
Senate Stances on Proposals of Bushes and Clinton on which House and
Senate Disagreed

President	Proposal	Ideological position by Senate favored			Change position by Senate favored		
		Liberal side	Conservative side	Not clear	Change	Status quo	Not clear
Bush 41	capital gains	X				X	
	S&Ls bailout			X			X
	deficit reduction	X			X		
Clinton (1)	economic stimulus		X			X	
	campaign finance		X			X	
	lobbying reform		X			X	
	motor voter		X			X	
	budget/energy tax		X			X	
Clinton (2)	fast-track trade		X		X		
	campaign finance		X			X	
	Social Security	X					X
Bush 43(1)	faith based	X				X	
	energy plan	X				X	
	Medicare drugs	X				X	
Bush 43(2)	estate tax repeal	X				X	
	Alaska drilling	X				X	
	malpractice suits	X				X	
	immigration	X			X		
Total		10	7	1	3	13	2

Source: Tables 3.1 and 3.2.

White House could apparently take or leave. Looked at one way,
the Democratic party's program of that year was as much Nancy
Pelosi's as Obama's. In that regard, there is an interesting analogy
to 1995. Then, Republican Speaker Newt Gingrich drove through

the House an ambitious, ideologically edgy "Contract with America" program that soon lost force and content in a sluggish Republican Senate. In 2009 a program driven by House Democrats advanced to a sluggish Democratic Senate.[108] There is symmetry in this analogy.

[108] See Naftali Bendavid, "House Democrats Gripe about Senate," *New York Times*, January 29, 2010, A4.

CHAPTER 5

Reform

This has been a long, sinuous journey through a sea of facts. Ambiguities and judgment calls have been many. Yet I hope that certain themes and thrusts have come through and that they have proven interesting and convincing.

A theme of microcosm, presented in chapter 1, has led the way. If the electoral constituencies of the presidency, the Senate, and the House have differed very little—at least as gauged through a deployment of the presidential vote as in chapter 1—what are the implications for policymaking? How should the three institutions be getting along? In chapter 2 I introduced a dataset of presidential requests to help wrestle with that question. For one thing, has the system biased its policy outcomes against Democratic presidents? That is a barely tractable question, yet one test seemed available in chapter 2, and I undertook it.

The answer seems to be: well, possibly yes. The pattern is cloudy, other factors may intrude, and it does not seem likely that any such bias has been widely perceived. But the answer may be yes. Yet I have little to say about the matter in this closing chapter, which addresses institutional reform. That is because we have not experienced major reform moves during recent generations that have addressed exactly this alleged problem—a joint House and Senate conservative tilt. Perhaps it is indicative that we have not. Dogs have not been barking. Perhaps a static of sentiment for switching to a parliamentary regime should count, but static it has only been. Given the alleged tilt, we might expect to see the Democrats pressing for a muscular presidency vis-à-vis Congress, and that was indeed a party motif from the 1930s through the 1960s, but since then it has been, if anything, a Republican motif. Here is a party symmetry across time. Perhaps the U.S. system of presidency, House, and Senate is so deeply anchored in law and custom that even questioning it makes no practical sense. Some ingredients of the Constitution are in stone. At any rate, reform at this deep structural level has not been on the table. The Democrats, like the Republicans, have put their overwhelming energy into popular mobilization within the existing system, as in 2008.

In chapters 3 and 4 I addressed an additional question: Have the House and Senate *differed* in positioning themselves vis-à-vis the presidency? That question quickly forked into two subquestions. The stricter one, true to the letter of the logic of chapter 1, probed for partisan disproportionality. Has there been a "partisan outlier disparity"? Have either the Democratic or the Republican presidents enjoyed disproportionate success in the Senate as opposed to the House in pressing their requests? That is, have the two chambers differed in their relative friendliness to the presidents of one party as opposed to the other? The answer to this formulation is a very clear no.

Yet in chapters 3 and 4 I also addressed a second, more general, subquestion: Have the presidents, regardless of party, encountered what might be called a "general outlier disparity" in pressing their requests? That is, has either of the two houses notably outpaced the other in giving the White House, regardless of which party has held it, trouble? Overwhelmingly, of course, the conflict waged in the nation's capital is partisan, and at least for this reason we would not expect to find a great deal of difference between a pattern of "partisan outlier disparity" and one of "general outlier disparity." And in fact, there is not much difference. But to go for the "general" was to introduce a bit of slack into the analysis. Occasionally, or to a certain degree, the dimensions of conflict in Washington, D.C., are not conventionally partisan, and to go for the general was to try to accommodate such idiosyncrasy (as regards, for example, the Senate filibuster and civil rights). Also, since I wanted to explore various theories or accounts of alleged institutional or representational waywardness (as regards, for example, the House's pre-1960s districting system), I thought it made sense to scout for any general interchamber disparities. Not to do so would have thrown away a good deal of interesting material.

At any rate, neither of the two chambers has posed a particular headache for presidents of one party as opposed to the other, and only by a surprisingly narrow margin has the Senate, by common reputation the outlier institutional naysayer, outpaced the House in disfavoring the presidents, period, regardless of the presidents' party affiliations. Moreover, the Senate's outlier edge in the latter measure, small though it may be, is not all that difficult to understand. For one thing, the civil rights issue, which used to crosscut the parties and bring on Senate filibusters, accounts for nearly half of it. Subtract that pre-1970s issue and the Senate's general outlier naysayer edge falls from 7 to 4 of the 184 White House requests—a decline from 3.8 percent to 2.2 percent of the total. That is pretty close to zero.

These House versus Senate results are at least consonant with chapter 1's "microcosm" prediction. There, I found that the House's median vote-share has differed on average from the national presidential vote-share by 1.1 percent, and the Senate's median has differed by 1.3 percent. That yields a trivial interchamber difference of 0.2 percent. What is the prediction? Consider a counterfactual. If there were no friction—that is, if it were true that every White House request happened to crystallize politicians along a standard Democrat versus Republican dimension, and if there existed no process wrinkles (such as the Senate filibuster) or representational wrinkles (such as the House's pre-1960s districting system)—the microcosm argument would predict House versus Senate outlier disparities—of either the partisan or the general variety—of zero or very close to it. In fact, the American system has certainly offered friction and wrinkles, yet the real empirical results have approached zero anyway.

Why is that? Why is the general outlier disparity so small? Why isn't there any partisan outlier disparity at all? The flesh of an answer is available, I hope, in the six accounts of theory and experience presented in chapters 3 and 4. In general, to repeat an argument from the beginning of chapter 3, there seems to have been a canceling-out effect. Certain process or representational features that might have veered one chamber or the other toward policy outlier behavior during the last sixty years have either favored the White House, and each of its two presidential parties, impartially or have come and gone, yielding the scene to other features that have cut the politics differently.

In addition, neither the House nor the Senate seems to have lived up to its reputation for antimajoritarianism—not even the Senate, notwithstanding its filibuster. In general, at least in the realm of White House requests, the "majoritarian postulate" has had a pretty good sixty years on Capitol Hill.[1] It is wickedly difficult to envision what differences it would have made in ultimate policy terms if either the House or the Senate, or both, had behaved in a seriously more antimajoritarian fashion during the last sixty years. The counterfactuals get tricky in a hurry. Faced by any such deviations, the parties, the politicians, the country's various interests, or the formal governmental institutions themselves might have adapted in various compensating ways. Yet, generally speaking, it seems a reasonable bet that the practical limits to antimajoritarianism exercised in both the House and the Senate have helped to tamp down any interchamber outlier disparities.

Here, then, is the general picture: The microcosm argument would predict cross-chamber symmetry. In actual historical practice, various deviations from symmetry seem to be accounted for

---

[1] See Krehbiel, *Information and Legislative Organization*, 16.

by particular wrinkles or distortions that are understandable. Yet the wrinkles or distortions have tended to cancel out, leaving a pattern of symmetry, or close to it, anyway.

All this is in the long run. Sixty years is a long time. That is the time frame spotlighted here in both chapter 2, with its probe for biases against Democratic presidents, and chapters 3 and 4, with their probe for interchamber disparities. The resulting patterns are important. The long-run performance of any political system is probably critical to its legitimacy. As regards the possible bias against Democratic presidents unearthed in chapter 2, the long run is the whole story. The basic structure of the Constitution is a constant, not a variable.

Yet the short run, the medium run, and the particular have significance, too. I have tried to address these realms in my recitation of wrinkles, distortions, and the like in chapters 3 and 4. In this chapter, one final argument remains to be made. It has three assertions and one judgment. First, in policy terms, various of those wrinkles, distortions, and the like have been, or at least have been seen to be, highly important. The Senate filibuster and the old House Rules Committee come to mind. The stories are well-known.

Second, in response to such assignments of importance, Americans have spent a great deal of time and energy advancing institutional or procedural reforms. Reform activity is endogenous to the system. In a way, this is a familiar point, but in a way it is not. The institutions or procedures, at least those short of constitutional fundamentals, are not insulated from tampering. They are works in progress. If you don't get your way, you can join a campaign to change the institutions. In particular, in the spirit of this study, you are free to target any of the three national elective institutions if you think it needs to be made more *properly representative*. That is, you might wish to target an institution if it is seen to deviate in policy terms from the median national viewpoint. Even more especially, you might target any such deviation if it is seen to be accompanied, somehow, by too much of an accumulation of institutional power. In that case, you might diagnose an alarming multiplicative thrust toward policy deviation that especially cries out for targeting. The "you" doing the targeting in these instances might be private interests, the political parties, or any of the formal institutions themselves feeling unfairly disadvantaged.

The third assertion is that such reform drives often work. They do not always work. Sometimes they fail or only partly work. Also, they can take agonizingly long to work. Yet a special kind of opening seems to be available. An argument that the national median viewpoint is being traduced can draw a receptive audience. A basic norm is at issue. Mobilization to close down any such violation may ensue. One way or another, such mobilization may be effective. If such wheels spin appropriately, the result for the system in the long run is homeostatic. Deviations by particular institutions are tamed back toward representational conventionality. In median-voter terms, a bent toward corrigibility is built in.

Those are the assertions. As for the judgment, it is that such reform efforts, accompanied by a track record in the aggregate that is both reasonably favorable and reasonably well-known, have been important to the legitimacy of the system. Over the last sixty years, the U.S. separation-of-powers system has offered not only a pattern of long-run balance, in the terms of chapters 1 through 4. It has also offered corrigibility, at least within a range short of abandoning the Constitution's basic design.

In chapter 1 I discussed two paradigmatic instances of such corrective activity—the British Reform Act of 1832 and the Seventeenth Amendment requiring direct election of U.S. senators.[2] (In some aspects, the Constitution *is* amendable.) In both cases, institutions seen to be off-median were swung into line. But such corrective activity seems to be unending. Waywardnesses arise. Nearly always there is cause for institutional reform of some kind.

Since World War II, to focus on the time span covered in this book, we have seen at least six corrective enterprises of this type that have enjoyed some measure of success. They have either

[2] On the campaign to enact the Seventeenth Amendment, see Kris W. Kobach, "Rethinking Article V: Term Limits and the Seventeenth and Nineteenth Amendments," *Yale Law Journal* 103 (1994), 1971–2007.

succeeded in a formal sense or else, by at least dramatizing problems and exerting pressure, helped swerve the course of policy. In these cases, the House or Senate has been targeted four times, the presidency twice.

From the Democratic or liberal side, there are four familiar stories. The first involves districting and apportionment. Growing skews in legislative representation stirred notice and alarm in the 1940s and 1950s. The median voter was being ignored. In a responding reform drive, which targeted the state legislatures as well as the House of Representatives, a movement of intellectuals, journalists, politicians, judges, and others tested the waters in the 1940s, honed strategies and generated publicity in the 1950s, then won its historic Supreme Court victories in the 1960s.[3] It was a textbook reform triumph. It had all the right ingredients. A deruralized House, as exhibited in figure 3.1, was one result.

A second liberal drive targeted the civil rights filibuster. In 1946, in the wake of World War II, President Truman raised the civil rights cause to the White House agenda. Yet, as before, Senate filibuster blockades kept occurring. Seven years later, in January 1953, a cross-party coalition of senators led by Clinton Anderson of New Mexico, specifically aiming to advance civil rights legislation, began a decade-long campaign to revise the Senate's rules on opening day so as to allow majority rule. Biennial dramas ensued. In a series of complicated test roll calls, the cause won twenty-one votes in 1953, thirty-eight votes in 1957, thirty-six votes in 1959, forty-six votes in 1961, and forty-two votes in 1963. This was a threat to the system. The South's filibuster game would be up, it was widely believed, if the Anderson cause crossed the 50 percent mark. Formally, this reform drive failed during the 1960s. Through

[3] The movement quality of the cause is discussed in Ward E. Y. Elliott, *The Rise of Guardian Democracy: The Supreme Court's Role in Voting Rights Disputes, 1845–1969* (Cambridge.: Harvard University Press, 1974), ch. 4. For the drive through the courts, see Ansolabehere and Snyder, *The End of Inequality*, part 2. Helping along this reapportionment (in the case of the U.S. House, just redistricting) cause were reform-oriented academic works such as Robert G. Dixon, Jr., *Democratic Representation: Reapportionment in Law and Politics* (New York: Oxford University Press, 1968); Robert B. McKay, *Reapportionment: The Law and Politics of Equal Representation* (New York: Twentieth Century Fund, 1965).

canny maneuvering, the Senate's leadership staved off a change in the chamber's rules. By successfully voting cloture, the Senate enacted the major civil rights laws of that decade anyway, in an absence of any important rules changes. But on the institutional side, the Anderson drive seems to have been a significant pressure ingredient in the accelerating civil rights cause of those times. It put the southern senators' feet to the fire. It seems a good bet that it would have formally prevailed, somehow, if the civil rights bills could not have cleared the Senate otherwise.[4]

Memorialized in often Homeric terms in skilled accounts is a third liberal reform drive—the successful effort to rein in the House's committee system during the 1950s, 1960s, and 1970s.[5] An alliance of academics, journalists, interest groups, and politicians spent a generation at the task. Liberal Democrats led the way, although the supportive coalitions tended to be cross-party.[6] In general terms, the House was targeted as a culpable antimajoritarian outlier owing to its customs, rules, and committee processes. Yet the matter was complicated. Was it the Democratic caucus majority or the House floor majority that was being thwarted?

[4] See Martin B. Gold and Dimple Gupta, "The Constitutional Option to Change Senate Rules and Procedures: A Majoritarian Means to Overcome the Filibuster," *Harvard Journal of Law and Public Policy* 28:1 (2004), 205–72, at 230–49; Robert Mann, *When Freedom Would Triumph: The Civil Rights Struggle in Congress, 1954–1968* (Baton Rouge: Louisiana State University Press, 2007), 35–36, 68–69, 137–38; John B. Gilmour, "The Contest for Senate Cloture Reform, 1949–1975," paper presented to the annual conference of the American Political Science Association, Chicago, August 31–September 3, 1995; *CQA 1953*, 313–14; *CQA 1957*, 655–56; *CQA 1959*, 212–14; *CQA 1961*, 408–9; *CQA 1963*, 373–76. After 1964, when Congress enacted the Public Accommodations Act by way of a successful cloture vote in the Senate, most of the steam went of the drive to revise the chamber's rules. See *CQA 1965*, 590.

[5] See, for example, Milton C. Cummings, Jr., and Robert L. Peabody, "The Decision to Enlarge the Committee on Rules: An Analysis of the 1961 Vote," ch. 11 in Robert L. Peabody and Nelson W. Polsby (eds.), *New Perspectives on the House of Representatives*, 2d ed. (Chicago: Rand McNally, 1969); Julian E. Zelizer, *On Capitol Hill: The Struggle to Reform Congress and Its Consequences, 1948–2000* (New York: Cambridge University Press, 2004), 56–60, 63–69, 85–91, 125–51; Nelson W. Polsby, *How Congress Evolves: Social Bases of Institutional Change* (New York: Oxford University Press, 2004), chs. 1, 2; David W. Rohde, *Parties and Leaders in the Postreform House* (Chicago: University of Chicago Press, 1991), 17–28.

[6] Eric Schickler, *Disjointed Pluralism: Institutional Innovation and the Development of the U.S. Congress* (Princeton: Princeton University Press, 2001), ch. 5; Eric Schickler, Eric McGhee, and John Sides, "Remaking the House and Senate: Personal Power, Ideology, and the 1970s Reforms," *Legislative Studies Quarterly* 28:3 (2003), 297–333.

Was the House floor majority really being thwarted much at all? At the margin, at least, it is plausible that the reforms of those decades, once executed, helped bolster the sovereignty of House floor majorities in fact as well as promise. Yet in retrospect, one result of it all might have been to trade in a slight committee-centered antimajoritarian bias for a slight party-centered antimajoritarian bias. For some Democratic reformers, the aim was a party cartel rather than House majoritarianism. The party's caucus and leadership, through reward-and-punish control of committee appointments, would be able to whip renegade members into line against their personal or constituency-induced ideal points.[7] Artificial floor majorities could thus be manufactured. This result no doubt came to pass, at least to a degree, although it did not help when Clinton's health-care reform came along.

Finally, although it occurred outside this book's discussion, the Democrats' drive to reform the presidential nominating system in the late 1960s and early 1970s qualifies as an instance. It resembled the drive for direct primaries in the early twentieth century targeting the elected institutions of the states. Chiefly at issue this time was the alleged antimajoritarian outlier stance of the Lyndon Johnson presidency regarding the Vietnam War. A clotted, elite-controlled Democratic nominating process would perpetuate that off-median stance and that war. A resort to majoritarian democracy was called for.[8] The nominating process was reformed.[9] The

[7] This aim followed the spirit of an influential midcentury tract, *Toward a More Responsible Two-Party System*, A Report of the Committee on Political Parties of the American Political Science Association (New York: Rinehart, 1950). The authors of this APSA report exhibited no interest whatever in policy control by the median U.S. House member. Emphasized instead was the need for the political parties to be able to devise and impose policies. In Congress, that would mean power centered in party leaderships and caucuses. It seems a good bet, although the authors of the report did not frame their case this way or perhaps realize what they were doing, that they were advancing party dictation over House majoritarianism in reaction to the rural skew of the House at that time. For liberals, which the APSA authors were, that skew made the median member of the House an unattractive figure.

[8] See, for example, Austin Ranney, *Curing the Mischiefs of Faction: Party Reform in America* (Berkeley: University of California Press, 1975), ch. 4; Nelson W. Polsby, *Consequences of Party Reform* (New York: Oxford University Press, 1983), part 1.

[9] Byron E. Shafer, *Quiet Revolution: The Struggle for the Democratic Party and the Shaping of Post-Reform Politics* (New York: Russell Sage, 1983).

validity of this case might be contested given a true eye for the national, or for that matter the Democratic party, median view of that time. Yet there was a good deal of intensity on the reform side, and democracy and majority rule were the manifest aims.

That is the liberal side. Since World II the conservative side has advanced two reform drives that resembled each other in grounding and thrust. The first was the campaign to limit presidents to two terms. It emanated in the Twenty-Second Amendment, which was approved by Congress in 1947 and ratified by the states in 1951. This important and indicative renovation seems to have occurred without much attention from academics or even journalists.[10] Homeric memorialization of it has been lacking. Why did the reform happen? A ban on any more Franklin D. Roosevelts was the obvious surface aim. I have not seen an elaborate rationale for the move, but here is a plausible construction of the conservatives' discontent. Whether or not FDR and Truman taken individually were in fact policy outliers (no doubt the conservatives believed that they were), there existed a policy outlier problem *over time*. It was a problem of over-time averaging. Republicans were not getting a fair shot at the presidency. As a historical generalization, it was true then, as it is now, that a party running an incumbent candidate manages to keep the White House roughly two-thirds of the time.[11] That is a high hurdle for an opposition

---

[10] For accounts, see David E. Kyvig, *Explicit and Authentic Acts: Amending the U.S. Constitution, 1776–1995* (Lawrence: University Press of Kansas, 1996), 325–34; Paul G. Willis and George L. Willis, "The Politics of the Twenty-Second Amendment," *Western Political Quarterly* 5:3 (September 1952), 469–82; Alan P. Grimes, *Democracy and the Amendments to the Constitution* (Lexington, Mass.: D. C. Heath, 1978), 113–24; Michael H. Klein, "The Twenty-Second Amendment: Term Limitation in the Executive Branch," Americans to Limit Congressional Terms, Washington, D.C., September 25, 1989. "The ratification of the Twenty-second Amendment was remarkable for the lack of media attention afforded it. Between 1947 and 1951, no items discussing the ratification battle or even the final passage of the Twenty-second Amendment appeared in the periodicals indexed in the *Readers Guide to Periodical Literature*. . . . No mention was made in the Washington or New York papers of the Congressional passage of the Amendment. The ratification process was not reported on at any length in the national press." Klein, 6–7.

[11] See David R. Mayhew, "Incumbency Advantage in U.S. Presidential Elections: The Historical Record," *Political Science Quarterly* 123:2 (Summer 2008), 201–28, at 212. In the elections of 1792 through 2008 (omitting the unusual contest of 1824), there is a clear contrast of in-party success records: 21–10 with incumbents running, 11–12 in open-seat

party. As of 1951, when a final jolt of popular support elevated the Twenty-second Amendment to ratification in the context of an unpopular Truman presidency, the country had witnessed four incumbent-led Democratic presidential victories in a row in 1936, 1940, 1944, and 1948. That kind of sequence had never happened before. The dice seemed to be loaded. There was a related reform thrust. During the New Deal and World War II, the executive branch had grown more powerful vis-à-vis the House and Senate, making for the perception of a multiplicative outlier problem. Unending Democratic control of the White House was bad enough, but an executive branch upgraded in power made things worse. Accordingly, just after World War II, the conservative side in Congress spurred another major reform, the Administrative Procedure Act of 1946, which placed a harness on executive discretion.[12]

A similar script played out a few decades later, this time involving the House of Representatives. By the mid-1980s, in the eyes of Republicans, that chamber had become a policy outlier institution that they no longer had a fair shot at. Worse yet, it was upgrading itself in power terms. A "constitutional crisis" was declared.[13] "The present-day Congress has become the most unrepresentative and corrupt of the modern era."[14] The House had become "an entrenched oligarchy, whose members have only a tenuous relationship to the voters who send them to Washington."[15] A "constituent service racket" had come to make House members nearly unbeatable.[16] "The success rate of incumbents running for reelection is profoundly threatening to the doctrine

circumstances. As of 1950 the historical contrast was less clear: 15–7 versus 10–7. But perhaps it, or at least the overall historical experience that went into it, was enough to spur an intuition.

[12] James E. Brazier, "An Anti-New Dealer Legacy: The Administrative Procedure Act," *Journal of Policy History* 8:2 (1996), 206–26; David H. Rosenbloom, "'Whose Bureaucracy Is This, Anyway,' Congress's 1946 Answer," *PS: Political Science and Politics* 34:4 (December 2001), 773–77.

[13] Gordon S. Jones and John A. Marini, "General Introduction," in Jones and Marini (eds.), *The Imperial Congress: Crisis in the Separation of Powers* (New York: Pharos Books, 1988), 1.

[14] Newt Gingrich, "Foreword," in Jones and Mariini (eds.), *The Imperial Congress*, x.

[15] Jones and Marini, "General Introduction," 8.

[16] Eric Felten, *The Ruling Class: Inside the Imperial Congress* (Washington, D.C.: Regnery, 1993), 211.

of separation of powers."[17] The resulting pathologies were said to be several. Powerful Democratic House members wired into the government bureaucracy never had their wires cut.[18] A culture of government spending was seen to be fed by unchecked careerism and insiderism.[19] A "Washington establishment" feeding on pork and casework, according to an influential nonpartisan analysis, had centered itself in the House.[20] Led by Newt Gingrich, a new generation of House Republicans plotted revolution starting in the mid-1980s.[21] The analogy between Gingrich then and liberal reformer Richard Bolling of a generation earlier is often missed. For both men, a House establishment needed to be destroyed in order to usher in better days.

In hindsight, the rise of House incumbency advantage in the 1960s probably backgrounded this Republican restlessness. Since the 1830s, no one had seen anything like an ultimately unbroken forty-year party hegemony in any of the elective national institutions. In House elections, the Nixon and Reagan eras had come and gone without breaking the Democrats' stride. It was curious. The House was supposed to be the popular, volatile body. Absent incumbency advantage, perhaps it would have lived up to that role. As noted in chapter 1, one study estimates that the perpetuation of a pre-1960s votes/seats translation ratio in House elections would have yielded Republican majorities in the lower chamber at least sometimes—probably in 1966, 1968, and 1984 and possibly also in 1980 and 1990.[22] As in the 1940s, here, at the least, was a policy outlier problem over time. In place, to use a

[17] Jones and Marini, "General Introduction," 7.
[18] Ibid., 9.
[19] James L. Payne, "Limiting Government by Limiting Congressional Terms," *The Public Interest* 103 (1991), 106–17; George F. Will, *Restoration: Congress, Term Limits and the Recovery of Deliberative Democracy* (New York: Free Press, 1992), 59–61, 185.
[20] Morris P. Fiorina, *Congress: Keystone of the Washington Establishment* (New Haven: Yale University Press, 1977).
[21] See William F. Connelly, Jr., and John J. Pitney, Jr., *Congress' Permanent Minority: Republicans in the U.S. House* (Lanham, Md.: Littlefield Adams, 1994), ch. 4; Dan Balz and Ronald Brownstein, *Storming the Gates: Protest Politics and the Republican Revival* (Boston: Little, Brown, 1996), 118–26; Schickler, *Disjointed Pluralism*, 242–46.
[22] Stephen Ansolabehere, David Brady, and Morris Fiorina, "The Vanishing Marginals and Electoral Responsiveness," *British Journal of Political Science* 22:1 (1992), 21–38, at 33.

phrase applied by V. O. Key, Jr., to a similar context, was something like a "sandbag on a safety valve."[23]

Not surprisingly, although it took them awhile, the Republicans came to settle on legislative term limits as one remedy for their plight. That could be one route to House control.[24] A confluence of populism and libertarianism as well as conservatism, the term limits movement drew endorsements from the Republican national platforms of 1988 and 1992 and the party's Contract with America in 1994.[25] Beyond the U.S. House, the seemingly impervious California State Assembly led by Democrat Willie Brown supplied a major secondary target.[26] Conservative money poured in. In state referenda aimed at Congress as well as the state legislatures, Republican voters lined up.[27] Many Republican congressional candidates term-limited themselves one by one, voluntarily. In the end, the term limits drive failed in a formal sense as regards Congress, but it seems to have served as a nontrivial pressure ingredient in the mix of considerations that led to Republican victory in the midterm election of 1994.

[23] Key's reference was to state governors of earlier times elected by large popular majorities yet stymied once in office by opposite-party legislative majorities. Key, *American State Politics*, 60.

[24] John B. Gilmour and Paul Rothstein, "Term Limitation in a Dynamic Model of Partisan Balance," ch. 9 in Bernard Grofman (ed.), *Legislative Term Limits: Public Choice Perspectives* (Boston: Kluwer Academic Publishers, 1996). "One need not be excessively cynical to believe that some of the Republican interest in reforms to weaken incumbency advantage . . . stems from the fact that most incumbents happen to be Democrats" (145).

[25] On the term limits drive in general: Stuart Rothenberg, "Transplanting Term Limits: Political Mobilization and Grass-Roots Politics," ch. 5 in Gerald Benjamin and Michael J. Malbin (eds.), *Limiting Legislative Terms* (Washington, D.C.: Congressional Quarterly Press, 1992); Erik H. Corwin, "Limits on Legislative Terms: Legal and Policy Implications," *Harvard Journal on Legislation* 28 (Summer 1991), 569–608, at 569–77; John David Rausch, Jr., "Understanding the Term Limits Movement," ch. 15 in Rick Farmer, John David Rausch, Jr., and John C. Green (eds.), *The Test of Time: Coping with Legislative Term Limits* (Lanham, Md.: Lexington Books, 2003); Jennie Drage Bowser and Gary Moncrief, "Term Limits in State Legislatures," ch. 1 in Karl T. Kurtz, Bruce Cain, and Richard G. Niemi (eds.), *Institutional Change in American Politics: The Case of Term Limits* (Ann Arbor: University of Michigan Press, 2007), 10–11.

[26] Charles M. Price, "The Guillotine Comes to California: Term-Limit Politics in the Golden State," ch. 6 in Benjamin and Malbin (eds.), *Limiting Legislative Terms*.

[27] Keith Boeckelman and Gina Corell, "An Analysis of Term Limitation Elections," ch. 11 in Grofman (ed.), *Legislative Term Limits*, 187, 192–93.

That event raises a side consideration. The main equilibrator in American politics is, of course, the electoral process itself. Elections are, among other things, occasions for voters to rein in presidents who have been pursuing off-median policies pleasing to their ideological bases. A homeostatic pattern can result.[28] Of particular relevance here, that kind of equilibration may obtain at least sometimes against majority parties in the House who press "party cartels" to the limit. Eric Schickler draws an analogy between House Republicans led by "Czar" Joseph Cannon around 1910 and House Democrats led by Speaker Jim Wright in the late 1980s. In both cases, the party-serving aggressiveness of these leaders infuriated the opposition and brought on, among other things, electoral retaliation.[29] Democrats denounced "Cannonism" in the elections of 1908 and 1910. Newt Gingrich, in one of his moves (there were others), dramatized a "House bank scandal" for the election of 1992.[30] The in-parties' electoral disasters of 1910 and 1994 were apparently helped along by these apt oppositional drives. The Pelosi Speakership was running that risk in 2009.

As a route to equilibration, however, institutional reform does vie with electoral victory. That is not likely to change. Reform causes spring to life. Off-center institutional tilts are not likely to be missed. Since World War II, we have seen at least the six drives discussed above, and we may see more.[31] As of today, at least two candidate drives lurk in the realm of potentiality.

[28] See Robert S. Erikson, Michael B. MacKuen, and James A. Stimson, *The Macro Polity* (New York: Cambridge University Press, 2002).
[29] Schickler, *Disjointed Pluralism*, 189, 193, 240–42, 254.
[30] On the place of the bank scandal in the 1992 campaign, see Michael A. Dimock and Gary C. Jacobson, "Checks and Choices: The House Bank Scandal's Impact on Voters in 1992," *Journal of Politics* 57:4 (November 1995), 1143–59. By 1992 Wright himself was already out of the picture, having resigned thanks to an ethics assault lodged by Gingrich.
[31] The six instances discussed here do not exhaust the experience of the last six decades. I could have discussed the drive to represent the District of Columbia in the Electoral College and the House of Representatives. I could have discussed legislative gerrymandering as it involves the House, although that practice, biased as it often is toward one party or the other in the crafting of particular state congressional delegations, has tended to balance out in party terms over space and time at the level of the full House. Possibly for this reason gerrymandering has not been targeted by a major reform movement associated with a particular party or ideology. I could have discussed campaign finance reform, but that cause has not dwelt on any disequilibrating waywardness alleged to be exhibited by any

One is reform or abolition of the Electoral College. A perennial option for reform, this old institution keeps rolling along. One reason for that, I argued in chapter 1, is the Electoral College's record of balance. On average during recent times, neither of the major parties has been advantaged or disadvantaged by it. Occasional small statistical disadvantage has brought occasional brief grumbling, but little else has occurred. Yet a reform cause could crystallize quickly. As remarked in chapter 1, a triggering event might be another 2000-type result that would arouse Democrats. In the American system, a party sensing disadvantage can be counted on to try to claw itself toward parity. On the specifics, there is no shortage of proposed remedies—from constitutional amendments through various designs for choosing electors by the individual states.[32]

Another obvious target is the Senate filibuster. By that I mean the enhanced institution of very recent decades that, in practice, accommodates "simply a minority veto" by forty-one senators.[33]

particular *one* of the three elective branches of the national government. That distinguishes campaign finance reform from each of the six instances I address here. More tenuously, I could have discussed congressional budget reform in the 1970s—partly the product of a perceived off-median policy tilt by the Nixon presidency as it tried to curb congressional spending by way of White House impoundment of funds. Not reached at all in this book's discussion is a rather different yet quite important realm of representation. The country's *national* institutions—its elected ones as well as its bureaucracies and courts—have drained vast power and authority from its *state and local* elected institutions during recent generations. Thanks to Tom Romer for alerting me to this matter. Whether this centralizing of power and authority has exacted, or eventually will exact, a significant price in U.S. system legitimacy is a question that academics and journalists rarely address. A persistent, counterbalancing reform movement has not arisen, although note the Ross Perot eruption of the early 1990s and the Tea Party uprising of 2009–10. There is certainly nervousness about D.C. Beltway power. On the steep upslope in the U.S. national government's role during the 1960s and 1970s, see Timothy Conlan, *New Federalism: Intergovernmental Reform from Nixon to Reagan* (Washington, D.C.: Brookings Institution Press, 1988). This American centralizing drift has not been unique: "The story of British local government during the past half-century is in large part a story of its cumulative loss of autonomy, its cumulative loss of freedom and its cumulative loss of power." Anthony King, *The British Constitution* (New York: Oxford University Press, 2007), ch. 7, quotation at 164.

[32] See, for example, Alexis Simendinger, James A. Barnes, and Carl M. Cannon, "Pondering a Popular Vote," *National Journal*, November 18, 2000, 3650–56; Alan B. Morrison, "A Better Way?" *National Journal*, January 4, 2003, 24–31; Edwards, *Why the Electoral College Is Bad for America*, 152–58; Koza et al., *Every Vote Equal.*

[33] Catherine Fisk and Erwin Chemerinsky, "The Filibuster," *Stanford Law Review* 49:2 (January 1997), 181–254, at 184.

This accentuated obstruction has not been in place long, and it may not last interminably. The histories of legislative bodies offer surprising quick changes in the content or interpretation of rules. "Majoritarian coups"—that is, on-the-spot moves by majorities to curb obstructive minorities—have occurred in, for example, the British House of Commons in 1881, the House of Representatives in 1890, and the Senate itself in 1908.[34] In the case of the Senate, an opening exists every two years for formal rules change at the beginning of a session;[35] yet another opening exists at any time for presiding officers to set "precedents."[36] Either route can be taken to chip away at obstructive practices. In either case, a presiding officer may make a ruling—for example, to suggest some possibilities, that the Constitution guarantees a fresh opportunity to revise chamber rules by majority vote as a session begins, or, to pose an especially ambitious example of establishing a precedent, that any additional debate on some specific motion under current consideration would be dilatory and thus for that very reason out of order.[37] This is not fantasy. Precedents are major weapons. A shakeup of Senate practices might be easy. On rulings from the chair, a presiding officer backed up by a committed floor majority can exert great influence. Current scholarship on Senate history supports these judgments. According to Gregory J. Wawro and Eric Schickler, "A simple majority of the Senate with the cooperation of a sympathetic presiding officer could curb obstruction."[38] According to Gregory Koger, "I find that simple majorities can determine the meaning of Senate rules"—that is, approve new interpretations that set precedents—"and that senators frequently make these

[34] See, for example, David R. Mayhew, "Supermajority Rule in the Senate," *PS: Political Science and Politics* 36 (2003), 31–36. On the two U.S. instances: Gregory J. Wawro and Eric Schickler, *Filibuster: Obstruction and Lawmaking in the U.S. Senate* (Princeton: Princeton University Pres, 2006), 51, 63.

[35] Gold and Gupta, "The Constitutional Option to Change Senate Rules and Procedures."

[36] Ibid., part 4; Gregory Koger, "The Majoritarian Senate: 'Nuclear Options' in Historical Perspective," paper presented at annual conference of American Political Science Association, Philadelphia, 2003.

[37] On the latter ambitious move, see Gold and Gupta, "The Constitutional Option," 260.

[38] Wawro and Schickler, *Filibuster*, 263. In general on the mutability of Senate Rules, chs. 3 and 11.

majoritarian decisions."[39] Koger concludes: "The persistence of filibustering in the Senate is more puzzling than previously thought. The majority of the Senate can eliminate obstruction at any time."[40]

If this is true, why has it not done so? At least four factors seem to have been holding the contemporary forty-one-senator veto in place.[41] First, like the Electoral College, the Senate filibuster has been affecting the parties more or less impartially. Starting in the 1980s, both sides have seen certain of their legislative drives win and lose. Also, on this evidence, either party getting blocked today can imagine blocking the other party tomorrow. Neither side has had special reason to take up arms against the filibuster.

Second, the White House's budget and trade instruments have been insulated from minority obstruction.[42] This is important. It is hard to believe that a supermajority hurdle for national budgets would have survived the politics of the last quarter century.[43] Moreover, the "reconciliation" option built into the budget process has offered a certain opportunism. Key party aims can be labeled budgeting and thus glide through on a preferred track. Again, Presidents can be tough and inventive. The Reagan White House engineered a surprising use of reconciliation in 1981, as did the Obama White House in advancing health care reform so as to skirt a filibuster in 2010.

Third, there is a familiar, fundamental reason that is not particular to recent decades. It extends back across two centuries.

---

[39] Koger, "The Majoritarian Senate," 1.

[40] Ibid., 14.

[41] One factor apparently *not* helping hold the process in place is any connection between state size and filibustering. Senators from small-population states, it is often speculated, have a special interest in preserving veto power for their constituencies. Nowhere else in the system do those states have such deployable clout. Yet Sarah A. Binder and Steven S. Smith have shown that, at least between 1918 and 1988, senators from the small states did not stand out statistically in opposing either cloture motions or reform of the cloture rule. Binder and Smith, *Politics or Principle? Filibustering in the United States Senate* (Washington, D.C.: Brookings Institution Press, 1997), 96–99.

[42] Ibid., 188–94.

[43] The state of California has such a supermajority hurdle for tax hikes and budgets. It is the deposit of referendum decisions. See Kevin O'Leary, "The Legacy of Proposition 13," *Time*, June 27, 2009, online; Kevin O'Leary, "How California's Fiscal Woes Began: A Crisis 30 Years in the Making," *Time*, July 1, 2009, online.

Senators enjoy their individual prerogatives to obstruct and are not eager to give them up.[44] Forced to make a choice, they will often trade away policy just enough to keep their prerogatives. It is a fine line. We saw it in the exertions of the Senate's "Gang of 14" who warded off the "nuclear option" by arranging a cross-party compromise on judicial nominations in 2005. Some Bush judges were approved. A shift to majority-rule procedures was staved off.[45] The system was preserved. To some degree, in short, shrewdly calibrated policy concessions can work to keep the Senate's procedures intact.

A fourth reason is speculative. Insofar as the Senate's obstructive minorities are parties—as opposed to factions or other formations—an interesting incentive arises. The leadership of a minority party in a legislative body has, among other things, a Downsian role.[46] Leaders like Bob Dole in 1993–94 and Tom Daschle in 1999–2000 may shy away from just parroting the policy positions of their already existent members. They may look toward having their parties take over the Senate. That means appealing to the national median voter—or close to that. That calls for suitable policy positioning. Sometimes, it can mean backing away from obstructive behavior even if the bulk of a party's caucus would prefer it. An instance might be Bob Dole, as Republican minority leader, refraining from staging a filibuster against the "Brady bill" to regulate handguns in the face of a wave of publicity during the Thanksgiving season of 1993.[47] Similarly, to

[44] See, for example, Wawro and Schickler, *Filibuster*, 273–74, 282.
[45] Ibid., 269–76.
[46] Anthony Downs, *An Economic Theory of Democracy* (New York: Harper and Row, 1957).
[47] "Republicans, aided by some Western and Southern Democrats, had the strength to continue blocking the bill in the Senate but were anxious to extract themselves from what had become an embarrassing stalemate. . . . Minority Leader Robert Dole embodied the conflicts among Republicans, and the Kansan seemed torn between his own political instincts and a fear of losing prestige among conservatives in his caucus. After days of recriminations, Mr. Dole tried to emphasize a gentler bipartisanship later, and when he met with reporters after the vote, he brought along Oregon Sen. Mark Hatfield, a GOP liberal who had backed the Brady bill. 'We were realistic,' said the Republican leader. 'It was in everybody's interest to get this issue behind us.'" David Rogers, "Brady Bill's Passage Illustrates Growth of Political Concern over Violent Crime," *Wall Street Journal*, November 26, 1993, A10. See also *CQW*, November 27, 1993, 3271–72.

pose a counterfactual, Dole in that same Congress, even if forty-one nay votes had been available, might have thought twice about trying to block a major Clinton health-care plan that had managed to both clear the House and win decisive public support.[48] Yet in that circumstance the forty-one nay votes might not have been available, either. Here is another kind of instance where policy concessions, so to speak, taken in the aggregate, might reduce the pressure for procedural reforms aimed at curbing obstruction.

Given these pulls toward stasis, what are the prospects? Wawro and Schickler state them nicely: "The prospects of moving toward majority rule will depend ultimately on whether the frustration of a majority party's agenda will become so troublesome that a floor majority will be motivated to bear the risks, uncertainty, and personal power costs of undertaking what has come to be known as the 'nuclear option.'"[49] A frustrated majority party is the key. One can imagine a scenario. A major White House program is backed by a Senate majority but runs into obstruction. The reconciliation process is not available. On the spot, a friendly vice president rules that debate has gone on too long and needs to stop. A majority of senators approve a motion to table an objection. Assisting this aim, a law school doctrine emerges that a guarantee of majority rule in the Senate has been implicit in a penumbra of the Constitution for over two centuries.[50] That might be it.

[48] Before public opinion soured on the Clinton health-care plan, Dole was apparently open to a compromise deal. But then opinion soured. See Johnson and Broder, *The System*, 35, 222, 345–46, 358–66, 371–73, 394–95.

[49] Wawro and Schickler, *Filibuster*, 264.

[50] Generally speaking, although the subject is complex, constitutional lawyers seem to be friendly to the idea of majority rule in the Senate. Fisk and Chemerinsky, for example, argue that it is unconstitutional for supermajority rule in the Senate to be "entrenched"—that is, for any Senate to foreclose a future Senate from reconfiguring its rules by majority vote. "The Filibuster," 245–54. Gold and Gupta argue that the "constitutional option" is available both at the openings of Senate sessions as well as in the everyday setting of precedents. That is, a presiding officer backed up by a floor majority is free to make rulings that favor majority rule. "The Constitution," parts 3 and 4. Robert Klotz reports the following regarding hearings held by the Senate in 2003: "During the hearings, eminent law professors suggested that the practice of allowing filibusters on judicial nominees could not be imposed by previous Senates on the current one. It, therefore, would be within the power of the 51 Republican Senators to uphold a point of order against the filibuster and proceed to govern by majority rule." Klotz, "The Nuclear Option for Stopping Filibusters,"

Yet public opinion winds would probably need to be favorable. Filibustering as a constraint on sovereignty by fifty-one senators is not necessarily unpopular.[51] The Senate cloture rule can be the median voter's best friend. A Senate majority party that tried to break the cloture rule to enact a major measure riding very low in public opinion would probably run into difficulty.

Note again that the filibuster practices of recent times have not posed a party asymmetry problem. That absence has probably helped keep the practices in place. Any growing perception that there *is* such a problem might help dislodge those practices. This could happen. For example, if one party in some durable, prominent, and convincing way should come to outpace the other in unsuccessfully pressing policies that break with the status quo, then the policy costs of obstruction would be party asymmetric— or least they would be widely seen to be asymmetric. In Britain, for example, the case for disempowering the House of Lords in the early twentieth century seems to have followed such a perception. But these days, the electorates of both Britain and the United States, notwithstanding the dissimilar governmental institutions of these countries, can recall both of their parties championing change at some times and the status quo at others. Ronald Reagan and Margaret Thatcher, the British promoter of a free enterprise society, were probably agents of change no less than, say, Lyndon B. Johnson or Clement Attlee, the mid-twentieth-century British promoter of a welfare state.[52] On the record, change on all sides can occur.

PS: Political Science and Politics 37:4 (2004), 843–46, at 843. A case for the unconstitutionality of today's Senate filibuster appears in Thomas Geoghegan, "Filibust!" *New York Times*, January 11, 2010, A15.

[51] In 2005, when the Republicans contemplated the "nuclear option" as a way to get their judicial nominees approved, "public opinion polling gave indications that the Republicans faced a potential backlash for going nuclear. A report by the Gallup Organization indicated that a majority of Americans opposed attempts to eliminate the filibuster." Wawro and Schickler, *Filibuster*, 273.

[52] Change brought by the Thatcher government is highlighted in a recent study of economic institutions, namely, public employment and labor union density, in eighteen OECD countries including the United States from 1960 through 2003. "The transformation of the United Kingdom under Margaret Thatcher has no equal [in any direction in any country]." Her time in office brought "a sharp decline in [Britain's] public sector . . . and also the most

Policy stability, however, can be valued also. Given today's American parties, the question does arise whether supermajority hurdles are necessarily a bad thing. From a system standpoint, there is a possible dark side to getting rid of the Senate filibuster. What if the Senate's obstructive activities of the last two decades really do index societal polarization? Then, what might strict majority rule in the Senate entail? In the long run, partisan symmetry in the system might not be undermined, but a good deal of back-and-forth policy volatility could ensue as majority parties come and go.[53] There are symmetries and symmetries.

Are there other reform causes? As regards Congress, one unending source of criticism is that institution's bent for pork-barrel spending. Benefits tailored to the state or district level by self-serving House and Senate members are attacked as wasteful spending. "Earmarks" are a current manifestation.[54] Presidents, whose constituency is nationwide, tend to criticize the practice. For the analysis here, however, pork-barreling does not present much of a party asymmetry problem. Granted, certain studies of the distribution of domestic federal outlays—a category somewhat broader than the "pork barrel" connotation—suggest that parties controlling Congress or the White House tend to favor their own congressional constituencies a bit.[55] Yet over time, a minority party enjoys a license to rise to majority status and gain its own edge. More important, benefits are customarily shared across the congressional aisle. Minority parties are not blanked. In 1987, for example, an omnibus highway bill laden with farflung

significant decline in union density in Europe. . . . In effect, with Thatcher's leadership, the UK became solidly classified as a liberal market economy." Jan-Emmanuel De Neve, "Endogenous Preferences: The Political Consequences of Economic Institutions," London School of Economics and Political Science, 2009, 22.

[53] For an argument along this line, see Jay Cost, "Why the Filibuster Is More Essential than Ever," *RealClearPolitics*, December 28, 2009, online.

[54] See, for example, Edmund L. Andrews and Robert Pear, "With New Rules, Congress Boasts of Pet Projects," *New York Times*, August 5, 2007, A1.

[55] See Steven D. Levitt and James M. Snyder, Jr., "Political Parties and the Distribution of Federal Outlays," *American Journal of Political Science* 39:4 (November 1995), 958–80; Christopher R. Berry, Barry C. Burden, and William G. Howell, "Proposal Power, the President, and the Geography of Federal Spending," paper presented at the annual conference of the American Political Science Association, Boston, 2008.

projects overcame a Reagan veto "on a massive, bipartisan 350–73 [House] vote." The Republican House minority leader, among others, voted aye to protect his own project.[56] The Transportation Act of 2005, "the most expensive public works legislation in US history," is said to have set "a new record for pork-barrel spending, earmarking $24 billion for a staggering 6,376 pet projects, spread among virtually every congressional district in the land."[57] Democrats were not ignored at that time of Republican government. In media accounts of pork-barreling, which may both reflect and shape public perceptions, the practice is not ordinarily seen as partisan. It is a congressional thing. "Hogs on the Hill" and "The Great American Pork Barrel" are typical headlines.[58] Individuals are singled out, as in "The Pork Barrel Barons."[59] Congressman Joseph McDade—a Republican serving during Democratic Congresses—brought an extravagant railroad museum, "Steamtown," to Scranton, Pennsylvania.[60] Congressman John Murtha won creative defense earmarks for Johnstown, Pennsylvania.[61] Senator Robert C. Byrd has famously loaded down West Virginia with benefits.[62] Senator Ted Stevens hustled for the "Bridge to Nowhere" in Alaska.[63] That is the tenor of the coverage.

[56] Diana Evans, *Greasing the Wheels: Using Pork Barrel Projects to Build Majority Coalitions in Congress* (New York: Cambridge University Press, 2004), 103.
[57] Jeff Jacoby, "The Republican Pork Barrel," *Boston Globe*, August 4, 2005, A17.
[58] Eloise Salholz with Ann McDaniel and Rich Thomas, "The Hogs on the Hill," *Newsweek*, April 13, 1992, 22–23; Ken Silverstein, "The Great American Pork Barrel: Washington Streamlines the Means of Corruption," *Harper's*, July 2005.
[59] Edward T. Pound and Douglas Pasternak, "The Pork Barrel Barons," *U.S. News and World Report*, February 21, 1994, 32–43.
[60] Brian Kelly, "A Tale of Piggery: Steamtown USA is a case study in the worst kind of pork-barrel politics," *Newsweek*, April 13, 1992, 24–25; James M. Perry, "GOP Congressman Shows How to Keep Power, Even While under Indictment for Corruption," *Wall Street Journal*, June 14, 1994, A16.
[61] John R. Wilke, "Murtha, Inc.: How Lawmaker Rebuilt Hometown on Earmarks," *Wall Street Journal*, October 30, 2007, A1. See also Carol D. Leonnig, "Murtha's Earmarks Keep Airport Aloft," *Washington Post*, April 19, 2009, online.
[62] B. Drummond Ayes, Jr., "Senator Who Brings Home the Bacon," *New York Times*, September 6, 1991, A16; Francis X. Clines, "How Do West Virginians Spell Pork? It's B-Y-R-D," *New York Times*, May 4, 2002, A1.
[63] Shailagh Murray, "For a Senate Foe of Pork Barrel Spending, Two Bridges Too Far," *Washington Post*, October 21, 2005, A8.

In the American system, pork-barreling may best be seen as a stable annoyance. It is an annoyance rather than a menace because it involves a quite small portion of the budget.[64] It is stable because members of an elected legislature are prone to "credit claiming" activities for their constituencies, and their constituents tend to appreciate that servicing.[65] And it is stable because it does not seriously violate the equilibrium of party symmetry. Still, the critique of pork-barreling is endogenous to the American system, too. It has a continual tamping-down role.

There is another facet of distributive politics. Party symmetry aside, at least in a direct sense, what about the Senate? In a familiar criticism, many critics blame that chamber where all states are equal for delivering higher government benefits per capita to states with smaller populations.[66] Unquestionably, it is a valid charge. This topic is a paradise for measurers. Cary M. Atlas and associates, in a high-side estimate covering 1972 through 1990, employing suitable control variables, report a $394 annual per capita spending gap between the largest and smallest states (California and, in 1990, Wyoming). Accommodated in their analysis are all federal expenditures on U.S. soil including outlays for entitlements and defense.[67] Frances E. Lee and Bruce I. Oppenheimer, in low-side estimates covering 1983 through 1990, also using suitable controls, report a $77 per capita spending gap

---

[64] See R. Douglas Arnold, "The Local Roots of Domestic Policy," ch. 8 in Thomas E. Mann and Norman J. Ornstein (eds.), *The New Congress* (Washington, D.C.: American Enterprise Institute, 1981), at 281–84; Robert M. Stein and Kenneth N. Bickers, *Perpetuating the Pork Barrel: Policy Subsystems and American Democracy* (New York: Cambridge University Press, 1995), 139–40.

[65] See Mayhew, *Congress: The Electoral Connection*, 2d ed., (New Haven: Yale University Press, 2004), 52–59.

[66] See, for example, Sanford Levinson, *Our Undemocratic Constitution: Where the Constitution Goes Wrong and How We the People Can Correct It* (New York: Oxford University Press, 2006), 49–62; Robert A. Dahl, *How Democratic Is the American Constitution?* (New Haven: Yale University Press, 2002), 162–64; Lynn A. Baker, "The Senate: An Institution Whose Time Has Gone?" *Journal of Law and Politics* 13:1 (Winter 1997), 21–102, at 30–42.

[67] Cary M. Atlas, et al., "Slicing the Federal Government Net Spending Pie: Who Wins, Who Loses, and Why," *American Economic Review* 85:3 (June 1995), 624–29. In table 2 on page 627, their relevant coefficient reads 787.13. It was calculated "on a biennial basis." I halved it. Excluded from the analysis are foreign-aid expenditures, international payments, and interest payments on the federal debt.

between California and Wyoming in nondiscretionary distributive spending (Congress writes the formulas) and a $35 gap in discretionary distributive spending (bureaucrats have leeway to allocate). These Lee and Oppenheimer results steer clear of entitlement policies like Social Security and Medicare, and defense. Transportation policy stands out as the chief small-state bargain.[68] In general, in Congress's formula legislation, a "fair shares" norm that awards each state at least something, regardless of its population size, seems to motor much of the favoritism.

In endeavors like this, is the Senate really the culprit? Recent research has traced the process in the enactment of the mammoth Transportation Act of 2005. A smoking gun emerged. In that enterprise it was indeed the upper chamber—the House did not do it—that generated the small-states favoritism.[69]

This unfairness is another annoyance, but is it a menace? Probably not. For one thing, there is no evidence of small-state favoritism in taxation, and little or none in redistributive entitlements.[70] Also, in a pattern relevant to total spending volume, the slope of the spending skew is apparently nonlinear. The very small states do well, but the expenditure differences per capita between the middle-sized and the large states are minimal. The "every state should get something" norm does that.[71] Most important, it seems

[68] Frances E. Lee and Bruce I. Oppenheimer, *Sizing Up the Senate: The Unequal Consequences of Equal Representation* (Chicago: University of Chicago Press, 1999), 158–59, 173–77. The value for transportation policy has a suitable control variable for state highway mileage.

[69] William R. Hauk, Jr., and Romain Wacziarg, "Small States, Big Pork," *Quarterly Journal of Political Science* 2 (2007), 95–106; Benjamin E. Lauderdale, "Pass the Pork: Measuring Legislator Shares in Congress," *Political Analysis* 16 (2008), 235–49, at 242.

[70] On taxation: Atlas et al., "Slicing," 627. On entitlements, Atlas et al., "Slicing," where the effect is relatively small: "The political magnitude as well as the statistical significance of the effect on federal spending of the variables reflecting representation tends to be smallest in the case of entitlements. This comports well with intuition, since spending on entitlements such as Social Security is less controllable and thus less easily targeted to a particular state" (628). Also on entitlements: Lee and Oppenheimer, *Sizing Up the Senate*, 173–83, where in an elaborate analysis no effect appears. In an examination by policy area, the latter authors, employing suitable control variables, find no significant geographic skew in the areas of agriculture (where payments go directly to individual farmers), health (which includes Medicare and Medicaid), or income security (which includes Social Security).

[71] See Lee and Oppenheimer, *Sizing Up the Senate*, 175.

a good bet that the American public does not see the small-state expenditure skew as a significant problem. This is for two reasons. First, overwhelmingly in American popular lore, pork-barreling seems to code as a general congressional matter, not as a small-states matter. You do not need to represent Vermont or Montana to aim for a Steamtown, and that is well-known. The impetus to credit claiming borders on universal, and both the upsides and downsides of it tend to be reckoned with accordingly. Second, the cost of the small-state skew is spread around. California may subsidize Wyoming, but California has vastly more subsidizers than Wyoming has beneficiaries. In the Lee and Oppenheimer calculation, individual Californians would have received roughly $10 more a year—that's all—if the sum of all federal discretionary and nondiscretionary benefits had been delivered on a national per capita basis absent any small-state skew.[72] In an Atlas and associates calculation, people in the larger-population states that were underrepresented in the Senate (that includes roughly one-third of the fifty states) forsook $35 per capita a year to subsidize people in the smaller-population states that were overrepresented there (that includes roughly two-thirds of the fifty states).[73] These imbalances hardly register on the scales. As inequities go, they are not of a size to incite alarm or even notice.

That is the end of this book's story. I should emphasize that it is a narrow and circumscribed story. Many kinds of arguments have been lodged—or might be—against the U.S. system of separation of powers. It is too messy. It is too confusing. It does not allow crisp, immediate decisions by majority rule. It shunts off too much power to the courts. It allows divided party control of the government—a kind of pathology all by itself.[74] It emanates in stasis punctuated by emergencies.[75] Its pork-barreling is not

[72] Ibid., 176.
[73] Atlas et al., "Slicing," 625–26. The figure in table 1 on 625 is $70 on a biennial basis. I halved it.
[74] James L. Sundquist, "The Crisis of Competence in Our National Government," *Political Science Quarterly* 95 (1980), 183–208.
[75] Walter Dean Burnham, *Critical Elections and the Mainsprings of American Politics* (New York: W. W. Norton, 1970).

really a minor matter. In general, over many decades and generations, it has resulted in poor policies. In recent times, it has brought an unlovely legislative branch.[76] Its parties can be unlovely institutions, too. It places too loose a leash on a president acting as commander in chief.[77] In terms of this work, it may allow a prying-apart bias against Democratic presidents as discussed in chapter 2. The matter is ambiguous.

Yet most of the imbalances I have analyzed in this work have *not* been major, permanent, systemic problems. More precisely, at least during recent generations, many alleged problems have proven to be nonexistent, short-term, limited, tolerable, or correctable. In general, representational symmetries across the parties have prevailed. That seems to be a fundamental and significant truth. In addition, the ancillary representational idiosyncrasies I have explored, chiefly regarding the Senate, do not seem to have caused much durable trouble either. A shrewd Burkeanism may inhere in the public on these matters. Consider the Senate. "New Yorkers, Californians, et al. seem to just shrug," one analyst concluded after reciting a familiar litany of arithmetic downsides that *might* stem from the Senate's, after all, quite odd geographic base.[78] Yet, in fact, the downsides do not seem to happen. The public's shrug is understandable.

[76] Thomas E. Mann and Norman J. Ornstein, *The Broken Branch: How Congress Is Failing America and How to Get It Back on Track* (New York: Oxford University Press, 2006).
[77] Hugh Heclo, "What Ever Happened to the Separation of Powers?" 153–64 in Bradford P. Wilson and Peter W. Schramm (eds.), *Separation of Powers and Good Government* (Lanham, Md.: Rowman and Littlefield, (1994).
[78] Daniel Lazare, *The Frozen Republic: How the Constitution Is Paralyzing Democracy* (New York: Harcourt Brace, 1996), 297–98.

APPENDIX

Sources for Presidential Proposals

Documented here are the sources used in preparing the list of 184 presidential proposals presented and weighted in table 2.1. Any reader wishing to see the exact basis for these inclusions and weightings may go back to the sources using this information.

For each presidential term, the sources are listed alphabetically by author. For each source, the proposals that ended up being included in table 2.1, if they received any relevant discussion at all in a particular source, are listed under the source in this appendix in the order of their appearance in table 2.1. The page numbers at which such discussion occurred are provided. This page documentation might seem to invite page counts as an indicator of White House interest or emphasis regarding the various proposals, yet any such use of the page data would be unwise. Relevant discussions on the pages range from elaborate to scanty, and page counts cannot reach the content of the discussions. Leaving aside certain trivial or cursory mentions in the texts (scattered references to the Clinton budget, for example, in the coverage of 1993–94), the page information here is intended to be a complete canvass. Absent mistakes of omission (no doubt there are some), it is a guide to all the relevant discussions, in all the sources, of the proposals listed in table 2.1.

How about also-rans? That is, presidential proposals that received some discussion in the sources but did *not* make the cut for table 2.1? Those that received discussion in at least two sources are listed here in a different way, for each presidential term, at the bottom of all the rest of each term's information. They are listed alphabetically by proposal, rather than by source, in each case documenting the sources in which relevant discussion took place along with page numbers. Why didn't these proposals make the cut? There were a number of reasons. Too few of the term's sources took an interest, or the discussions were cursory, or the president was reported to be not really very interested, or the White House was taking defensive action somehow on a proposal that originated on Capitol Hill, or an announced White House aim never did emanate in a concrete proposal. Also-rans that came especially close to the cut included child care under Bush in 1989–90, and anti-Communist loyalty legislation under Eisenhower in 1953–54. I had trouble sorting Nixon's energy proposals in 1973–74 into yeses and no.

Through 2002, all except two of the proposals included in table 2.1 are discussed in at least two sources. Those two, both items from 1985–86, are a balanced-budget amendment and an agriculture plan discussed only by Reagan himself in his memoirs. *Congressional Quarterly Weekly* enters the picture for 2005–06.

TRUMAN: 1949–50

Robert J. Donovan, *Tumultuous Years: The Presidency of Harry S. Truman, 1949–1953* (New York: W. W. Norton, 1982), p. 24, ch. 11: civil rights 24, 119, tax hike 123, Taft–Hartley 24, 120–22, education 24, 123–25, health insurance 24, 126, agriculture 122–23, omnibus housing 24, 127, minimum wage 127, social security 125–26.

Robert H. Ferrell, *Harry S. Truman: A Life* (Columbia: University of Missouri Press, 1994), ch. 14: civil rights 296–97, tax hike 288, 290, Taft–Hartley 288, 290, education 289, health insurance 290–91, agriculture 288, 289, housing 288, 290, minimum wage 288, social security 288, executive reorganization 288.

Harold F. Gosnell, *Truman's Crises: A Biography of Harry S. Truman* (Greenwood, Westport, Conn.: 1980), ch. 34: civil rights 444, 446–47, tax hike 440–41, Taft–Hartley 443, education 443, 445, health insurance 443–44, agriculture 442–43, 445, omnibus housing 443–44, minimum wage 445, social security 445, 449, CVA 445, 448–49, middle-income housing 445, 448, rent control 441, displaced persons 445, executive reorganization 441, trade 441.

Donald R. McCoy, *The Presidency of Harry S. Truman* (Lawrence: University Press of Kansas, 1984), ch. 8: civil rights 166, 167–68, tax hike 176, 178–79, Taft–Hartley 166, 173–74, education 166, 182–83, health insurance 166, 173, agriculture 166, 183–85, omnibus housing 166, 172, minimum wage 166, 175, social security 166, 175, CVA 175, rent control 166, 172, executive reorganization 167, trade 166.

Richard E. Neustadt, "Congress and the Fair Deal: A Legislative Balance Sheet," pp. 15–42 in Alonzo L. Hamby (ed.), *Harry S. Truman and the Fair Deal* (Lexington, Mass.: D. C. Heath, 1974): civil rights 29, 30, tax hike 19, Taft–Hartley 29, 30–31, education 29, health insurance 29–30, agriculture 31–32, omnibus housing 29, minimum wage 29, social security 29, middle-income housing 32, displaced persons 29.

David B. Truman, *The Congressional Party: A Case Study* (New York: John Wiley and Sons, 1959), ch. 2: civil rights 19, 24, 29–30, 33–35, Taft–Hartley 19–24, 29, education 19–21, health insurance 19, 22–23, agriculture 19, 24, 27, 29, housing 19, 20, 23–24, minimum wage 19, 25–26, social security 19, 27, 35, CVA 19, 32, middle-income housing 28–31, rent control 19–20, 28–29, 34, displaced persons 28–29, 32, executive reorganization 19, trade 19, 26, Defense Department 22.

Harry S. Truman, *Memoirs*, vol. 2, *Years of Trial and Hope* (Garden City, N.Y.: Doubleday, 1956), pp. 17–24, 53, 59, 179–84, 262–68, 283–84: civil rights 179–84, health insurance 17–24, agriculture 262–68, Defense Department 53.

William Frank Zornow, *America at Mid-Century*, vol. 1, *The Truman Administration* (Cleveland: Howard Allen, 1959), ch. 7: civil rights 114–15, tax hike 119–21, Taft–Hartley 117, education 117, health insurance 117, agriculture 116, omnibus housing 115, minimum wage 117, social security 115, CVA 117, middle-income housing 116, rent control 115–16, displaced persons 116, executive reorganization 116, trade 118, Defense Department 118.

Not included:
- —anti-inflation controls: Gosnell 439, Neustadt 19
- —basing point: Gosnell 445, D. B. Truman 27–28
- —Clayton Act: Ferrell 288, McCoy 181–82, Neustadt 29, D. B. Truman 40
- —National Science Foundation: Gosnell 445, Neustadt 29, D. B. Truman 31
- —small business help: Gosnell 445, Neustadt 32–33
- —St. Lawrence Seaway: Gosnell 443–44, 445, Zornow 117

EISENHOWER: 1953–54

Stephen E. Ambrose, *Eisenhower*, vol. 2, *The President* (New York: Simon and Schuster, 1984), pp. 48, 85–86, 115–18, 155–60, 199–202: profits tax 85–86, tax code 158, housing 158, social security 48, 115, 158, health insurance 157, 199, agriculture 159–60, Taft–Hartley 48, 116–18, 158, atomic energy 157, St. Lawrence 158, post office 116, 200, displaced persons 48, 115–16, Hawaii 157, trade 48, 155–56, 201–02.

Robert J. Donovan, *Eisenhower: The Inside Story* (New York: Harper and Brothers, 1956), pp. 60–61, 65, 76–78, 143, 145, 172–77, 224–29, 273–75: profits tax 60–61, tidelands 75, tax code 274–

75, housing 143, 174, 224, 228, 274, social security 143, 172–74, 228, 274, health insurance 228, 273, 275, agriculture 228, 273, 274, Taft–Hartley 143, 175–76, 228, 275, St. Lawrence 65, 76–78, 143, 274, Hawaii 143, 275, trade 229, 274.

Dwight D. Eisenhower, *Mandate for Change, 1953–1956* (Garden City, N.Y.: Doubleday, 1963), chs. 8, 12, 15: profits tax 201–3, tidelands 195, 203–8, 218, tax code 297–98, 299, 303, housing 295, 303, social security 295, 303, health insurance 295, 303, agriculture 287–90, 294, 299, 300, 303, Taft–Hartley 195–99, 291–92, 294, 303, atomic energy 294, 303, St. Lawrence 287, 301–3, post office 195, 196, 199–201, 300, 303, displaced persons 216–18, Hawaii 195, 218, 295, 303, Colorado River 388, trade 195–96, 208–11, 292–94, 299, 303.

Chester J. Pach, Jr., and Elmo Richardson, *The Presidency of Dwight D. Eisenhower* (Lawrence: University Press of Kansas, 1991), pp. 53–58: profits tax 53, tidelands 56, tax code 54, housing 56, social security 56, health insurance 56, agriculture 55, atomic energy 56, St. Lawrence 58, Hawaii 58, Colorado River 56–57.

Merlo J. Pusey, *Eisenhower the President* (New York: Macmillan, 1956), ch. 11: profits tax 210, tidelands 219, 220–23, tax code 217, 244, housing 217, 226–27, social security 211, 217, 227–28, health insurance 208, 229–30, agriculture 217, 223–25, Taft–Hartley 217, 230–31, St. Lawrence 219, 220, Hawaii 207–8, Colorado River 220, trade 217, 245–47.

Gary W. Reichard, *The Reaffirmation of Republicanism: Eisenhower and the Eighty-Third Congress* (Knoxville: University of Tennessee Press, 1975), chs. 5–7: profits tax 103–7, tidelands 149–53, tax code 110–12, housing 123–29, social security 129–33, health insurance 133–35, agriculture 138–42, Taft–Hartley 143–46, atomic energy 153–57, 159–63, St. Lawrence 164–74, displaced persons 85–87, trade 77–84.

Zornow, *America at Mid-Century*, vol. 2, *The Eisenhower Administration*, ch. 4: profits tax 44, tidelands 44–45, tax code 46–47, housing 46, 47–48, social security 46, 47, health insurance 46, 48, agriculture 46, 47, Taft–Hartley 45, 46, 48, atomic energy 46, 47, St. Lawrence 45, 46, 48, post office 45, displaced persons 45, Hawaii 45, 48, trade 45.

Not included:
- —18-year-old vote: Ambrose 158, Eisenhower 295, 303
- —Communism/disloyalty: Ambrose 157, Eisenhower 287, 303
- —Hells Canyon: Pach and Richardson 57, Pusey 220, Reichard 176–77
- —highways: Ambrose 159, Eisenhower 303
- —unemployment insurance: Eisenhower 303, Pusey 228, Zornow 46

EISENHOWER: 1957–58

Ambrose, *Eisenhower*, vol. 2, *The President*, 388–91, 406–7, 412–13, 458–59: budget 388–91, civil rights 406–7, 412–13, NDEA 459, Defense Department 458, NASA 458–59.

Dwight D. Eisenhower, *Waging Peace, 1956–1961* (New York: Doubleday, 1965), chs. 5, 6, 10, pp. 323–25: budget 127–32, civil rights 153–62, NDEA 239, 242–43, Alaska 323–25, Defense Department 239, 244–53, school construction 132, 138–40, 242, NASA 239, 257, Hawaii 323–25.

Rowland Evans and Robert Novak, *Lyndon B. Johnson: The Exercise of Power* (New York: New American Library, 1966), chs. 7–9: budget 181–84, civil rights ch. 7, Defense Department 141–42, trade 142.

Ivan Hinderaker, "The Eisenhower Administration: The Last Years," ch. 4 in Jack W. Peltason (ed.), *American Government Annual, 1959–60* (New York: Henry Holt, 1959): budget 88, civil rights 88, Defense Department 82–84, NASA 84, trade 84–87.

Pach and Richardson, *Presidency of Eisenhower*, chs. 6, 7: budget 167–69, civil rights 147–48, agriculture 177, NDEA 172, 178, Alaska 180, Defense Department 178–79, NASA 179–80.

Zornow, *America at Mid-Century*, vol. 2, *The Eisenhower Adminis-tration*, ch. 8: budget 116, 119, civil rights 116–17, agriculture 129–30, NDEA 129, Alaska 119, 129, Defense Department 127, 128, trade 119, 127, Hawaii 119, 129.

Not included: no entries

KENNEDY: 1961–62

Robert Dallek, *An Unfinished Life: John F. Kennedy, 1917–1963* (Boston: Little, Brown, 2003), chs. 10, 11, 14, 15: unemployment benefits 379, depressed areas 334, 378–79, education 379, 495, Medicare 379, 495–96, minimum wage 334, 379, housing 334, 379, HUD 377–78, agriculture 379, social security 334, 379, trade 510, tax credit 378.

James M. Giglio, *The Presidency of John F. Kennedy* (Lawrence: University Press of Kansas, 2006), chs. 5–7: unemployment ben-efits 128, depressed areas, 99, 105–6, 128, education 99, 103–4, 122, Medicare, 99, 104–5, 119, 122, minimum wage, 99, 102–3, 119, 128, housing, 99, 106, 128, HUD, 106–7, 122, manpower retraining, 108, agriculture 110–14, 122, social security 107, 128, trade 107–8, 141, tax credit 136, drugs 108, civil rights, 122, 186–87.

Marian D. Irish, "The Kennedy Administration—Appraisal at the Halfway Mark," ch. 2 in Jack W. Peltason (ed.), *American Government Annual, 1963–1964* (New York: Holt, Rinehart and Winston, 1963): unemployment benefits 42, 43, depressed areas, 412, education 41, 43, 57, Medicare 42, 43, 57, minimum wage 42, housing, 42, HUD 42, 43, 57, manpower retraining 43, agriculture, 42–43, 57, social security 42, trade 43, 47–48, Comsat 43.

Louis W. Koenig, "Kennedy and the 87th Congress," ch. 5 in Ivan Hinderaker (ed.), *American Government Annual, 1962–1963* (New York: Holt, Rinehart and Winston, 1962): unemployment benefits 76, depressed areas 73, 74, education 73, 74, 78–80, Medicare 73, 74, 78, minimum wage 73, 74–75, housing 73, 75–76, social security 73, 76.

Allen J. Matusow, *The Unraveling of America: A History of Liberalism in the 1960s* (New York: Harper and Row, 1984), chs. 2–4: depressed areas, 97, 100–101, education 97, 105–7, Medicare 97, minimum wage 97, 98–99, housing 97, 102–3, manpower retraining 97, 103–4, trade 35–36, tax credit 35, Comsat 37, drugs 37–38, civil rights 67.

Michael O'Brien, *John F. Kennedy: A Biography* (New York: St. Martin's, 2005), chs. 28, 29, 31: depressed areas 580–81, education 565–67, Medicare 568, 583, minimum wage 564–65, manpower retraining 580–81, trade 580–81, 640, tax credit 641, Comsat 580–81, 641, drugs 580–81, civil rights 599.

Herbert S. Parmet, *JFK: The Presidency of John F. Kennedy* (New York: Dial Press, 1983), pp. 94–97, 205–9, 257: depressed areas 97, 206, education 97, 205, 206, Medicare 97, 206, 208, minimum wage 97, 206, housing 97, 206, HUD 206, manpower retraining 206, agriculture 206, social security 97, trade 206, 208, 209, tax credit 94, 209, Comsat 208, civil rights 206, 257.

Theodore C. Sorensen, *Kennedy* (New York: Harper and Row, 1965), chs. 14, 16, pp. 474–75, 481–82: unemployment benefits 397, depressed areas 397, 404, education 357–62, Medicare 342–44, minimum wage 352, 397, housing 397, HUD 481–82, manpower retraining 404, agriculture 342, 397, 402–3, social security 397, trade 410–12, tax credit 401–2, drugs 352–53, civil rights 474–75.

Not included:
   —college aid: Dallek 379, Irish 42, 43, O'Brien 565
   —juvenile delinquency: Giglio 107, 119, Matusow 107, 110
   —tax reform: Dallek 379, Giglio 122, Irish 43, O'Brien 580–81
   —water pollution: Dallek 379, Giglio 107, Parmet 97

JOHNSON: 1965–66

Vaughn Davis Bornet, *The Presidency of Lyndon B. Johnson* (Lawrence: University Press of Kansas, 1983), chs. 6, 10: ESEA 121–24, 227, Medicare 127–28, 222, VRA 129, 221, higher education 122, 124–27, highway beautification 139, 142, 143, arts and humanities 122, heart, cancer, stroke 122, Taft–Hartley 245, agriculture 246, HUD 122, 243, water quality 141, immigration 245, Department of Transportation 134, 243, model cities 134, 235–36, open housing 134, 231.

Robert Dallek, *Flawed Giant: Lyndon Johnson and His Times, 1961–1973* (New York: Oxford University Press, 1998), chs. 4, 6: ESEA 192, 195–203, Medicare 192, 203–11, VRA 211–21, antipoverty 227, highway beautification 229, 230, arts and humanities 230, Appalachia 192, HUD 228, water quality 229–30, rent supplements 228–29, immigration 192, 227–28, Department of Transportation 300, 313–16, model cities 300, 313, 317–22, open housing 300, 324–27.

Evans and Novak, *Lyndon B. Johnson*, chs. 22, 25: ESEA 491–92, 498, Medicare 491, 492, 498, VRA 493–97, Appalachia 498, Taft–Hartley 500, 559, 572, omnibus housing 493, agriculture 493, HUD 493, rent supplements 500, 559, 561, immigration 492–93, Department of Transportation 559, model cities 559, open housing 559, D.C. home rule 500, 559, 561.

Lyndon Baines Johnson, *Vantage Point: Perspectives of the Presidency, 1963–1969* (New York: Holt, Rinehart and Winston, 1971), chs. 7, 9, 15: ESEA 206–12, 322–23, Medicare 212–19, 323, VRA 161–66, 323, antipoverty 220–21, higher education 219, heart, cancer, stroke 220, HUD 329, water quality 337–38, Department of Transportation 329, model cities 330, open housing 176–77, D.C. home rule 323.

Matusow, *Unraveling of America*, chs. 6–8: ESEA 153, 221–23, Medicare 153, 226–27, VRA 153, 181, 184–87, immigration 202, open housing 206–7.

Alfred Steinberg, *Sam Johnson's Boy: A Close-up of the President from Texas* (New York: Macmillan, 1968), chs. 70, 71: ESEA, 698, 705, 716, Medicare 698, 705, 708–10, 716, VRA 705, 706–8, 716–17, antipoverty 698, higher education 717, highway beautification 706, 711–14, arts and humanities 698, Appalachia 705, Taft–Hartley 719, omnibus housing 710–11, agriculture 710, HUD 698, 706, immigration 698, 706, 717, model cities 722.

Irwin Unger and Debi Unger, *LBJ: A Life* (New York: John Wiley and Sons, 1999), chs. 17, 18: ESEA 337, 338, 343–47, Medicare 338, 362–67, VRA 355–59, higher education 337, 338, 381–82, highway beautification 337, 343, 380–81, arts and humanities 337, 374–76, heart, cancer, stroke 337, 338, Appalachia 339, Taft–Hartley 367–68, 384, omnibus housing 362, 390–91, HUD 337, 343, 374, water quality 339–40, 343, 376–77, rent supplements 367, 384, 390–91, immigration 338–39, 377–79, Department of Transportation 401, model cities 380, 402–4, open housing 380, 394–95, D.C. home rule 367, 384.

Randall B. Woods, *LBJ: Architect of American Ambition* (New York: Free Press, 2006), chs. 27, 28, 31–33: ESEA 558, 562, 563–67, 667, Medicare 558, 561, 562, 568–73, 667, VRA 558, 561, 562, 583–87, antipoverty 562, 649–51, 652, 667, 686, higher education 567–68, highway beautification 664, 665, 667, arts and humanities 659, 667, heart, cancer, stroke 667, Appalachia 563, 667, Taft–Hartley 563, 668, 686, HUD 653, 667, water quality 663, immigration 558, 561, 562, 660–61, Department of Transportation 688–89, model cities 686, 690–92, open housing 686, 697–99.

Not included:
- —four-year House terms: Dallek 300, Evans and Novak 557–58, 572, Woods 686
- —clean air 1965: Bornet 141, Dallek 65, 229–30, Unger 377, Steinberg 698
- —clean air 1966: Evans and Novak 559, Woods 663
- —excise tax cut: Dallek 194, Steinberg 698, 706
- —minimum wage: Unger 401, Woods 687, Steinberg 722

—Teacher Corps funding: Evans and Novak 559, Unger 390–91

—truth in packaging: Dallek 300, 316, Unger 391

—water quality 1966: Evans and Novak 559, Woods 663, 686

NIXON: 1969–70

Stephen E. Ambrose, *Nixon*, vol. 2, *The Triumph of a Politician, 1962–1972* (New York: Simon and Schuster, 1989), chs. 12–18: FAP 268–69, 291–94, 314–15, 366–67, 391, 407, tax reform 290–91, revenue sharing 297, 328, SST 397–98, D.C. crime 261.

Rowland Evans, Jr., and Robert Novak, *Nixon in the White House: The Frustration of Power* (New York: Random House, 1971), chs. 3, 5, 7, 8, 12: FAP 213, 223–33, 376, tax reform 131, 186, 194–201, 211–12, 214–23, revenue sharing 380, SST 53, 376, postal service 131, D.C. crime 56–57.

Michael A. Genovese, *The Nixon Presidency: Power and Politics in Turbulent Times* (New York: Greenwood, 1990), ch. 3: FAP 76, 78–80, 94, revenue sharing 77–78, 94, drugs 89–90, D.C. crime 89.

John Robert Greene, *The Limits of Power: The Nixon and Ford Administrations* (Bloomington: Indiana University Press, 1992), chs. 2, 3: FAP 47–51, 71, revenue sharing 62–63, SST 71.

Richard M. Nixon, *The Memoirs of Richard Nixon* (New York: Grosset and Dunlap, 1978), pp. 414–15, 424–28, 430, 521, 670–71: FAP 415, 424–28, 670–71, tax reform 414, 521, 670, revenue sharing 671, SST 430, postal service 414, drugs 414, 671.

A. James Reichley, *Conservatives in an Age of Change: The Nixon and Ford Administrations* (Washington, D.C.: Brookings, 1981), chs. 5, 7, 8, 10: FAP 90, 97, ch. 7, 157, tax reform 90–91, 208–11, revenue sharing 97, 138, 154–57, SST 87, 211–12.

Melvin Small, *The Presidency of Richard Nixon* (Lawrence: University Press of Kansas, 1999), chs. 6, 7: FAP 185–89, tax reform 156,

205, revenue sharing 188, 194–95, postal reform 195–96, DC crime 159.

Not included:
—voting rights: Ambrose 370, Evans and Novak 129–31, Small 166

NIXON: 1973–74

Stephen Ambrose, *Nixon*, vol. 3, *Ruin and Recovery, 1973–1990* (New York: Simon and Schuster, 1991), chs. 1, 3, 7–9, 11–13: 1973 budget 13–14, 22, 61–63, trade 170–72, emergency powers 279, energy department 187, Alaska pipeline 218, 221, 266, 278, energy R&D 187, 221, 266, natural gas deregulation 187, 218, 221, 303, speed limits 266, 279, 291, health insurance 304, 318, 340.

Genovese, *Nixon Presidency*: trade 65–66.

Allen J. Matusow, *Nixon's Economy: Booms, Busts, Dollars, and Votes* (Lawrence: University Press of Kansas, 1998), 1973 budget 216–19, emergency powers 262, 263, Alaska pipeline 252, 263, daylight savings 262, 263, natural gas deregulation 252, speed limits 262, 263.

Nixon, *Memoirs*, pp. 764–68, 979–80, 982–86: 1973 budget 764–66, emergency powers 984, energy department 983, Alaska pipeline 984, 985, daylight savings 984–85, energy R&D 983, natural gas deregulation 983, 984, speed limits 983–85, health insurance 979.

Reichley, *Conservatives in an Age of Change*, chs. 10, 11: 1973 budget 227–28, 246.

Small, *Presidency of Nixon*, pp. 147–48, chs. 6, 7: trade 147–48, cabinet department 202, Alaska pipeline 202, daylight savings 202, energy R&D 202, natural gas deregulation 202, speed limits 202, health insurance 192.

Not included:
—deepwater ports: Ambrose 187, Nixon 984
—environmental standards (relaxation of): Ambrose 221, 266, Matusow 252, 262
—surface mining: Ambrose 187, 221, Nixon 984

CARTER: 1977–78

Peter G. Bourne, *Jimmy Carter: A Comprehensive Biography from Plains to Presidency* (New York: Scribner, 1997), chs. 22, 25: reorganization 373, 375, emergency natural gas 375–76, water projects 373, 415, 419, omnibus energy 373, 375–77, 416, CPA 373, ethics 373, economic stimulus 374, 419, welfare reform 373, 417–18, 420, agriculture 419, Department of Energy 373, 377, social security 373, 419, hospital costs 373, airline deregulation 418.

Jimmy Carter, *Keeping Faith: Memoirs of a President* (Fayetteville: University of Arkansas Press, 1995), pp. 69–113: reorganization 73, 74–75, 92, emergency natural gas 98, water projects 82–84, omnibus energy 73, 92, 96–112, ethics 92, economic stimulus 79, 82, tax reform 88–89, 113, welfare reform 88, Department of Energy 73, 103, hospital costs 89–90, 92, airline deregulation 73, 93, 113, civil service 73, 92, 113, Department of Education 73, 80–81.

John Dumbrell, *The Carter Presidency: A Re-Evaluation* (New York: St. Martin's), 1993, chs. 1–4: reorganization 4, 45, water projects 4, 40–41, omnibus energy 4, 5, 40, 41, 43, 45, 53, CPA 5, 44, ethics 4, 54–55, economic stimulus 4, tax reform 4, 44, welfare reform 4, 44, Department of Energy 4, hospital costs 4, 43, 53, airline deregulation 41, civil service 5, 41, 54–55, Department of Education 53.

Garland A. Haas, *Jimmy Carter and the Politics of Frustration* (Jefferson, N.C.: McFarland, 1992), ch. 2: water projects 75–77, 90, omnibus energy 67–71, CPA 74, economic stimulus 89–90, tax

reform 92–93, welfare reform 80, Department of Energy 70, social security 73, hospital costs 81, airline deregulation 71–72, civil service 73.

Haynes Johnson, *In the Absence of Power* (New York: Viking, 1980), chs. 1, 5–7: reorganization 21, 155, water projects 158–60, omnibus energy 21, 153, 185–93, 221–25, 227, 231, 233, 292–93, CPA 233–41, 290, ethics 21, economic stimulus 161, tax reform 153, 290, welfare reform 152–53, 290, civil service 193–98, 233, 250–55, 293.

Burton I. Kaufman, *The Presidency of James Earl Carter, Jr.* (Lawrence: University Press of Kansas, 1993), chs. 1, 3, 5, 6, 8: reorganization 28, 32, emergency natural gas 32–33, water projects 28, 30–31, 51–52, omnibus energy 2, 28, 33–35, 57–58, 59, 66–68, 81, 107–9, CPA 28, 32, 66, ethics 28, economic stimulus 28, 29, 31, 52, tax reform 58–59, 81, 100, 101–2, 109, welfare reform 28, 52–55, 59, 102, agriculture 55–57, 73, Department of Energy 28, 57, social security 28, 72, 81, hospital costs 28, 100–1, civil service 2, 101.

Not included:
    —housing and community development: Bourne 418–19, 420, Dumbrell 99, Haas 73, Kaufman 28, 74
    —strip mining: Bourne 418, Carter 92, 112

REAGAN: 1981–82

Nigel Ashford, "The Conservative Agenda and the Reagan Presidency," ch. 9 in Joseph Hogan (ed.), *The Reagan Years: The Record in Presidential Leadership* (New York: Manchester University Press, 1990): ERTA 192, OBRA 193–94, federalism 195, S&Ls 198, balance budget 196, school prayer 210, tuition tax credits 210, TEFRA 193, abortion 211.

Lou Cannon, *President Reagan: The Role of a Lifetime* (New York: Public Affairs, 2000), chs. 7, 10, 12, 16, 17, 22: ERTA 93, 150, 198–99, 221, 236, 238, 438–39, OBRA 93, 150, 198–99, 203–4,

219–20, S&Ls 238, 740–42, IRS rules 459–61, school prayer 730, TEFRA 153, 198, abortion 729–30.

Robert Dallek, *Ronald Reagan: The Politics of Symbolism* (Cambridge: Harvard University Press, 1984), chs. 3, 4: ERTA 65–69, OBRA 65–68, federalism 100–1, 121–23, balance budget 95, 105–6, 108, IRS rules 79–80, school prayer 95, 123–25, tuition tax credits 123–25, school busing 123–25, TEFRA 108–11, 119, abortion 123–25.

John Ehrman, *The Eighties: America in the Age of Reagan* (New Haven: Yale University Press, 2005), ch. 2: ERTA 54–55, OBRA 54–55, TEFRA 57–58, 61.

David Mervin, *Ronald Reagan and the American Presidency* (New York: Longman, 1990), ch. 5: ERTA 110–13, 120, 123–24, OBRA 106–10, 112, 116–17, 123–24, school prayer 123, school busing 123, abortion 123.

William E. Pemberton, *Exit with Honor: The Life and Presidency of Ronald Reagan* (Armonk, N.Y.: M. E. Sharpe, 1997), chs. 5, 7: ERTA 95–104, OBRA 95–104, S&Ls 130, TEFRA 104, 127–28.

Ronald Reagan, *An American Life* (New York: Simon and Schuster, 1990), chs. 37, 43, 46, 47, 50–52, epilogue: ERTA 231–33, 234, 265, 279, 284–88, 298, 311, 315, 324, 333, 335, 349, OBRA 234, 265, 279, 284–86, 298, balanced budget 320, 321, 323, 337–38, 726, TEFRA 314–15, 317–22 passim.

Michael Schaller, *Reckoning with Reagan: America and Its President in the 1980s* (New York: Oxford University Press, 1992), chs. 2–4: ERTA 35, 41–46, 57, OBRA 35, 41–46, S&Ls 35, 108–10, balance budget 39, 47, school prayer 35, 39, school busing 39, TEFRA 47, abortion 35, 39, 57, 92, 95.

Jules Tygiel, *Ronald Reagan and the Triumph of American Conservatism* (New York: Pearson Longman, 2004), ch. 8: ERTA 124–27, OBRA 125–27, S&Ls 134–35, TEFRA 134, abortion 134.

Not included: no entries

REAGAN: 1987–88

Ashford, "The Conservative Agenda": TRA 192–93.

Cannon, *President Reagan*, chs. 12, 18: TRA 236, 238, 488–89, 499–500.

Ehrman, *The Eighties*, ch. 4: TRA 133–35.

Mervin, *Ronald Reagan*, ch. 6: TRA 133–40.

Pemberton, *Exit with Honor*, ch. 7: TRA 144–46.

Reagan, *An American Life*, chs. 51, 52, 66, 69, epilogue: TRA 332, 333–35, 349, 536, agriculture 343–45, balanced budget 337–38, 726.

Schaller, *Reckoning with Reagan*, ch. 2: TRA 64

Tygiel, *Ronald Reagan*, ch. 10: TRA 172

Not included: no entries

BUSH 41: 1989–90

Ryan J. Barilleaux and Mark J. Rozell, *Power and Prudence: The Presidency of George H. W. Bush* (College Station: Texas A&M Press, 2004), ch. 2: flag burning 33, clean air 25, education 23, 24–25, drugs 25, deficit reduction 33–35.

Michael Duffy and Dan Goodgame, *Marching in Place: The Status Quo Presidency of George Bush* (New York: Simon and Schuster, 1992), ch. 3, 4, 8, 9: disabilities 79, 80, 86, 99–100, clean air 79, 80, 86, 87, S&Ls bailout 58, capital gains 88, 98, 217, drugs 80, 86, 88, 103–4, deficit reduction 58, 80, 81–82, 220–21, 233–37.

John Robert Greene, *The Presidency of George Bush* (Lawrence: University Press of Kansas, 2000), chs. 5, 6: flag burning 63–64, disabilities 74–75, clean air 74–75, 76–78, S&Ls bailout 81–83, education 68–70, capital gains 80, 81, drugs 72–74, deficit reduction 83–88.

David Mervin, *George Bush and the Guardianship Presidency* (New York: St. Martin's, 1996), chs. 4, 6, 9: disabilities 90, 93, 98–101, 110, 205, clean air 93, 94–98, 110, 205, S&Ls bailout 92, education 90, 205, capital gains 149–51, drugs 90, deficit reduction 127–57.

Herbert S. Parmet, *George Bush: The Life of a Lone Star Yankee* (New York: Scribner, 1997), chs. 19–21: flag burning 400–401, 402–4, disabilities 424–25, clean air 421, S&Ls bailout 382, 394–96, 430, 438–40, capital gains 421, 470, deficit reduction 381–82, 429–35, 468–71.

Paul J. Quirk, "Domestic Policy: Divided Government and Co-operative Presidential Leadership," ch. 3 in Colin Campbell and Bert A. Rockman (eds.), *The Bush Presidency: First Appraisals* (Chatham, N.J.: Chatham House, 1991): clean air 74, 85–87, S&Ls bailout 69, 74, education 73, 75, 82–83, capital gains 76, 78, drugs 73, 75, 83–84, deficit reduction 73, 76–82.

Barbara Sinclair, "Governing Unheroically (and Sometimes Unappetizingly): Bush and the 101st Congress," ch. 6 in Campbell and Rockman (eds.), *The Bush Presidency*: disabilities 171, clean air 160, 169, 171, S&Ls bailout 160, education 160, 171, capital gains 166, drugs 160, deficit reduction 174–81.

Robert J. Thompson and Carmine Scavo, "The Home Front: Domestic Policy in the Bush Years," ch. 9 in Ryan J. Barilleaux and Mary E. Stuckey (eds.), *Leadership and the Bush Presidency: Prudence or Drift in an Era of Change?* (Westport, Conn.: Praeger, 1992): education 150, 156–61, drugs 152–56, deficit reduction 151.

Not included:
  —child care: Barilleaux and Rozell, 24, Mervin 205, Sinclair 160, 169–70, 171

CLINTON: 1993–94

William C. Berman, *From the Center to the Edge: The Politics and Policies of the Clinton Presidency* (Lanham, Md.: Rowman and Littlefield, 2001), ch. 2: budget 20–21, 23–26, 32, 41, stimulus 24, 25, family leave 21, 32, motor voter 32, EITC 24, 25, 26, 31, Brady bill 28–29, 32, NAFTA 29–30, 32, 41, welfare reform 39, health care 26–28, 32–33, 39, 40, lobbying 41, campaign finance 41, crime 39–40, GATT 30.

Bill Clinton, *My Life* (New York: Vintage, 2004), chs. 29, 31–42: budget 452, 458–63, 488, 491–92, 493–96, 496–97, 513, 522, 525, 530, 533–38, 556, stimulus 461, 499–500, 514, family leave 490, 496, 513, 556, motor voter 513, 556, EITC 494, 513, 556, 557, AmeriCorps 496, 513, 547, 556, Brady bill 496, 557–58, NAFTA 540, 546–47, 557, welfare reform 576, 602, 621, Goals 2000, 496, 576, 590, health care 482–83, 492, 499, 514, 539–40, 547, 548–49, 555–56, 567, 576–78, 582, 594–95, 596, 601–2, 610, 612, 620–21, lobbying 496, campaign finance 496, crime 496, 556, 576, 582, 595–96, 610–12, GATT 636.

Richard E. Cohen, *Changing Course in Washington: Clinton and the New Congress* (New York: Macmillan, 1994), chs. 3–6, 8–10: budget 49, 66–67, 70–86, 93–100, 111–15, 123–25, 136–42, 180–81, 192–200, 203–12, stimulus 80, 85, 95–96, 124, 125–30, family leave 69–70, motor voter 122, EITC 80, AmeriCorps 191, 201, NAFTA 191, 203, 222, health care 49, 222, 223–26, lobbying 174–75, campaign finance 106–7, 133, 174–75, 191, crime 222.

Michael Foley, "Clinton and Congress," ch. 2 in Paul Herrnson and Dilys M. Hill (eds.), *The Clinton Presidency: The First Term, 1992–96* (New York: St. Martin's, 1999): budget 27, 29–31, stimulus 27–29, 33, family leave 25–26, 32, motor voter 25–26, 32–33, Brady bill 33, NAFTA 32, health care 31–32, 33, lobbying 32, campaign finance 32, 33, crime 33, GATT 33.

Nigel Hamilton, *Bill Clinton: Mastering the Presidency* (New York: Public Affairs, 2007), chs. 2, 6, 9, 12–14, 19–21, 25, 26, 30, 37, 44,

45: budget 17–22, 55, 80–82, 93–97, 107–8, 123, 159–72, 309, stimulus 55–56, 100, 103, 105, 106, 117, family leave 174, 309, AmeriCorps 174, 309, Brady bill 309, NAFTA 176–80, 228–30, 309, health care 56–62, 99–100, 173–74, 181–84, 219–27, 261–66, 301–4, crime 302–3, 309, GATT 365, 369.

John F. Harris, *The Survivor: Bill Clinton in the White House* (New York: Random House, 2005), chs. 1, 2, 7, 8, 10, 22: budget 4–6, 18–25, 29–30, 77, 78, 86–93, stimulus 29, 84–86, family leave 17, EITC 23, 84, 87, AmeriCorps 94, NAFTA 95–96, 101, welfare reform 93–94, health care 20, 25, 110–19.

Joe Klein, *The Natural: The Misunderstood Presidency of Bill Clinton* (New York: Doubleday, 2002), chs. 2, 3, 5: budget 48–53, 54–55, stimulus 57, EITC 55–57, AmeriCorps 55, NAFTA 57–58, 79–81, health care 117, 119–27.

Paul J. Quirk and Joseph Hinchliffe, "Domestic Policy: The Trials of a Centrist Democrat," ch. 9 in Colin Campbell and Bert A. Rockman (eds.), *The Clinton Presidency: First Appraisals* (Chatham, N.J.: Chatham House, 1996): budget 268–71, 272–73, 283, stimulus 269, 271–72, family leave 267, 283, motor voter 267, 283, AmeriCorps 267, 283, Brady bill 267–68, 283, welfare reform 279–81, 283, health care 274–77, 283, crime 277–79, 283.

Barbara Sinclair, "Trying to Govern Positively in a Negative Era: Clinton and the 103rd Congress," ch. 3 in Campbell and Rockman (eds.), *The Clinton Presidency*: budget 88, 101–3, 104–9, 120, stimulus 88, 102, 103–4, 118, family leave 100, 120, motor voter 100, 118, 120, EITC 120, AmeriCorps 118, 120, Brady bill 118, 120, NAFTA 88, 109–11, 113, 120, welfare reform 88, Goals 2000 120, health care 88, 111–18, 120–21, lobbying 119, campaign finance 119, crime 88, 116, 119, 120, GATT 119.

Martin Walker, *Clinton: The President They Deserve* (London: Vintage, 1997), chs. 7, 8, 10, 13, 14: budget 172–74, 181–83, 186–87, 307–9, 312–15, 318, stimulus 181, 187–88, 191, 307, 309, 314, family leave 180, 318, motor voter 318, EITC 182, 315, 318, AmeriCorps 185, NAFTA 224, 285–86, 288, 291–94, 316–17,

318, welfare reform 183–84, 185, 321, Goals 2000 321–22, 327, health care 176, 183, 185, 214–15, 218–24, 316–17, 319–20, 322, 325, 328, lobbying 328, campaign finance 328, crime 318, 322, 324–25, 327, GATT 285–86, 288, 297–98.

Not included:
—abortion: Cohen 201, Sinclair 120
—college loans: Clinton 513, 556, Cohen 201, Sinclair 120
—education 1994: Clinton 623–24, Sinclair 119, 120
—mining law: Foley 32, Walker 328
—safe drinking water: Foley 32, Sinclair 119
—Superfund: Sinclair 119, Walker 328
—telecommunications: Foley 32, Sinclair 119, Walker 328

CLINTON: 1997–98

Berman, *From the Center to the Edge*, ch. 4: balanced budget 73, 74–75, 87–88, CHIP 74, teachers 81, 87–88, trade 74, 77–78, 79, social security 80, 87, minimum wage 81, immigrant aid 74–75, child care 79, 81, campaign finance 78.

Clinton, *My Life*, chs. 40, 47–49: balance budget 743, 744, 745, 754–55, 760–61, 770, 825, CHIP 620, 744, 745, 754, 755, 761, 770, 825, higher education 743–44, 745, 754, 755, 770, teachers 743, 777, 814, 820, 822, 825, trade 744, 769, social security 777–78, 814, 820, 822, minimum wage 813, 814, 820, 822, patients 772, 777, 798, 814, 820, 822, immigrant aid 743, 754, 761, child care 743, 771, 777, campaign finance 741, 743, 778–79, 820.

Harris, *The Survivor*, chs. 24, 25, 30, 31, 33: balanced budget 253, 261–63, trade 298, social security 299, 311, minimum wage 311, patients 311, 325, immigrant aid 253.

Klein, *The Natural*, prologue, ch. 6: balance budget 158–61, CHIP 159–60, higher education 159, trade 16, social security 7, 18–19, immigrant aid 160.

Paul J. Quirk and William Cunion, "Clinton's Domestic Policy: The Lessons of a 'New Democrat,'" ch. 9 in Colin Campbell and Bert A. Rockman (eds.), *The Clinton Legacy* (New York: Chatham House, 2000): balanced budget 212, 215, CHIP 212, 218, higher education 212, teachers 212, social security 213.

Not included:
—tobacco regulation: Clinton 820, Harris 311

BUSH 43: 2001–2

Peri Arnold, "One President, Two Presidencies: George W. Bush in Peace and War," ch. 7 in Steven E. Schier (ed.), *High Risk and Ambition: The Presidency of George W. Bush* (Pittsburgh: University of Pittsburgh Press, 2004): tax cut 148–49, education 148, 149–50, energy 150, Patriot Act 155–56, Homeland Security Department 156–57.

John P. Burke, *Becoming President: The Bush Transition, 2000–2003* (Boulder, Colo.: Lynne Rienner, 2004), chs. 3–8: tax cut 54, 60, 61, 91, 121–22, 123, 131, 132, 133, 135, 136–38, education 54, 57–59, 60, 88, 123, 131, 132, 133, 135, 138–41, 189, 223, faith-based 54, 60–61, 82, 122, 123, 132, 133, 141–45, 189, energy 98, 132, 148–49, trade 122, 223, Medicare 131–32, 146–47, Patriot Act 185–86, 223, airline security 185, 223, Homeland Security Department 186–88, 223.

Robert Draper, *Dead Certain: The Presidency of George W. Bush* (New York: Free Press, 2007), chs. 5–7: tax cut 117, 118–20, 127, education 113–18, 127, 169, faith-based 127, Medicare 127, stimulus 166, Patriot Act 166, airline security 166, 169, rebuild New York City 127, Homeland Security Department 170–72.

John C. Fortier and Norman J. Ornstein, "President Bush: Legislative Strategist," ch. 6 in Fred I. Greenstein (ed.), *The George W. Bush Presidency: An Early Assessment* (Baltimore: Johns Hopkins University Press, 2003): tax cut 139, 140, 145, 146–47, 147–51, 153,

155–56, 170, education 139, 140, 145, 146–47, 151–53, 155–56, 170, faith-based 146, 154, energy 154, trade 160–63, Medicare 139, 140, 146, Patriot Act 157, 159, airline security 157–58, rebuild New York City 157, Homeland Security Department 140, 163–67, 172.

John E. Owen, "American-Style Party Government: Delivering Bush's Agenda, Delivering the Congress's Agenda," ch. 7 in Iwan Morgan and Philip Davies (eds.), *Right On? Political Change and Continuity in George W. Bush's America* (London: Institute for the Study of the Americas, 2006): tax cut 140, 141, 142, 145, education 140, 141, 142–43, faith-based 141, 143, energy 141, trade 141, Medicare 140, 141, 143, 146, stimulus 144, Patriot Act 144, airline security 144, rebuild New York City 144, Homeland Security Department 144, 145, 147.

Andrew Rudalevige, "George W. Bush and Congress in the Second Term: New Problems, Same Results?" ch. 5 in Robert Maranto, Douglas M. Brattebo, and Tom Lansford (eds.), *The Second Term of George W. Bush: Prospects and Perils* (New York: Palgrave Macmillan, 2006): tax cut 83–84, education 83–84, faith-based 83, energy 84, trade 85, Medicare 83, stimulus 85, Patriot Act 85–86, airline security 85, rebuild New York City 85, Homeland Security Department 86.

Barbara Sinclair, "Context, Strategy, and Chance: George W. Bush and the 107th Congress," ch. 5 in Colin Campbell and Bert A. Rockman (eds.), *The George W. Bush Presidency: Appraisals and Prospects* (Washington, D.C.: Congressional Quarterly Press, 2004): tax cut 110, 111–15, 117, education 110, 111–12, 115–17, 122, faith-based 120, 127, energy 121, 122, 124, 127, trade 124, 125, 127–28, Medicare 127, stimulus 125–26, Patriot Act 123, 124, 128, airline security 124, rebuild New York City 123, Homeland Security Department 128, 129, 130.

Not included:
   —agriculture: Burke 223, Owen 145
   —airline bailout: Draper 127, Owen 144
   —Alaska drilling: Burke 176, Owen 141

—campaign finance reform: Burke 223, Fortier and Ornstein 154

—corporate accountability: Burke 223, Owen 143, Sinclair 127

—patients' bill of rights: Burke 146–47, Fortier & Ornstein 146, 154, Owen 140, 143, Rudalevige 84

—social security reform: Burke 54, 122, 132, Fortier and Ornstein 146

—terrorism insurance: Burke 223, Owen 144

BUSH 43: 2005–6

Dan Balz, "Bush's Ambitious Second-Term Agenda Hits Reality," ch. 2 in John C. Fortier and Norman J. Ornstein (eds.), *Second-Term Blues: How George W. Bush Has Governed* (Washington, D.C.: American Enterprise Institute and Brookings Institution Press, 2007): social security 17, 18, 19, 22, 23, 26, 27, 31–34.

Draper, *Dead Certain*, chs. 16, 20, epilogue: social security 293–94, 295–304, energy 309, CAFTA 309, Katrina 411–12, immigration 372–77, 412.

Fred Greenstein, "George W. Bush: The Man and His Leadership," ch. 3 in Fortier and Ornstein (eds.), *Second-Term Blues*: social security 56, 57, class action 56, 57, bankruptcy 56, 57, energy 57, CAFTA 57, high schools 56, Patriot Act 59, immigration 59.

Geoffrey Hodgson, "President Bush's Second Term Agenda," ch. 1 in Morgan and Davies (eds.), *Right On?*: social security 22–25, 38, extend tax cuts 22.

Owen, "American-Style Party Government": social security 155, 156, 157, 158, class action 155, 156–57, bankruptcy 155, 156–57, energy 155, high schools 155, 156, Patriot Act 158, deficit reduction 157–58, extend tax cuts 155, 157, immigration 155.

Rudalevige, "George W. Bush and Congress": social security 92, 93, class action 92, 93, bankruptcy 93, high schools 92, 93, Patriot Act 93–94.

Congressional Quarterly Weekly, 2005: social security 112, 170, 175, 304, 550, 828, 1147, 1238–39, 2888, class action 175, 230–37, 460, 824, 2890, bankruptcy 824, 2890, energy 305, 1017, 1084, 2108–10, CAFTA 1063, 1523, 1656, 1759, 2047, 2111–13, high schools 305, 492, Patriot Act 932–33, 1902, 1970, 2044, 3325, deficit reduction 305, 2912, malpractice suits 305, Alaska drilling 2108, extend tax cuts 305, Katrina 2492–96, 3401, immigration 305, HSAs 175, 305, repeal estate tax 305, 1013, 1518, 2189.

Congressional Quarterly Weekly, 2006: social security 14–16, 80, 82, 342–43, 2600, 2601, 3364–65, class action 14–16, 81, 109, bankruptcy 14–16, 81, energy 14–16, 81, 113, 122, CAFTA 14–16, 81, 112, 121, high schools 3168–69, Patriot Act 14–16, 80, 82, 116, 342, 493, 600, 703, 3360, deficit reduction 14–16, 117, 290, 347, malpractice suits 342–44, 1334–35, Alaska drilling 35, 80, 84, 122, 342, 700, 764, 3344, extend tax cuts 82, 342–44, 1326–27, Katrina 14–16, 489, immigration 343, 828, 912, 974–75, 1169, 1400–2, 1473, 1785, 1880, 2315, 2470, 2600, 3324, 3326, 3357, military tribunals 80, 1881, 1966, 2390, 2458–60, 2554–55, 2600, 2624–25, 3324, 3342–43, HSAs 342–44, 3287–88, 3353, repeal estate tax 1621, 1788, 1876, 2176–78, 2319–20, 2600, 3367–68.

Not included: no entries from Balz through Rudalevige above

Abramowitz, Alan I., 152n
agriculture policy, xviii, 51, 60, 130–32, 188n70; under Carter, 124n4, 131; under Eisenhower, 130–31, 141; under Johnson, 131; under Kennedy, 125, 131; under Reagan, 124n4, 131–32; under Truman, 48, 63, 76, 124n4, 130, 135n
Alabama: and 1960 election, 4–5, 10n, 18n41, 21; demonstrations in, 36, 52n37
Alaska, 186; oil in, 48, 144, 157; statehood for, 18n40, 29n55, 31n, 48, 53, 64n88
Anderson, Clinton, 171–72
Ansolabehere, Stephen, 15n33, 30n, 114n34, 17n, 176n22
Atlas, Cary M., 187, 188n70, 189
Bailey, Stephen K., 106n, 108n26, 116
banking policy, xv, 34, 124n4, 140n59, 155, 160n107
Baucus, Max, 12–13, 61, 61n, 70–71, 77
Bawn, Kathleen, 100n19
Beard, Charles, xiv
Binder, Sarah A., 13n32, 146n74, 151n81, 152n82, 181n41
Bolling, Richard, 64, 107, 124n4, 176
Borah, William, 32–33, 119
Brady, David W., 30n, 176n22
Brady bill, 182–83
Britain, xviii, 26, 179n31, 184–85; Reform Acts in, 1–2, 14, 170, 180
budgets: of Clinton, 10–11, 49, 50, 133; of Eisenhower, 124n4; of Nixon, 124n4; of Reagan, 10, 11, 35, 141, 142. *See also* deficit reduction; reconciliation process

Burnham, James, 5n16
Burns, James MacGregor, xvii, 64, 107, 111n30, 160n107
Bush, George H. W., 7–9, 54–55; and capital gains tax, 144, 146, 153; and deficit reduction, 49, 81, 138, 140
Bush, George W., 58n70, in 2007–8, 137, 139–40, 140n57 and 59, 142, 144, and judges, 182; and Medicare drugs, 53–54; and Social Security, 37–38, 40, 65, 75; and tax cuts, 10, 12, 35, 58n70, 61, 76
California, 116–17, 177, 181n; population size of, 17, 26, 188, 189
campaign finance, 178n31; reform of, 34, 139n53, 144, 162
Campbell, James E., 153n85
Carey, John W., 141n60
Caro, Robert A., 154–55, 157
Carter, James, 53, 157n97; and energy policy, 49–50, 76, 88; style of, 51–52, 55–56, 59, 66
Census, 112n32, 158–59
Chemerinsky, Erwin, 144n66, 145n70, 151n81, 179n83, 183n50
cities: and policy 53, 110, 114, 114n, 150n79, 155, 157; and representation, 24–26, 114n, 116
civil liberties, 34, 37, 70, 139–40, 142
civil rights policy, 156; after 1960s, 128, 129, 157–58; before 1945, 85, 98–99, 100–1, 156; under Eisenhower, xv, 98–100; and filibuster, 70, 85, 98–101, 143–44, 147–49, 167, 171–72; under Johnson, 36, 53, 98–99; under Kennedy, 52n37, 85, 86n6, 129, 143n; under Truman, xv, 63, 81, 98–99

125; under Obama, xv, 60n76, 76, 76n105, 133

environmental policy, xv, 34, 51–52, 60n, 76, 76n, 133

Erikson, Robert S., 75n99, 178n28

executive branch, 41; design of cabinet departments in, 37, 53, 124, 125, 129, 135n46, 136n49; regulation of, 160n107, 175. *See also* postal reform

expenditures, 155, 157, 176; pork barrel, 185–90; Reagan cuts in, 49, 58, 138–39

federalism policies: centralization in, 179n31; as new federalism, 87n8, 125n6; as revenue sharing, 53, 126; regarding tidelands oil, 149–50

Fenno, Richard F., Jr., 5n17, 56n56, 86n7, 109n27, 157n98

filibustering: on civil rights, xix–xx, 85n5, 86n6, 98–101, 129, 143–44, 147–49, 154, 167; general pattern of, 142–54; in House of Representatives, 53n43, 109, 129; and intensity, 100, 151–53; on labor-management relations, 159, 161; not undertaken, 146–51, 154; reform of, 171–72, 179–85; since 1980s, 13n, 85n5, 144–45, 151–54, 162, 179–80

Fiorina, Morris P., 13n32, 30n, 152n84, 176n20, 22

Fisk, Catherine, 144n66, 145n70, 151n81, 179n83, 183n50

Florida, 4, 18, 21–22, 24

Foley, Tom, 126, 131n36

foreign policy, xv, 36–37, 60n75, 140n57

Frymer, Paul, 7–9

Geoghegan, Tom, 88n10, 155, 157, 160n107

gerrymandering: partisan, 24, 112n32, 115, 178n31; prorural, 114–15; of states, 2–3, 30–32. *See also* rotten boroughs

Gillmour, John B., 146, 177n24

Gingrich, Newt, 142, 163–64, 175n14, 176, 178

Hacker, Jacob S., 72n98

Hawaii: statehood for, 18n40, 31n, 53, 64n88, 86n6, 128

health care policy, 155, 157; under Carter, 156, 157n97; under Clinton, 35, 38, 39, 48, 49, 59n72, 74, 75, 85n5, 87n8, 124n4, 135, 144n68, 156, 173, 183; under Eisenhower, 38, 86n6, 123, 134; under Nixon, 38, 87n8, 128, 156; under Obama, xv, 35, 38, 61n, 74, 109, 133, 157, 162–63, 181; as rationalizing designs, 60, 76; under Truman, 38, 49, 63, 65, 125, 156

Hertzberg, Hendrik, 155–56, 157n97

Hollings, Ernest, 158n100

hospital cost containment, 127, 136

House of Representatives: as antimajoritarian, 101–15, 121–42; conservative tilt of, 101–15; Democratic hegemony in, 29–30, 175–77; as first mover, 86–87; reform of, 172–73, 175–77; role of Speaker in, 137, 140n57; rural tilt of, 111–15

housing policy, 114, 157; under Eisenhower, 102, 104, 107, 124n4; under Kennedy, 48, 135n46, 147; under Johnson, 147; and Taft, 106, 109–10; under Truman, 103–6, 109–10, 120, 129, 135n46, 146n76

immigration policy, 37, 128, 129, 137

incumbency advantage: for House members, 29–30, 175–77; for presidents, 174–75

intensity, 100, 101n, 119, 143–44, 148–50, 151–53, 161

Jacobson, Gary C., 18n39, 153n85, 178n30

Jeffords, James, 28n53, 58n70

Johnson, Lyndon B., 41, 48, 52n37, 53, 54, 98–99, 151n80, 173, 184

Kamarck, Elaine, 77

Kendall, Willmoore, 5n16 and 17

Kennedy, John F., 109; election of, 4–5, 21; proposals of, 9–11, 48–49, 62–63, 70

Key, V. O., Jr., 5, 16n35, 17n37, 21n44, 177

King, Anthony, 179n31

Koenig, Louis, 116

Koger, Gregory, 100n19, 180–81

Krehbiel, Keith, xvii, 35n, 83n, 130n, 132n, 145, 152n, 168n